...NS IN EUROPE
1848–1849

Martial Ro...

The Revolutions in Europe
1848–1849
From Reform to Reaction

Edited by

R. J. W. EVANS

and

HARTMUT POGGE
VON STRANDMANN

OXFORD
UNIVERSITY PRESS

OXFORD
UNIVERSITY PRESS

Great Clarendon Street, Oxford OX2 6DP

Oxford University Press is a department of the University of Oxford.
It furthers the University's objective of excellence in research, scholarship,
and education by publishing worldwide in

Oxford New York

Athens Auckland Bangkok Bogotá Buenos Aires Cape Town
Chennai Dar es Salaam Delhi Florence Hong Kong Istanbul Karachi
Kolkata Kuala Lumpur Madrid Melbourne Mexico City Mumbai Nairobi
Paris São Paulo Shanghai Singapore Taipei Tokyo Toronto Warsaw

with associated companies in Berlin Ibadan

Oxford is a registered trade mark of Oxford University Press
in the UK and in certain other countries

Published in the United States
by Oxford University Press Inc., New York

British Library Cataloguing in Publication Data
Data available

Library of Congress Cataloging in Publication Data
Data available

ISBN 0-19-820840-5 (hbk)
ISBN 0-19-924997-0 (pbk)

1 3 5 7 9 10 8 6 4 2

Typeset by John Waś, Oxford
Printed in Great Britain
on acid-free paper by
TJ International Ltd., Padstow, Cornwall

Preface

THE chapters in this book began life as a lecture series held in Oxford at the beginning of 1998 to commemorate the sesquicentenary of the outbreak of the revolutions of 1848: the first, and still to this day the only, simultaneous European-wide collapse of traditional authority, and an event which we believe to possess seminal importance for the subsequent history of the continent. The lectures were revised for publication over the next months, 150 years after the struggle of the new revolutionary regimes to establish themselves. They go to press just 150 years after the apparent failure of the revolutionary experiment. They will appear in print 150 years on from the point when the old order seemed—but how fleetingly, as time would show!—to have been reasserted.

Most of the contributors are present and past members of the Faculty of Modern History at Oxford. We are very grateful to David Saunders for making good so willingly and effectively our lack of expertise on the Russian front, and to Timothy Roberts for sharing with us the fruits of his recent dissertation on the place of the United States of America in the story of 1848. We should also like to express warm thanks to Teena Stabler, who has handled most of the administrative tasks with great dexterity, and to Richard Laver, for placing his skills as an indexer at our disposal.

R.J.W.E.
H.P. v. S.
October 1999

Contents

Chronology

1846

Feb.	Peasant revolt in Galicia
16 June	Election of Cardinal Mastai-Ferretti as Pope Pius IX
winter 1846–7	Severe famine in western Europe

1847

10 Sept.	Meeting of south-west German democrats at Offenburg articulates 'people's demands'
10 Oct.	Meeting of south-west German liberals at Heppenheim calls for German unification, without violence
4–29 Nov.	Sonderbund war in Switzerland
7 Nov.	Hungarian diet opened at Pressburg (Pozsony)

1848

12 Jan.	Revolt in Palermo
10 Feb.	Constitution in Naples
17 Feb.	Constitution in Tuscany
22–6 Feb.	Revolution in Paris; abdication of Louis-Philippe; establishment of National Workshops
24 Feb.	Publication of *Communist Manifesto* in London
27 Feb.	Popular meeting at Mannheim; reform demands passed
2 Mar.	Universal manhood suffrage proclaimed in France
3 Mar.	Kossuth's revolutionary speech to Hungarian diet
4 Mar.	Constitution (Statuto) granted in Piedmont-Savoy
12 Mar.	Electoral law in Belgium
13–15 Mar.	Insurrection in Vienna; Metternich resigns; convocation of constituent assembly (Reichstag)
14 Mar.	Constitution in Papal States
15–21 Mar.	'March Days' in Berlin; violent clashes between army and people; constituent assembly summoned; Prussia to be 'absorbed into' Germany
18–22 Mar.	'Five Days' of Milan: insurrection there and in Venice, where republic proclaimed; Piedmont declares war on Austria
21–4 Mar.	Denmark annexes Schleswig; revolt of local Germans; formation of provisional government
26 Mar.	Nicholas I condemns revolutionary 'events in western Europe'

30 Mar.	Beginning of hostilities in Schleswig
31 Mar.–3 Apr.	Pre-Parliament (Vorparlament) at Frankfurt
10 Apr.	Chartist demonstration in London
11 Apr.	April Laws ratified in Hungary; Palacký's letter of refusal to participate, as a Czech, in the forthcoming German national assembly
12–20 Apr.	Republican uprising in Baden led by Friedrich Hecker
23 Apr.	Elections to French national assembly
25 Apr.	Constitution in Austrian lands
29 Apr.	Pope Pius IX proclaims neutrality
4 May	Constituent assembly meets in Paris; (Second) French Republic proclaimed
15 May	Neapolitan parliament summoned but dispersed; collapse of revolt there
15–17 May	Renewed insurrection in Vienna; dynasty flees to Innsbruck
18 May	German national assembly, elected by universal male suffrage, meets in Frankfurt
22 May	Prussian constituent parliament assembles in Berlin
2–17 June	Slav Congress in Prague; disturbances quelled by Windischgrätz
21–7 June	Revolution in Wallachia
23–8 June	'June Days' in Paris: street violence; suppression of National Workshops; General Cavaignac head of government
28 June	Provisional government set up in Frankfurt
5 July	National assembly meets in Pest
22 July	Reichstag assembles in Vienna
19–20 July	Seneca Falls (NY) convention on women's rights
25 July	Battle of Custoza: Radetzky defeats Charles Albert
29 July	Small and ill-conceived Irish rising fails in County Tipperary
6–9 Aug.	Milan recovered by Austrians; Austro-Piedmontese armistice
12 Aug.	Austrian emperor returns to Vienna
28 Aug.	First war for Schleswig-Holstein concluded with armistice of Malmö between Prussia and Denmark
5–18 Sept.	Armistice of Malmö rejected, then accepted by majority of Frankfurt assembly; revolt of minority in favour of German rights in Schleswig
12 Sept.	New constitution in Switzerland
17 Sept.	Jellačić invades Hungary

21 Sept.	Outbreak of second republican uprising in Baden, led by Gustav Struve
25–8 Sept.	Wallachian revolution suppressed
6–31 Oct.	Revolution in Vienna; dynasty flees to Olmütz (Olomouc); quelled by Windischgrätz
3 Nov.	New constitution in the Netherlands
4 Nov.	New French constitution
9 Nov.	Execution of Robert Blum in Vienna
16–25 Nov.	Insurrection in Rome; flight of Pius IX
2 Dec.	Abdication of Emperor Ferdinand of Austria; succeeded by Franz Joseph
5 Dec.	Military occupation of Berlin; Prussian constituent assembly dissolved; dictated (*oktroyiert*) constitution
10 Dec.	Presidential election in France: victory of Louis Napoleon

1849

9 Feb.	Establishment of Roman Republic
4–7 Mar.	Dictated (*oktroyiert*) constitution in Austria; Reichstag dissolved
23 Mar.	Battle of Novara; Radetzky again defeats Charles Albert
27 Mar.–3 Apr.	Frankfurt constitution; assembly offers crown to king of Prussia; offer effectively rejected
31 Mar.–10 July	Second war for Schleswig-Holstein
14 Apr.	Habsburgs deposed as rulers of Hungary
14–28 Apr.	Recognition of German constitution by twenty-eight German states; but Prussian king officially rejects crown
23 Apr.	Arrest and condemnation of Petrashevtsy in Russia
3–9 May	Uprising in Dresden (Richard Wagner participated)
4 May	Frankfurt assembly demands general acceptance of German constitution; fight to save it in Saxony, Baden, and the Palatinate
13 May	Elections to French Legislative Assembly
5 June	New constitution in Denmark; rump of Frankfurt assembly (Rumpfparlament) meets at Stuttgart
17 June	Russian armies invade Hungary
18 June	US President nominates envoy to Hungarians; military dissolution of Stuttgart rump parliament
1–2 July	Fall of Roman Republic
23 July	Capitulation of Baden revolutionary army in fortress of Rastatt
9–13 Aug.	Final defeat of Hungarian armies and capitulation by Görgey
28 Aug.	Fall of Venetian Republic

3 Oct.	Surrender of last Hungarian fortress, Komorn (Komárom)

1850

20 Mar.	Erfurt parliament convened by Prussia; Austria excluded
16 May	Reconstitution of German Confederation
2 July	Peace treaty between Prussia and Denmark
11 Sept.	Freiinwalde arbitration: Mecklenburg's modern constitution revoked
29 Nov.	Convention of Olmütz; Prussia abandons plans for a German union without Austria

1851

2 Dec.	*Coup d'état* of Louis Napoleon
5 Dec.	Arrival of Kossuth in America
31 Dec.	Silvester Patent in Austria; absolutism restored

Central Europe in 1848–1849

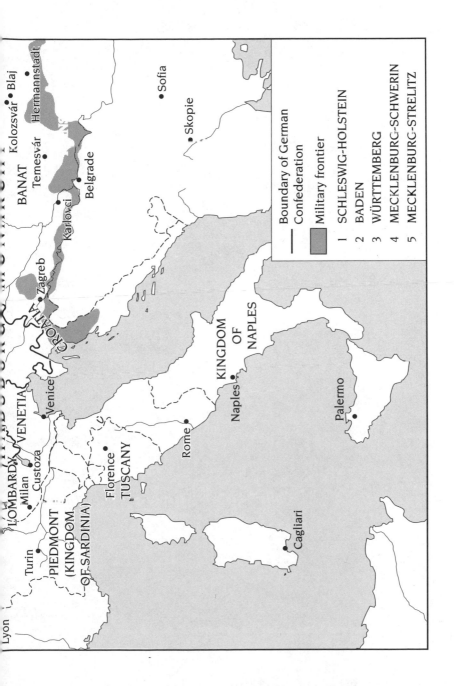

Boundary of German
Confederation
Military frontier

1 SCHLESWIG-HOLSTEIN
2 BADEN
3 WÜRTTEMBERG
4 MECKLENBURG-SCHWERIN
5 MECKLENBURG-STRELITZ

Lyon

Turin

PIEDMONT
(KINGDOM
OF SARDINIA)

Milan
LOMBARDY
Custoza

VENETIA

Venice

Florence
TUSCANY

Rome

KINGDOM
OF
NAPLES

Naples

Cagliari

Palermo

Sofia

Skopie

BANAT

Kolozsvár
Blaj

Temesvár
Hermannstadt

Belgrade

Karlovci

Zagreb

CROATIA

I

1848–1849:
A European Revolution?

HARTMUT POGGE VON STRANDMANN

RARELY has an event in European history been so much hoped for, predicted, or anticipated, as well as dreaded and feared, as the revolution of 1848–9.[1] Many contemporary observers thought a revolution would break out in Belgium, Britain, or possibly even in France because of poverty, rising social tensions, the expulsion of people through emigration programmes, and the economic crisis of the mid-1840s. Only a few expected a wholesale revolution to grip either Germany, the Habsburg empire, or Italy. There was a saying before 1848 that revolutions were made in France, that they were thought and theorized about in Germany and that the situation in England was characterized by fear of revolution and measures to prevent its possible outbreak. Concomitant with the predictions and the saying existed another conviction that a revolution would not be restricted to one or two countries. According to this view it was generally expected that given time the entire continent might be set on fire. Yet it was not clear whether there would be a European revolution or a series of different revolutions in Europe. Whatever the expectations, the anticipated revolutions would have one thing in common, namely that they happened roughly at the same time.

When the revolution eventually broke out in Paris, it swept eastwards through Germany and the Habsburg monarchy within a very short space of time only to be stopped at the western boundaries of tsarist Russia. It also reinvigorated the revolutionary movement in Italy, which had started a few weeks earlier without causing a Euro-

---

[1] Eric Hobsbawm, *The Age of Revolutions, 1789–1848* (New York, 1962), 361–2.

pean chain reaction.[2] Many contemporaries regarded the events in
Paris as the beginning of a European revolution and believed in
the formation of a revolutionary front against the *anciens régimes* of
central and eastern Europe. Some even advocated a revolutionary
war against tsarist Russia. However neither the initial enthusiasm
for certain general aims, nor general revolutionary exuberance nor
the temporary collapse of most of the *anciens régimes* is a sufficient
reason to interpret the revolution as a united and common action.
What is, then, the case for calling it a European revolution, if one
bears in mind that each country was dominated by a different political system and that the national question, although crucial for all the
other countries involved, was not an issue of the revolution in Paris?

Different political systems and different nationalist manifestations were not sufficient to deflect from the fact that the entire
continent became embroiled at varying levels of intensity. Europe
still appeared as a revolutionary entity. Yet not all European states
experienced their own revolution. Some remained quiet because of
a system of strong repression as in the case of Russia. Others, like
Britain, relied on preventive measures such as reformist legislation
or the employment of a large police force in the form of special constables. Others relied on the introduction of a liberal constitution
to stave off revolutionary threats, as in Denmark and the Netherlands. Given that the remaining west-European states of Belgium,
Sweden, Spain, and Portugal did not experience any serious upheaval, it follows that the concept of a European revolution could be
questionable. Moreover, does it make sense to use the label 'European revolution' if only four major countries—France, Germany,
the Habsburg empire, and Italy—were directly involved?

Although these four countries experienced a major revolutionary upheaval, all the others were strongly affected by what happened in Paris, Vienna, Berlin, and Rome. So some of the outsiders
even turned their passiveness into active intervention, as in the
case of the Russian counter-revolutionary invasion of Hungary in
1849. Russian intervention was the exception, but Britain and Russia watched, for instance, the German revolution and its national
aspirations very carefully and let their reactions be known diplo-
matically. They also observed Paris for any signs that the French

---

[2] Simonetta Soldani, 'Annäherung an Europa im Namen der Nation: Die italieni-
sche Revolution 1846–1849', in Dieter Dowe *et al.* (eds.), *Europa 1848: Revolution
und Reform* (Bonn, 1998), 125–66 at 142–6.

might repeat the revolutionary expansion of the 1790s. A more active diplomatic pressure, mainly from Britain and Russia, brought to an end the German-Prussian war against Denmark over the duchies of Schleswig and Holstein. The effects of foreign politics were also felt on the domestic scene in Germany. The armistice of Malmö led to nationalist reactions, which in turn ignited growing social tensions and disillusionment amongst peasants, artisans, and rural workers. The result was social protest movements in Silesia, Saxony, and some Rhenish cities, where even the demand for a 'social republic' was heard for the first time. Serious rioting also occurred in Frankfurt, which led to the second wave of revolutionary violence, mostly in the south-west of Germany.[3] In addition to military intervention and diplomacy, some of the less revolutionary powers became involved by offering asylum to political refugees. This affected mostly Britain and Switzerland, and to a lesser extent Belgium and the Netherlands. Occasionally refugees stayed on in these countries, but often they moved to the United States or were allowed to return to their home countries later.

There is another area which highlights the extent to which European nations in this period were increasingly interlinked. Even if the revolution was concentrated in four countries, yet the whole of Europe became involved by means of greatly improved communications. Railway and telegraphic links had improved significantly, so that news could travel faster across national boundaries than during any previous revolution. The growing interest in news is illustrated by the explosion of political and other publications. The number of political newspapers in Prussia alone increased by 56 per cent between 1847 and 1850 and in Austria by 79 per cent once press censorship was abolished. The vastly extended circulation of newspapers, placards, caricatures, posters, songs, and illustrated papers created something of a revolutionary culture which was appreciated by a growing number of people. In Germany, for instance, estimated levels of literacy had reached approximately 80 per cent.[4]

The European character of the revolution was also expressed in a Berlin poster, during the optimistic early phase, in which the 'masses' were invited to a republican public meeting on 3 April 1848.[5] The public notice started with 'vive la république' and 'hur-

[3] Wolfram Siemann, *Die deutsche Revolution von 1848/49* (Frankfurt, 1985), 161–5.
[4] Ibid. 114–24.
[5] Lothar Gall (ed.), *1848: Aufbruch zur Freiheit* (Berlin, 1998), 110–11.

rah for the republic' and then went on to announce that speeches would be held in German, French, and English. The meeting was organized in honour of the 'great European revolution' and the text of the poster ended with cheers to the 'European revolution' and the 'new world'. Obviously the concept of a European revolution was alive and some people believed in it, but their hopes were soon to be undermined by the national and regional complexities determining the revolutionary outcome in each country or region. Nevertheless, one can discern five themes which underlay the revolution, but which varied in strength and intensity from country to country and region to region. There was first of all the widespread opposition to the *anciens régimes*; secondly, the bid for greater political participation and reforms. Thirdly, the social question had become much more urgent than ever before. Fourthly, the assertion of national self-determination and the attempt to set up independent nation states played a vital role in central, eastern, and southern Europe. Finally, the slowly growing success of the counter-revolution was to affect all revolutionaries across the four countries regardless of whether they were moderate liberals, democratic radicals, or even socialists.

In the eyes of contemporaries, however, the concepts of liberty and solidarity figured strongly and characterized the first phase of the revolution in Europe. In view of the power of these catchwords, it may not be surprising that already at the first anniversary of the outbreak of the revolution in Paris, in February 1849, Frédéric Sorrieu published a coloured lithograph called *The Triumph*.[6] The middle of the picture is dominated by a memorial dedicated to the 'martyrs of freedom' from the years 1793, 1830, and 1848. Two processions move to the memorial. The large one is headed by the statue of freedom on a horse-drawn chariot holding the torch of the Enlightenment in her hand. The statue is flanked by freedom fighters, dressed in the national colours of the different European freedom movements. The other procession, a smaller one, is led by some women. Their inclusion is to show that women played an important role in 1848. Even at the time when the revolution had been defeated in France and when the conservative forces were heading for victory in Berlin and in the Habsburg Monarchy, the idea of the European revolution was still alive and the appeal to

[6] Ibid. 112–13. This lithograph was part of a series of three which dealt with the revolution.

solidarity still existed. Sorrieu's widely publicized lithograph may have expressed nostalgia for international co-operation in the face of the emerging force of nationalism during the past twelve months. Initially nationalism had not been regarded by many revolutionaries as a term opposing freedom and solidarity. Only when the nationalist movements turned against each other did they tend to undermine the appeal of international solidarity and liberty in central Europe. If, in this later situation, nationalisms proved to be decisively divisive, it showed that the first euphoric phase also had a strong symbolic character, expressed by the rather Utopian term 'spring of the peoples'.

A closer examination of the beginning of the revolution reveals that it was dominated by the first three of the five broad themes mentioned above. In addition, the outbreak of the revolution in February and March 1848 appears synchronized. It seems evident that neither the war of 1847 in Switzerland, nor the uprising in Cracow, nor the rebellion in Palermo triggered a Europe-wide revolution. It is also doubtful whether these events provided an impulse for developments in France. But they may have contributed to a rise in general expectations that the outbreak of a revolution in Europe was imminent. In this situation the so-called 'knife and fork' revolution in Paris galvanized the other countries into action when dissatisfaction with the political regime in Paris had reached its peak. It was the signal from Paris in February which triggered the publicly voiced demands for reforms which found mass support in the Habsburg lands, in Italy, and in Germany. The escalation of activities found a widespread echo not only in the major cities but also in the countryside among the peasantry, the artisans, and the rural and urban workers. Whether the involvement of the lower strata of society was a sign of political mobilization rather than the consequences of the prevailing disastrous economic situation still needs further clarification. But the analysis of collective violence undertaken by the Tillys points to 1848–9 as a turning-point away from hunger and starvation as the cause of violent action and towards political motives as the source of collective violence.[7] In any case, the initial harmony among the social groups pushing for reforms may give the impression that the revolution in those four countries pursued

---

[7] Siemann, *Deutsche Revolution*, 42–8. Siemann quotes Richard Tilly, 'Unruhen und Proteste in Deutschland im 19. Jahrhundert', in the latter's *Kapital, Staat und sozialer Protest in der deutschen Industrialisierung* (Göttingen, 1980), 143–74.

similar aims. But this was not the case. In Paris social issues were much more prominent than in Germany or in the Habsburg Monarchy, where constitutional and national questions were paramount in the early phase. But because of these differences the image of a European revolution was not and should not be abandoned.

There is one further point which has been made against the concept of a European revolution. In contrast to 1789 or 1917, the 1848 revolution did not have a centre. Of course Paris initiated the chain reaction and was regarded by many as the capital of the revolution, but after the June Days, incidentally not the epitome of a class struggle, the centre of gravity moved eastwards to Germany and finally even to Hungary. Recent interpretations of the revolution of 1848 have confirmed the view that there were several centres and that the revolution was characterized by regional variations or, as Charles Pouthas has put it, by the 'sum of local events'.[8] So at a certain level it seems possible to speak of a European revolution, but this statement ultimately depends on whether common or different elements are emphasized.

So far the five themes as well as the synchronism, the early symbolism, and the improved communications have been mentioned to underline the common elements of the revolution. Let us briefly consider whether even the run-up to the outbreak of the revolution showed common features. First of all there was a widespread and general expectation of a revolution to come. The ground was so well prepared intellectually by Europe-wide reform discussions and demands that the forbidding of a banquet became the spark which triggered revolutionary action in Paris. Without the expectation of a revolution and an increasingly tense atmosphere it could not have spread so quickly, overriding the different political, economic, and social conditions prevailing in each country or region. The anticipation of revolution went hand in hand with a loss of confidence in the existing governments. Furthermore, the discussion about a forthcoming revolution was so pervasive that it seems possible to consider it as a direct cause of the revolution.

Secondly, all the existing regimes gave in initially and made concessions, at least in the early phases, to some of the revolutionary demands, in order to prevent a radicalization along the lines of the dreaded first French Revolution of 1789. Especially in France the

---

[8] Charles Pouthas, 'Die Komplexität von 1848', in Horst Stuke and Wilfried Forstmann (eds.), *Die europäischen Revolutionen von 1848* (Königstein, 1979), 17–29.

monarchy had lost its confidence in handling the revolutionaries in February 1848. However, the other monarchies managed to survive, largely because republican threats did not have sufficient public support. One explanation for the loss of governmental authority may be that before February 1848 governments had seen the revolution coming for some considerable time and felt that they were losing their long struggle against rising liberalism and nationalism. This was especially true for Metternich, who fled Vienna without putting up much of a struggle to stay in power. In February and March 1848 it may have been difficult to foresee that the conservative forces would ultimately win in 1849 and 1850. But at what point did the conservatives begin to regain courage and confidence to win the struggle?

The failure of Chartism in London may have come too early to comfort the conservatives, but the June Days in Paris gave encouragement to those who advocated the use of violence against the revolution. By that stage it had become reassuringly clear to some reactionaries that neither the apparatus of the state nor the levers of the economy had moved into the hands of the revolutionaries. Even if the tide began to turn after the June Days, it took months before a conservative victory was in sight. When it was finally achieved, it turned out to be a Pyrrhic victory for the conservative forces, because the political, economic, and social agenda of the 1860s was determined by the issues of 1848–9.[9] This does not mean that the revolution was ultimately victorious, but some of its long-term effects may appear as a vindication of the revolution of 1848.

A third common feature of the pre-revolutionary period was the growing political movement against the Vienna Settlement of 1815. The foreign political and domestic solutions of 1815 lost their appeal in the face of the rising tide of nationalism and liberalism. However, in the end the revolution did not change the international situation and the European powers returned to the status quo ante.

In looking back at the European revolutions of the late eighteenth, nineteenth, and twentieth centuries, it is now possible to say that none of the great revolutions succeeded in the long run. Even the Bolshevik Revolution of 1917 ultimately proved to be unsuccessful. The long-term failure of the European revolutions does

---

[9] Heinz-Gerhard Haupt and Dieter Langewiesche, 'Die Revolution in Europa 1848: Reform der Herrschafts- und Gesellschaftsordnung—Nationalrevolution— Wirkungen ', in Dowe *et al.* (eds.), *Europa 1848*, 11–41.

not imply that their effects were not of tremendous importance. The revolution of 1848 may not have the same significance as those of 1789 or 1917, but its lasting repercussions belie the impression of its short-term failure. One of the major achievements of the revolution was the abolition of feudal rule in the countryside. In particular, most of the Habsburg lands experienced a modernization of their agrarian constitution. As for Germany, it is now generally agreed that its political parties had their origins in the revolution. Furthermore, all German states—except Mecklenburg—have enjoyed a representative constitution since 1848 and the 'basic laws' of Frankfurt influenced the Weimar constitution of 1919 and became part of the constitution of the Federal Republic after 1949. Social groups became much more conscious of their role in society, and the general level of political mobilization grew considerably. All this makes up the 'complexity of 1848', a term with which Charles Pouthas has characterized that revolution. Although it is not difficult to go along with his emphasis on the complexity of the revolution, it does not follow that his rejection of the term 'European revolution' should be equally accepted.

Pouthas went a step further when he argued that the revolutions of 1848 had nothing in common except their name. This minimalist interpretation does not make sense because the common elements discussed above are neglected and no comparison is made. In the words of the Berlin historian Hartmut Kaelble, 1848 was the most international of all revolutions and thus by definition the most European.[10] Despite the divisive nationalisms of the revolution and regional variations, common factors, including common causes and common consequences, played a vital part in the revolutionary development. The revolution of 1848 was more than the summary of revolutionary and counter-revolutionary events in each country. This revolution formed the watershed between the eighteenth century and the restorative years after 1815 on the one side, and the dominating issues of the second half of the nineteenth century on the other.

[10] Hartmut Kaelble, '1848: Viele nationale Revolutionen oder eine europäische Revolution?', in Wolfgang Hardtwig (ed.), *Revolution in Deutschland und Europa 1848/49* (Göttingen, 1998), 260–78.

2

Liberalism, Nationalism, and the Coming of the Revolution

R. J. W. EVANS

In late November 1847 the 15-year-old Archduke Ferdinand Maximilian of Habsburg unburdened himself to his confessor. Ever since first hearing about 1789 and the French Revolution, he revealed, he had been prey to a secret fear that a similar storm would blow up again, depriving him of his title and the Catholic Church of its authority. He asked the confessor to note down his intuition, and promised to remind him of it in later life.[1]

Indeed, storms lay just around the corner for the house of Austria, and for other European dynasties. They were unleashed only weeks afterwards. Moreover, 1848 and its legacy would indeed blow Ferdinand Maximilian himself away in the fullness of time. As the luckless Emperor Maximilian of Mexico he died there before a firing squad in 1867. The confessor, who had stayed at home (though ironically his name was Columbus), shared in the concurrent discomfiture of the Catholic establishment in the Habsburg lands, as reformist governments cut away its privileges.

The first French Revolution set an agenda, the stuff whether of daydreams or of nightmares, for the nineteenth century. It established France as the touchpaper for future international explosions. No one could doubt, once successive regimes across Europe broke down in the early months of 1848, that these were 'revolutionary' events in the sense understood since 1789. Above all, the famous, almost totemic, acts associated with the destruction of the French

[1] Elisabeth Kovács (ed.), *Geheime Notizen des Joseph Columbus, 1843–8* (Vienna, 1971), 130.

ancien régime—the National Assembly, the storming of the Bastille, the Declaration of the Rights of Man, the abolition of feudalism—simultaneously gave birth, in their modern form, to the two foremost streams of political ideology, liberal and national, which dominated the programmes of 1848, and whose subsequent influence swept the continent and beyond, extending as far as Maximilian's Mexico by the 1860s.

These two ideologies, then and later, interacted continuously with one another. Liberalism stood, in essence, for the free development of individuals and groups, guaranteed by responsible government. Nationalism asserted the claim to primacy of a particular political group, the national community. The first French Revolution mobilized and focused these sets of ideas. On the one hand, it established new constitutional structures from 1789 onward and made possible political participation at all levels. On the other hand, it asserted that the 'principle of all sovereignty resides in the nation',[2] such that the *nation française* took over the place of the monarchy by 1793 as the organizing principle of the state.

Like no previous political movement, the first French Revolution proved quickly and dramatically exportable. Not for nothing had France exerted such a puissant cultural and linguistic hegemony over Europe in the age of Enlightenment. Now her transformatory ideas were retailed across the continent, winning manifestations of sympathy and co-operation from Ireland to Poland. Yet France had also possessed the strongest eighteenth-century army, and this soon meant that the revolution was exported in a more and more debased form: liberty imposed by French troops with small groups of local collaborators; the national cause that of France writ large. From 1799 constitutionalism became a charade and the nation a vehicle for the ruthless military dictatorship of Napoleon Bonaparte. Besides, a third political force unleashed in the 1790s, radical and violent, helped to defeat the purpose of much of the initial revolutionary programme.

Thus the French example generated more and more negative responses outside France; and progressively French aggression, alongside its domestic consequences, actually set back elsewhere the very ideas it claimed to embody. Powerful reformist tendencies

---

[2] 'Le principe de toute souveraineté réside essentiellement dans la nation': 'Declaration of the Rights of Man and the Citizen', in *French Revolution Documents*, ed. J. M. Roberts (2 vols.; Oxford, 1966), i. 171–4.

had, after all, already been at work in some *ancien régime* societies, where governments enacted greater equality before the law, measures of peasant emancipation, enhanced religious tolerance, wider education provision, and so forth. Such changes had been espoused by some in existing representative institutions, from Great Britain to Sweden or even Hungary. Whether or not parliamentary arrangements came into play, swelling public debate ensued about proto-liberal issues, for example in the German and Italian states. At the same time patriotic sentiments were engaged, as concomitant both to some of these government programmes and to forms of critique, even open opposition, generated in different societies, from the Netherlands to Russia.[3]

All this activity was ruthlessly curbed by the mid-1790s, with tough restrictions enforced on every form of communication and association, inside and outside the new imperial French frontiers. Those controls would yield a flashpoint for future discontent—a direct line leads from them to the organs of censorship and repression brought low in the first phase of disturbances in 1848. Yet for the moment they were widely accepted by all the foremost sections of society, defending property or church, dynasty or homeland.

The eventual collapse of the Napoleonic empire, though it owed something to disillusion among progressives within France and a great deal more to patriotic sentiments in the countries of the anti-French coalition, seemed to the victors to vindicate such reactionary measures and to require their continuation. Hence the restoration in 1815 of a 'legitimate' Europe. The peacemakers at Vienna had priorities which were conservative, patriarchal, and devout; they aimed to secure monarchy as a ruling institution, aristocracy as a social ordering, and the churches as guardians of cultural values. But their intention was by no means simply to renew the *status quo ante*. Even for France this held good: the Bourbons were permitted to return only when a settlement with the authoritarian Bonaparte proved impossible. Outside a France reduced to her 1790 frontiers, the chief strategy was to prevent any future disturbance—putatively of a revolutionary kind—from that quarter.

France was in fact in decline from 1815 onwards, by comparison with the other main states of Europe. The latter, however, hardly

[3] Useful introduction to this subject in Otto Dann and John Dinwiddy (eds.), *Nationalism in the Age of the French Revolution* (London, 1988).

perceived this. They feared *revanche*, and not altogether without reason, although the threat of it only re-emerged after 1848, ironically when the French people's own realization of that decline led them to bring back a Bonaparte as their ruler. Meanwhile, political change in France henceforth played itself out on a domestic, and mostly a Parisian, stage only. Yet in 1830 (as we shall see) instability in French affairs again bid fair to set Europe alight. By 1848 it did so—but France proved unable to influence the course of the resultant events abroad.

The international order settled at Vienna was guaranteed, first and foremost, by the two principal restorative powers, Britain and Russia. The basically constitutional system of the one played with reaction under Lord Liverpool, while the basically reactionary system of the other toyed with constitutionalism under Tsar Alexander I. But whereas British restraints were exercised only at home, and not even very effectually there, Russian controls, proclaimed through the manifesto of international solidarity between throne and altar known as the Holy Alliance, became part of a much broader policing operation. They underpinned the reconstructed balance in central Europe, whose paramount features were the German Bund or Confederation and a congeries of likewise subordinate Italian states, both presided over by an Austrian regime existentially concerned about both liberal and national forces, though not perceiving them yet as a concerted threat.

The symbol, and more than just the symbol, of the restoration was Prince Clemens Metternich, foreign minister and chief confidant to the Austrian emperor, Francis I. That was so not least because the influence of this conservative aristocrat, who proclaimed all Europe to be his fatherland, spanned exactly the whole period between the Congress of Vienna and the year 1848. The principal influences upon Metternich, however, lay further back. As a youth in the Rhineland, he had experienced at first hand the Revolution of 1789, initially from the periphery in Strasbourg, then at the sharp end when French armies invaded the Austrian Netherlands, where his father was governor. From that point on, Metternich placed himself definitively in the service of the arch-reactionary Francis.

Like his sovereign, Metternich thus became implacably opposed to ideas of change. All reform, on his jaundiced analysis, would lead directly to anarchy. Yet there was discernment in his position too. He accepted reliable new vehicles for conservatism—hence his years of ultimately fruitless negotiation with Napoleon. By the same token he wanted Europe's conservative regimes to be capable and reasonably benign. He looked to counter liberalism with proficient paternalism, nationalism with regional oligarchy. Moreover, as a man formed by the culture of the Enlightenment, he entertained a deep mistrust of the religious and other kinds of enthusiasm, the Romantic and organic notions, of right-wing intellectuals in the years around 1815.

Crucially for our purposes, Metternich identified Austrian security interests with those of Europe as a whole, a policy which was perhaps not inappropriate, once given the over-exposure of the Habsburg monarchy on the international stage. For decades he sought to protect the stability of Europe to the advantage of stability within Austria. By 1848 that stood revealed as a bankrupt strategy; indeed, by then it served only to ensure that the revolution, once it had dislodged its prime scapegoat in Vienna, would be a Europe-wide one.

In the shorter term, stability nevertheless proved in some ways remarkably easy to achieve after 1815. There has been endless debate about how far the comparative tranquillity of the restoration years was due to the soundness of the settlement itself, and how far to the efficiency of the arrangements for policing it. On the whole it did not rest upon terror, and the regimes, cultivating a dynastic, even patriarchal, image, were not—did not try to be—very tough. Louis-Philippe's envious comment may be recalled: 'Republics are lucky: they can shoot people.'[4]

Rather, liberal and national impulses were initially much weaker still, able to mobilize only small and still inchoate groups of students, nascent commercial interests, ex-Napoleonic officials, and the like. Operative republicanism stood at a long-time low. It survived merely in Switzerland and a few midget states, including the handful of remaining free cities in Germany and the new puppet municipality of Cracow. Elsewhere even the severest critics of individual rulers rarely extended their censure to monarchy as a whole.

The only immediate threat seemed to emanate from the third force of the revolutionary tradition, from radical and Utopian groups. These were usually incompetent, strong enough only for brief challenges to the local balance. Being—of necessity—secret

---

[4] Schroeder, *European Politics* (see Introductory Reading), 707; cf. 573, 799, and *passim*; cf. Emsley (see Introductory Reading), and Mack Smith in this volume.

societies, they owed a clear debt to, and sometimes embodied a
direct continuity with, earlier Freemasonic lodges. Thus their real
or presumed existence fed refurbished versions of those conspiracy
theories which the paranoia induced by the French Revolution had
begotten.

This postwar European order was, however, always vulnerable at
the edges. The collapse of Iberian authority in South America had
alarming repercussions, not just for Spain and Portugal. Mindlessly
reactionary government in southern Italy soon became the despair
of Metternich. Serbs and after them Greeks engaged in messy but
partly successful risings against Turkish rule. Then the Poles, who
rebelled against Russian overlordship, and to some extent also the
Hungarians, who came close to open confrontation with the Habsburgs, showed how constitutional and patriotic sentiments could
already be combined in an inflammatory mix. These developments
were followed with growing enthusiasm by progressive opinion
across the continent; but in 1830 it was two sets of events in the
heart of Europe's existing revolutionary zone which ushered in a
new phase.

The 'July Days', which witnessed the replacement of the Bourbon by the Orleanist dynasty, proved to be a tightly controlled
coup d'état within the French establishment. They were nevertheless also a powerful liberal statement, opening up a programme
of individual and corporate freedoms which forthwith acquired its
own momentum. The July Revolution in Paris provided a powerful
stimulus to constitutional change elsewhere, most conspicuously in
Great Britain, with calls for broader suffrage, at least to reflect shifting property relations. The repercussions of simultaneous events
in the Low Countries were still further-reaching. Belgium's claim
to independence provoked an international crisis, whose resolution in favour of the creation of a new sovereign state with notable
constitutional guarantees for its citizens afforded also spectacular
encouragement to national separatist goals. If 'nationalism' as a
principle was not yet strong enough to assert its rights—Belgians
notoriously formed no straightforward 'nation' in a modern sense—
it had become clear that the repression of groups conscious of some
kind of national identity could seriously impair Europe's stability.

In the 1830s, therefore, oppositional forces took heart. They
were also more inclined to define themselves in generational terms:

'Young Europe', as a vague sodality of the 'young' patriots in different countries, sought intellectual renewal, with stress on individual liberties, legal equality, educational meritocracy, and social justice. Such ideals attracted especially the greater number of students emerging from revamped systems of higher education, with a string of newly dominant metropolitan universities: Berlin and Munich, Madrid and London. Metternich, typically just off target, predicted that the foundation of the last of these would ensure revolution in England.[5]

Youth movements were only one part of the surge during the 1830s in associational activity of all kinds, often with an implicitly liberal agenda. Indeed, in some sense such activity was liberal by definition, as a focus for bourgeois organizational talent and a probing of the limits of state control. Police and censorship anyway found themselves increasingly unable to cope with a progressively more mobile and educated population; and their efforts were not helped by the huge French breach in the entire 'continental system' of Holy Alliance restraints, since the rule of Louis-Philippe, however devious and heavy-handed, was never authoritarian. France became a refuge for *émigrés* of all kinds, particularly dissident Poles and Italians. Across central Europe, self-aware national communities, likewise beginning to gain an institutional base, were associated with much of this ferment and with its characteristic values—middle-class, intellectual, forward-looking, sociable, literary, and musical.[6] In the absence of coherent and cohesive official ideologies, the cultural initiative passed into other hands.

Two further dimensions of the new climate of ideas need to be noted. The first is economic. Commercial and industrial groupings belonged centrally to the corporative life of the day, and they tended to favour economic liberalism, with the German Zollverein, or Customs Union, as its most prominent vehicle. But national elements were hardly less important: *laissez-faire* might quickly be trumped by the threat of foreign competition. By the early 1840s Friedrich List (not to be confused with his contemporaneous close namesake, Franz Liszt, though both were idols of the rising anti-

[5] Sked in *Europe's Balance* (see Introductory Reading), 176; cf. Lenore O'Boyle, 'The Problem of an Excess of Educated Men in Western Europe, 1800–50', *Journal of Modern History*, 42 (1970), 471–95.

[6] Serviceable introductions to this in Hroch, *Social Preconditions* (see Introductory Reading) and Józef Chlebowczyk, *On Small and Young Nations in Europe: Nation-forming Processes in Ethnic Borderlands in East-Central Europe* (Wrocław, 1980).

establishment) became the acknowledged pioneer of a doctrine of national markets.

The second dimension is religious. Liberals were often anticlerical. Yet the faithful anyhow constituted less and less of an automatic bastion of the existing order. Besides the freethinking Protestant contribution to Young Germany, there were outstanding liberal Catholics from France to Hungary, and national Catholic movements, especially in Italy, with the emergence of Gioberti, and in the German Confederation, where the *Deutschkatholiken* came to direct their fire against both spiritual and secular hierarchies. Even more conservative kinds of Catholic organization could challenge state authority, as they did in Prussia and in Ireland by the end of the 1830s. Only Orthodox peoples remained, in ecclesiastical terms, very largely quiescent.

These European societies of the decades before 1848 also included substantial numbers of Jews. Whereas the tender plant of Jewish legal emancipation, which had been sown before 1789 and ripened by Napoleonic regimes, now languished under unsympathetic restoration states, the process of assimilation, at least to the extent of close involvement in financial and capitalist ventures, continued apace. Jewish influence was not necessarily reformist at all points—we now know a good deal about its support for Metternich-style governments and individuals;[7] and anti-Semitism might be unleashed *pari passu*. Yet on the whole significant symbiosis between liberals and Jews developed in antagonism to the political status quo, and sometimes already on an explicitly national platform.

The recrudescence of strong opposition by the 1840s was underpinned and stimulated by socio-economic transformation on an ever more dramatic scale, whose implications were deeply divisive. Here, as in the political sphere, changes which had commenced before the first French Revolution exerted a slow but lasting impact, notably eighteenth-century legislation to enhance the lot and broaden the horizons of the lower classes, which went with persistent population rise in the still semi-feudal countryside. An agricultural boom during the Napoleonic years was sustained in certain sectors thereafter; but the sharp rise in numbers of landless labourers and the exten-

[7] Niall Ferguson, *The World's Banker: The History of the House of Rothschild* (London, 1998), 131–43, 163–72, 246–72, 374–89, 400–13, and *passim*.

sion of commercial farming often exacerbated peasant difficulties. Meanwhile the gradual undermining of the manorial system continued, even in Russia, though official action in that direction remained very limited and piecemeal.

Villagers drifted to the towns, where industrial enterprise, with textile production as its leading sector, expanded to absorb some of this new labour force. Most spectacular of all, of course, was the new age in communications, where steamboats vied with locomotives and with breakthroughs in civil engineering as the most dazzling achievements of the day. All this presented a stark threat to traditional trades, and especially to guild organizations, still thriving across much of the Continent. It also generated elements of an industrial underclass or 'proletariat', a notion which, like that of the 'masses', gained ground from the 1820s onward. The claims made by, or on behalf of, that class became an essential ingredient in the prehistory of 1848.

Socialist ideas were at least as much a part of existing revolutionary discourse as a response to current discontent. They flourished with corresponding strength in France; but their echoes could be heard clearly enough elsewhere, and the 'spectre' of international communist subversion was readily conjured by those who stood under the spell of conspiracy theory. As percipient an observer as Tocqueville thought such ideas crucial to the collapse of France in 1848; and the *Communist Manifesto*, issued on the eve of revolution by Karl Marx and Friedrich Engels, with its precocious insights into social change, is a remarkable and revealing document of its time, however sanguine—and sanguinary—its prescriptions.[8] Not least of socialism's problems were its very varied and sometimes contradictory aspirations. Did it favour communitarian or individual property rights? And what kind of (central) authority? Were its ideals urban or rural? Democratic programmes embracing universal suffrage, republicanism, and perhaps some rights for women overlapped with socialist ones, but only up to a point.

Nevertheless, the cumulative effect of social dislocation and radical thought was to create, in larger cities across much of the continent, the preconditions for modern urban riot and for the distinc-

---

[8] Alexis de Tocqueville, *Recollections*, ed. J. P. Mayer and A. P. Kerr (Eng. trans.; London, 1970), esp. 11 ff., 61 ff. Two new and commemorative editions of the *Communist Manifesto*, one by Eric Hobsbawm, the other by David McLellan, appeared in 1998, in London and Oxford respectively.

tive ritualized forms—from barricades to the so-called 'cats' music' (*Katzenmusik*) or charivari—which accompanied it. Although rural protest remained much more widespread before 1848, it was upris- ings in the towns which made revolution possible. There, social and economic misery could more easily be channelled towards cultural and political goals.

By the mid-1840s Europe had entered the years of 'pre-revolution'. The notion must be used with care. In German central Europe 'Vormärz', 'pre-March [of 1848]', became the universal designa- tion for the period—but naturally only after the event. Widespread expectations of some kind of significant power shift were further nourished by the disastrous harvest failures and industrial slump between 1845 and 1847. Yet the incidence of collapse, when it came, proved also intensely surprising. The most appalling con- ditions, in Ireland, yielded no significant protest movement; while the most politicized urban campaign, British Chartism, proved a damp squib. On the whole the material corner had already been turned by 1848, with new technology—crops, breeds, machines, communications—on hand to lift considerably the miasma of sub- sistence existence in both town and countryside during the third quarter of the century.

We must also pay attention to the immediate triggers, which linked together spontaneous popular unrest and well-matured élite grievance in places where the political ice was already at its thinnest. We can identify a chain of the most important of them. In 1846 the wildest bout of mass savagery, a *jacquerie* in the Habsburgs' Polish province of Galicia, where peasants, summoned to support a na- tional rising, butchered hundreds of their own lords instead, sug- gested the desperate need for action against social deprivation, and the large rewards open to those who acted first. The same year saw the election as pope of Pius IX, who promptly announced a pack- age of reform proposals for his government in Rome to reconstruct one of Europe's worst tyrannies. In late 1847 religious and political tensions in the relatively free societies of the Swiss cantons spilled over into a brief conflict, the Sonderbund war, which, widely inter- preted as a contest between conservatives and liberals, led swiftly to victory for the latter. By the end of that year discontent with the limp and corrupted Orleanist regime in France began to be focused on an ostensibly innocent, but in fact cunningly seditious, series of public banquets.

The final trigger, less conspicuous, but more general in its operation and deadly in its impact on the now terminally vulnerable states of the Vormärz, was insolvency. Tax shortfalls from the years of hardship and overstretched military budgets to maintain the status quo played havoc with the finances of governments too feeble and inept to have broadened their base for revenue creation. Creditors now demanded constitutional assurances. Suddenly diets and other representative bodies regained their legitimacy, and proved to be full of critics with liberal and national agendas. Opposition came out into the open, forging links—at least temporary ones—across classes and borders, finding sustenance even within the narrow and effete establishments, and thus diminishing further the power of the latter to defend themselves.

Time had eventually run out for Metternich. His obstinate presumption that all reform must lead inexorably to revolution now, after so many years of inaction, turned into a self-fulfilling prophecy. It thus became too late to test the converse urging of Metternich's British counterpart Palmerston—a man equally concerned to preserve the international order—that the only way to stave off revolution lay in constitutional concessions.[9] Such concessions might well have saved the first main casualty of 1848, the Orleanist regime in France, where liberals were the foremost threat, with socialists in the wings. They might also have rescued the petty despotisms in Italy, where in January and February of that year the rights of subjects were still advanced in a mainly provincial context. But when the Juggernaut reached Austria too, in March, disorder was compounded, as nationalist demands overlay and challenged liberal ones, again with a potent dash of extremer ideologies in the background. Vienna, symbol of peacemaking in 1815, stood in 1848 for turmoil and violence.

In the great complexity of developments during 1848 and 1849 which this book explores lies a fascinating interplay of the particular and the general. The authors who here examine the main settings for revolutionary turbulence—France, Italy, Germany, and the Habsburg lands—all point to the importance of specific fac-

---

[9] Jasper Ridley, *Lord Palmerston* (London, 1970); Muriel E. Chamberlain, *Lord Palmerston* (Cambridge, 1987); cf. Mack Smith and Mitchell in this volume.

tors in their story. France, though its initial change of government provided a crucial impulse to others, furnished, as Geoffrey Ellis stresses, no model: its pattern of social and regional breakdown, climaxing in the June Days, the most bloodthirsty single episode in the year's saga of violence, was definitely *sui generis*. The movements in Italy, described by Denis Mack Smith, while operating within a very loose national framework, were fragmented and ill-directed, heroic and ludicrous by turns, split between republican and monarchist loyalties. Germany's reformers, by contrast, the subject of Hartmut Pogge von Strandmann's chapter, made a clear bid for national unity, but could not or would not eliminate vested interests, and found themselves driven into armed conflict over the borders of the prospective state, before being dispossessed by the regimes they thought they had superseded. That happened in the Habsburg lands too; but there diversity proved much stronger than unity, though not necessarily separatist in intention, till the imbroglio issued in civil war and protracted carnage on a scale unmatched elsewhere.

In the rest of Europe dislocation was more limited. That applied where the prime bugbears of reformers—oppressive rule and national subjugation—were either absent, because some form of broad political representation and loyalty to a common sovereign and/or fatherland had already taken root, or not yet objects of contention, for want of a sufficiently broad-based, educated, and urbanized society and articulate peasant discontent. Yet no part of the continent was immune from the effects of 1848, and that constitutes the best evidence for the revolution as equally a general, international force. Two kinds of case need to be considered.

The great powers of west and east, the United Kingdom and Russia, stood on the sidelines, but their common fear of contamination brought them back, for the first time since the days of Napoleon I, to parallel responses, if not co-ordinated ones, to the European situation. In Britain, as Leslie Mitchell shows, the constitutional-social challenge of Chartism was quelled in April with massive deployment of the volunteer militia, and the national-social one in Ireland was likewise easily seen off, helped by a substantial presence of the regular army and by the hopeless debilitation of the mass of the population. Simultaneously in Russia the government introduced frantic measures against a much-exaggerated foe—for radicals were exceedingly few—which culminated later in its notorious sadism against the Petrashevsky circle (including the young Dostoevsky); a policy which, so David Saunders argues, proved clearly counter-productive.

In other countries of Europe the impact of 1848, while sufficiently subdued or lacking in larger consequences for us to have accorded them no separate treatment here, was more positive. Switzerland had been inoculated by the events of the previous year—yet 1848 yielded its new constitution, the foundation stone of the modern confederation. In the Low Countries too, recent experience of conflicts in the 1830s helped prevent serious disturbance. French agitation quickly spilled over into Belgium, but was shrewdly contained by the authorities. A legion of Walloon workmen took the train from Paris to spread revolution at home; but their carriages were uncoupled and redirected to a branch line, where they could be easily disarmed. Thus was graphically shown how the new technology might serve conservative ends. The ruler of the Netherlands hurriedly issued a more progressive constitution to head off discontent further north.[10]

In Iberia the year 1848 was hardly worse in terms of public order than others during the chronicly troubled reign of Queen Isabella (and of Queen Maria in Portugal, for that matter). But the fall of the French monarchy unleashed fresh factional struggles in Spain within Cortes and army. There were elements of farce, as when an attempted *coup d'état* in late March had to be delayed while the would-be revolutionaries enjoyed their lunch; but periodic turbulence continued through the rest of the year, as the military government manœuvred between dissident groups on left and right, and sought to advertise its own reformist credentials. Moreover, the repressive arm of the premier, General Narvaez, was real enough. Of Narvaez it is claimed that on his deathbed, asked whether he forgave his enemies, he replied there was no need to, since he had had them all shot.[11] In that sense, at least, as Louis-Philippe might have said, he was a good republican.

March 1848 precipitated demonstrations in both Scandinavian kingdoms. In Denmark the reformist 'Casino ministry' held power

---

[10] E. H. Kossmann, *The Low Countries, 1780–1940* (Oxford, 1978), 179–205; for the train episode: Bartier in Fejtő, *1848* (see Introductory Reading), 165.

[11] Raymond Carr, *Spain, 1808–1939* (Oxford, 1966), 227–46; cf. J. Quero Molares in Fejtő, *1848* (see Introductory Reading), 143–59.

for a time, and a constitution introduced in 1849 sharply curtailed time-honoured traditions of royal authority; Sweden too, where political reform began earlier in the decade, and even its outlying and populist dependency of Norway, experienced unrest for a time.[12] But all this was soon overshadowed by the crisis over Schleswig-Holstein, the Danish-controlled provinces which the Frankfurt Parliament sought to bring under German rule. The invasion of Danish territory by Prussian troops dramatically altered the terms of the contest in the Baltic region, even though international pressure was rapidly brought to bear to halt it.

Meanwhile something similar, *mutatis mutandis*, was taking place in the Balkans. There the main theatre of strife was the Romanian principalities, whose intellectuals had been heavily influenced by French culture. In Moldavia a dissident boyar (i.e. aristocratic) group already staged an abortive putsch in March. Further south in Wallachia matters took longer to come to the boil, but radicals returning from the Parisian barricades were gradually able to mobilize support from peasants and from the urban masses of Bucharest. In June they assumed power and installed a responsible ministry, only to be riven by discord in their own ranks. Here too, local developments soon became part of the wider picture as foreign invasion produced a denouement. First Turkish and then Russian troops dispersed the revolutionaries. Those Russian troops, comparatively invisible as pacifiers of their own Ottoman backyard, where the tsar already exercised rights of protectorship, were shortly to be employed, to the consternation of many, in extinguishing the independence of Hungary.[13]

In these two cases then, Germans in Jutland and Russians along the lower Danube, foreign incursion affected the course of events in 1848, though in the first instance it carried revolutionary slogans with it, and in the second, counter-revolutionary ones. In a third

[12] Introductions in David Kirby, *The Baltic World, 1772–1993* (London, 1995), 75 ff.; W. Glyn Jones, *Denmark: A Modern History* (Beckenham, 1986), 28 ff.

[13] On the Romanian revolution, so often overlooked by western historians of 1848: John C. Campbell, *French Influence and the Rise of Roumanian Nationalism* (New York, 1971); Cornelia Bodea, *The Romanians' Struggle for Unification, 1834–49* (Bucharest, 1970); latest summary in Keith Hitchins, *The Romanians, 1774–1866* (Oxford, 1996), 231–49. There was a clear linkage between the movements among Romanians in the principalities and those within the Habsburg monarchy (discussed in ch. 8 below), though one by no means as close as is implied in Bodea's title. The second and larger Russian invasion of Hungary actually took place from Polish territory, but the point made here stands.

case, that of the Piedmontese in Habsburg northern Italy, invasion failed. Where nationalities straddled borders, some contagion was inevitable: between principalities in Germany or Italy; through the lands of the former Polish kingdom; across the porous frontiers of the northern Balkans. Yet overall it is characteristic of the year of revolution that the international order held firm. The collapse of a 'Metternichian system' within states coincided with a remarkable sturdiness of the diplomatic structures established at Vienna in 1815. Certainly those structures were buffeted; certainly the tide of affairs suggested certain future outcomes—Austrian inadequacy to continued leadership in Germany, perhaps, or a Russian bid for hegemony in the Balkans. But when international relations themselves broke down in their turn, in 1854–6, 1859–60, 1866, and 1870–1, no spectacular domestic instability resulted (save only the short-lived experiment of the Paris Commune).

Those fierce wars, in Russia, Italy, Germany, Austria, and France, which upset the Viennese balance and ushered in the later nineteenth-century pattern of European power relations, brought no domestic revolution in the lands where they were fought precisely because the enabling revolution had already taken place. Instead, they acted as midwife to a delayed realization of the main goals of 1848. With that we engage the much-misunderstood issue of the significance and consequences of the upheavals described in this volume.

The year 1848 has often been pronounced a defeat. A. J. P. Taylor once famously described it as the turning-point when Europe failed to turn.[14] Yet that is a serious misunderstanding. Although the revolutionaries—too often unfairly stigmatized by posterity as bungling conspirators or unworldly professors—were divided, dispersed, and put to the sword, and although much of the *ancien régime* appeared to be re-established in the aftermath, sometimes with an enhanced capacity for authoritarian and alien rule, there is much evidence here of immediate and lasting achievements: universal suffrage in France; constitutions in parts of Germany and

---

[14] In *The Course of German History*, 2nd edn. (London, 1951), 68. In his *Revolutions and Revolutionaries* (London, 1980), 13, Taylor admits that he took the phrase from G. M. Trevelyan. In fact, Taylor's effervescent analysis of the revolution in Fejtő, *1848* (see Introductory Reading), and elsewhere is far more positive than this aphorism would suggest.

Italy; national rights, at least on paper, even in Austria; peasant emancipation and law reform, fiscal and commercial innovation. By the time the political status quo was restored—not till 1850 or 1851 in some places—much had already been incorporated into the old-new regimes.

Far more important, however, were the delayed repercussions. The 1850s saw a strong material advance, but political and ideological stagnation over most of the continent. Within a decade the unstable post-revolutionary governments began to crumble, a process promptly catalysed by the wars just mentioned. In France the Republic was refounded, and proved remarkably durable. Germany and Italy underwent unification; and a liberal nationalism, or national liberalism, for all its limitations, marked indelibly the progress of the two integrated realms over the next half-century. Austria likewise became a constitutional state, and the claims of its national communities enjoyed extensive recognition: whereas the Magyars alone, along with the well-entrenched German Austrians, gained scope for fully autonomous development in the Dual Monarchy, the other national programmes, above all those of the Czechs and the Croats, took mature form along the lines prefigured in 1848.

Of course there was failure too in 1848. One aspect of it lay precisely in the *perception* of failure. The high ideals of liberty and fraternity seemed betrayed by the outcome, and legends of heroism and self-sacrifice were born. This applied more specially to the radical programmes of that year: the genuine revolutionaries, as opposed to those liberal and national moderates who had revolution thrust upon them, indeed gained very little, either then or over the next half-century. When the first major anniversary of 1848 was commemorated fifty years on, while the new liberal and ethnic establishments celebrated their by then increasingly threadbare accomplishments, democrats and socialists, as well as radical nationalists in the tradition of Lajos (Louis) Kossuth, the greatest tribune of the revolutionary year, still demanded the fulfilment of their goals. Fifty years further on, in 1948, it was widely thought, in hope or in apprehension, that their hour had finally struck.

These constructive memories of the revolution show its continuing power to mobilize and underpin reform projects down into our own day: Robert Gildea's analysis of them here extends to some of the numerous commemorative occasions during 1998. In France and Germany, Italy, and the various successor states to the Habsburg monarchy 1848 is still present history. At the same time its impact, as this collection also tries to demonstrate, ranged more broadly: a first manifestation of kinds of parallel and interlocking change across the face of modern Europe and beyond. From Russia, where despite—or because of—Nicholas's obscurantist response the reform of serfdom, with all its structural implications, could now be delayed no longer, that impact stretched in some degree even across the Atlantic, with the liberation of slaves in the French colonies as its most powerful material statement. White male citizens of the United States might—like many of the English—feel, as Timothy Roberts and Daniel Howe make clear, that they had perfected a polity which had nothing to learn from the ideals of 1848. Yet issues of human rights, representation, and national identity would never be the same again in the New World either, as poor Ferdinand Maximilian of Habsburg was soon to discover to his cost.

INTRODUCTORY READING

Jonathan Sperber, *The European Revolutions, 1848–51* (Cambridge, 1994), is the best available general survey, particularly good in its wide-ranging analysis of causes and consequences. A dated but still useful work, itself now part of the classic historiography of the subject as the proceedings of a high-profile conference held one hundred years after the event, is François [Ferenc] Fejtő (ed.), *The Opening of an Era, 1848: An Historical Symposium* (London, 1948). Two further accessible treatments are Jean Sigmann, *1848: The Romantic and Democratic Revolutions in Europe* (London, 1973), and Peter N. Stearns, *The Revolutions of 1848* (London, 1974).

For the French Revolution as an international affair, R. R. Palmer, *The Age of Democratic Revolutions* (2 vols.; Princeton, 1959–64), remains a controversial but comprehensive survey. The age of restoration is now helpfully introduced by Michael Broers, *Europe after Napoleon: Revolution, Reaction and Romanticism, 1814–48* (Manchester, 1996); while C. H. Church, *Europe in 1830: Revolution and Political Change* (London, 1983), does the same for the prelude to 1848. Eric Hobsbawm's *The Age of Revolution: Europe, 1789–1848* (London, 1962), remains an outstanding treatment from a left-wing perspective.

The international situation can be studied in Alan Sked (ed.), *Europe's Balance of Power, 1815–48* (London, 1979), and the later chapters of Paul W. Schroeder's sparkling but contentious *The Transformation of European*

Politics, 1763–1848 (Oxford, 1994). For the German Confederation see now Brendan Simms, *The Struggle for Mastery in Germany, 1779–1850* (London, 1998). Accessible approaches to Metternich in his European context are Constantin de Grunwald, *Metternich* (Eng. trans.; London, 1953), and Guillaume de Bertier de Sauvigny, *Metternich and his Times* (Eng. trans.; London, 1962). For the form of state control so intimately associated with Metternich, see the good introduction by Clive Emsley, *Policing and its Context, 1750–1870* (London, 1983).

Literature on the great intellectual-political movements of the day tends to be either too theoretical for these purposes or else concentrated on particular countries. But see, for liberalism: Anthony Arblaster, *The Rise and Fall of Western Liberalism* (Oxford, 1984), and the excellent case-study by James J. Sheehan, *German Liberalism in the 19th Century* (Chicago, 1978); for nationalism: John Breuilly, *Nationalism and the State* (Manchester, 1982), Mikuláš Teich and Roy Porter (ed.), *The National Question in Europe in Historical Context* (Cambridge, 1993), and Miroslav Hroch, *Social Preconditions of National Revival in Europe* (Eng. trans.; Cambridge, 1985); and for socialism the early chapters of Carl Landauer, *European Socialism: A History of Ideas and Movements from the Industrial Revolution to Hitler's Seizure of Power* (2 vols.; Berkeley and Los Angeles, 1959), vol. i, and Hobsbawm (above).

Finally, economic change is documented for the whole continent in *Documents of European Economic History. i. The Process of Industrialization, 1750–1870*, ed. S. Pollard and G. Holmes (London, 1968), and analysed for all but Britain in A. Milward and S. Saul, *The Economic Development of Continental Europe, 1780–1870* (London, 1979); while Jerome Blum, *The End of the Old Order in Rural Europe* (Princeton, 1978), is a likewise wide-ranging account of peasant conditions. See also, most recently, Mikuláš Teich and Roy Porter (ed.), *The Industrial Revolution in National Context* (Cambridge, 1996).

3

The Revolution of
1848–1849 in France

GEOFFREY ELLIS

THE French revolution of 24–6 February 1848 was not in fact the
first of the many uprisings in Europe during that momentous year.
Those troubles had started in the Italian peninsula, when a revolt
in Palermo on 12 January had quickly spread to the Neapolitan
mainland of the Kingdom of the Two Sicilies, forcing Ferdinand II
to grant a constitution on the 29th of that month. The grand duke
of Tuscany had followed suit on 17 February, and after similar
rumblings in Piedmont-Savoy, King Charles Albert was also to
grant a Statute on 4 March. All the same, these were largely regional
events, with little impact outside Italy at the time, and it would
surely be perverse of me to challenge the long-established historiographical tradition that the February Revolution set off the great
wave of uprisings or reform movements which were to engulf so
many other European states during the course of 1848–9. Indeed,
the political cataclysm in France has always provided the crux of
the great contrasting ideological reconstructions of 1848.

On the one hand, we have the image of a therapeutic chain
reaction, as it were a 'kiss of life' passed on successively among
insurgents across state frontiers, as expounded by radicals and socialists. On the analogy of the 'springtime of the peoples', this
might be called the '*Germinal*' thesis; and if that sounds rather
self-consciously Zolaesque on my part, it is meant to. On the other
hand, there is the dark pessimism of the 'virus' or 'contagion' thesis,
which conservatives have preferred. 'When France has a cold, all
Europe sneezes,' Prince Metternich once famously said, although
the immediate object of his remark had actually been the French

revolution of 1830. In that and the following year the Belgians had revolted against Dutch rule, successfully as it turned out; the Poles against Russian rule, unsuccessfully as it turned out; while in parts of central Italy the leaders of some secret societies had made a feeble and ultimately vain attempt to challenge the Habsburg dominion there. Even if the causal links between these and the July Revolution in France were clearly established, which is by no means the case, they hardly match the sheer scale of the Continental repercussions which followed the February Revolution in Paris in 1848.

I specify the revolution *in Paris*, because that is where nearly all of the most dramatic and decisive action in France then occurred. Thus, adapting Metternich's earlier metaphor, one might say that the cold which set the rest of Europe sneezing so curiously out of season in the 'springtime of the peoples' had been incubated, first and foremost, in the French capital. Yet its population of a little over one million then accounted for only 3 per cent of the French total of some 35.5 million.[1] From there, the effects spread quickly to other capital cities: to Munich (4 March), Vienna (13 March), Buda-Pest (15 March), Venice and Cracow (17 March), Milan and Berlin (18 March), where insurgents confronted the armed forces across barricades. In these early weeks at least, the state or provincial capitals *were* indeed the principal foci of revolution, and very clearly Paris *had* set the pace. Jonathan Sperber, in his detailed account of the subject, goes so far as to call Paris 'the capital city of European politics, the center of the hopes of the party of movement'.[2] The barricades and the liberty trees of Paris, it seemed, were powerful symbols for all Europe to emulate. The irony is that provincial France *was* to be directly involved in the course of events during 1848, but its main influence was to be felt rather later, and then chiefly on the side of the reaction which led to the terrible watershed of the June Days. The essential conservatism of provincial France, especially in defence of existing property rights, the foundation of the wider public perception of 'law and order', and even of the 'moral order' of society, was to prove much more than a match for the reforming visions of the socialists and radicals who had gained a brief hold on power in the Provisional Government during the early weeks of the Second Republic. In the end, it was this

[1] B. R. Mitchell, *European Historical Statistics 1750–1970*, abridged edn. (London and Basingstoke, 1978), 4, 14.
[2] Jonathan Sperber, *The European Revolutions 1848–1851* (Cambridge, 1994), 114.

same provincial conservatism, rooted much more in small-scale peasant proprietorship than in the dynamic functions of bourgeois capitalism, that was to give Louis Napoleon Bonaparte his massive popular mandate in the presidential elections of December 1848. The official census of 1846 had revealed, after all, that just over three-quarters (75.6 per cent) of the French population still lived in *communes* of less than 2,000 inhabitants.[3]

And yet, for nearly eighteen years the monarchy of Louis-Philippe had seemed to satisfy those same conservative interests of the propertied classes, especially after his appointment as foreign and effective first minister in 1840 of François Guizot, whose term of office is usually associated with a *laissez-faire* economic policy and its celebrated exhortation: *Enrichissez-vous*—'Get rich!' It is true that the franchise under the July Monarchy had been restricted to about a quarter of a million inhabitants, i.e. to the official *notables* of the legal nation, those (some 5 per cent of the adult male population) who paid 200 francs or more in direct taxes. This had excluded the mass of the peasantry, the urban artisans, and most of the *petite bourgeoisie*. Popular agitation for a wider participation in the political process had been slow to form, however, and even then had not managed to organize itself effectively until quite late in the day. The failed artisan uprisings of 1832, 1834, and 1839, provoked by immediate social and economic malaise rather than by any coherent plan to deliver Utopia, had embarrassed but not seriously threatened the Orleanist regime. Louis Napoleon's two attempted *coups d'état*, first at Strasbourg in October 1836, and then at Boulogne in August 1840, had been little more than pathetic fiascos. As late as August 1846, the government had done well in the parliamentary elections, actually increasing its support in many constituencies. Yet, only eighteen months later, it had fallen beyond recall, as both Louis-Philippe and Guizot sought exile in England. Clearly, something rather fundamental had gone wrong during the intervening period.

But what exactly? It is tempting to look for the cause of the February Revolution in precisely the wider social and economic malaise which had threatened to undermine the July Monarchy at earlier stages of its history. The evidence for such an explanation is weighty; indeed, we now know much more about the scale and economic intricacies of the problem than contemporaries did.

[3] Georges Dupeux, *French Society 1789–1970* (Eng. trans.; London, 1976), 10.

It appears, in particular, that real wages in most of the artisanal trades had actually been declining, albeit only slowly, in the order of perhaps 10 to 15 per cent according to William Sewell, between the 1820s and the 1840s.[4] More immediately, the failure of the cereal harvests of 1845 and 1846, exacerbated by the notorious potato blight, had led to a sharp rise in food prices, obliging many marginal farmers and small urban traders to take out emergency loans. Although the plentiful grain harvest of 1847 had reduced food prices somewhat during the following winter, so at least easing the immediate fear of famine, it provided little relief to those already heavily in debt, and it had even less effect on the widening business slump which had set in from the end of 1846. As for that, the same *laissez-faire* policies which had heralded the start of the great railway boom in France, along with all its speculative excesses in the stock markets, also allowed a counter-cycle to run its course, and this had the predictable repercussions on all those with outstanding loans or who desperately needed new credit. The value of stocks fell, and bankruptcies multiplied. Moreover, as the purchasing power of artisans and the poorer peasants declined, so their demand for industrial and commercial goods shrank, which in turn led the larger employers to trim their commitments in the labour markets.

This lethal combination of lower real wages and higher unemployment, especially among the industrial workforce, compounded by a general crisis in business confidence during the winter of 1847–8, might have been enough to alarm even a more far-sighted and better-prepared regime than that of Louis-Philippe. We need not doubt that the mood of the French people during that winter was generally sullen, and perhaps also ready for political change. On the other hand, the peasantry was not an active revolutionary force in February 1848. Its part in the overthrow of the king and his ministers was, at best, passive. Feudalism had been abolished long since in France, officially during the Great Revolution, and its definitive legal extinction dated from Napoleon I's Civil Code of 1804. Millions of peasants had joined the bourgeoisie in the purchase of national lands confiscated from the Church and the *émigrés* during the 1790s, and most of them were now established as a proprietary class instinctively hostile to the prospect of more radical social

---

[4] William H. Sewell, Jr., *Work and Revolution in France: The Language of Labor from the Old Regime to 1848* (Cambridge, 1980), 160.

change. If the revolution of 1848 really was a popular movement, the people whose action mattered most were urban dwellers.

Nevertheless, one may well ask whether the militancy of the urban artisans would have been enough to bring down the July Monarchy. The doctrine of inevitable 'class struggles' according to the *Communist Manifesto* of Marx and Engels had only just been born. French socialism itself had a longer pedigree—it appears that Pierre Leroux was the first to use the term 'socialist' in France, in 1832—but some of its strands were pacifist rather than revolutionary. Their ideology was communalist in an older, Utopian sense, rather than Communist in the newer sense of state ownership of the means of production and state control over the distribution of the gross national product. Étienne Cabet and his band of so-called 'Icarians' had been active in the dissemination of socialist theory during the 1840s, but their emphasis had been on the peaceful and more equitable distribution of resources through self-sufficient and self-managed producers' co-operatives, not on 'class war'. Some at least of these early socialists were also profoundly religious men, and their iconography could even depict Jesus Christ as the first, exemplary sans-culotte.[5] Most of them had a loathing of violence and bloodshed. Louis Blanc, whose *Organisation du travail* had already gone through five editions between 1840 and 1848, provided a foundation stone for another variant of French socialism, at once more *étatiste* and hierarchical in its controlling functions; but it had not yet popularized the idea of 'the right to work'. Pierre-Joseph Proudhon, too, had already gained prominence as a still more radical socialist firebrand, perhaps; but rhetorical flourishes such as 'property is theft', enunciated in the first chapter of his polemical tract *Qu'est-ce que la propriété?* of 1840, had not yet gained their later resonance among supporters. Auguste Blanqui, for his part, was another who believed that political reform alone would never be enough to deliver his brave new world, and that fundamental social reform must be the ultimate goal. We know from contemporary print-runs that all of these socialist or radical publicists of the 1830s and 1840s, and a good many others besides, were widely read at the time. Yet the plain fact remains that few urban artisans had been willing to march as foot soldiers for their several

[5] Pamela M. Pilbeam, *Socialism in France: The Future in the Past?* (Inaugural Lecture Presented at Royal Holloway, University of London, on 29 October 1996; Egham, 1997), 6.

causes much before the extraordinary events of 1848. In that sense, the February Revolution was not a carefully prepared political plot hatched by the French Left against an unpopular government. The element of calculated pre-planning was minimal. The behaviour of even the most committed revolutionaries was reactive, not pre-conceived, and they were themselves astonished by the speed with which the course of events changed and carried them along.

All this suggests that the socialist theorists and their support-ers among the artisan militants, even if they had managed to co-ordinate a plan for disciplined revolutionary action, would not have been able to unseat an established constitutional regime by their own force alone. The missing factor in my account so far is, of course, the role of the liberal and republican bourgeoisie. The bandwagon of the 'banquet campaign', a movement designed to get round the laws against political association under the guise of con-vivial gatherings, had gathered momentum as from July 1847, again most notably in Paris. Its binding principle was electoral reform, specifically universal manhood suffrage, and much of its rhetoric laid claim to the legacy of the Great Revolution of 1789, which has often been construed as the 'Rights-of-Man' legacy. In fact, it was much more radical, since the demand for universal manhood suffrage extended well beyond the distinction between 'active' and 'passive' citizens current in political practice during most of the 1790s. Nevertheless, the 'banquet campaign' was manned from the start by men of predominantly middle-class origin, and it had what proved to be a very significant foothold in the National Guard. It also had the support of the opposition press, of men like Alphonse de Lamartine and the publicists of *Le National*, whose compara-tively moderate demands for political reform gave it a wider appeal among the educated public.

The immediate trigger of the revolution of 24–6 February was Guizot's decision on the 21st to ban a mass reform banquet planned for the following day in the twelfth arrondissement of Paris. The popular demonstrations before the Chamber of Deputies which then followed next day were dispersed by a regiment of dragoons, in the event without casualties. But the wider deployment of royal troops on the 23rd, and the over-reaction of a line regiment that evening as angry crowds gathered outside the Ministry of Foreign Affairs, chanting 'à bas Guizot!', left eighty dead and wounded in the boulevard des Capucines. And so the die was cast, as popular protests multiplied on the 24th. One immediate effect was that the frustrated banqueteers joined forces with the militant artisans, with the leaders of the secret societies, and with others who supported the cause of the radical newspaper *La Réforme,* to demand a republic—a step which had not seemed inevitable or indeed even likely only a few weeks earlier. In the immediate context of the February Revolution, the rallying of many of the prominent republican and liberal bourgeoisie to the popular movement was a crushing blow to Louis-Philippe and his ministers.

So far, at least, one section of the French bourgeoisie had participated in the events which started the process that brought the monarchy down. But what of another, and economically more powerful, section: the financial, commercial, and industrial magnates, many of whom had also been associated with earlier liberal causes, and all of whom actually had the vote under the July Monarchy? Their part in forcing the abdication of the Bourbon king, Charles X, during the July Revolution of 1830 is well known. Two of them, the bankers Jacques Laffitte and Casimir Perier, had gone on to head the earliest ministries of the new reign, although neither of them lived to see the fall of Louis-Philippe. Where were their likes, the men of *la haute banque,* whom Charles Morazé has called 'les bourgeois conquérants',[6] in February 1848? The short answer is: lying low, and smarting from the deepening economic depression which had subdued them. In such dismal times, they were either unable or unwilling to offer any lifeline at which Louis-Philippe might have grasped in his hour of desperate need. We are thus left with a nice irony. The class which had been so decisive by its presence in July 1830 was most conspicuous by its absence in February 1848. It *was* to rally within a few months, and to rally fast behind the new leaders of the anxious propertied establishment; but by then it was too late for the house of Orleans.

Now, in all fairness, it must be said that Louis-Philippe never put that lifeline to the test. He made no last public appeal for the support of the capitalist bourgeoisie or, for that matter, of the propertied classes in a wider sense. He had no time to do so. Like others, he was caught wholly unawares by the sheer pace of events. His decision to dismiss Guizot on 23 February and to offer in rapid succession, first Count Louis Molé, then Adolphe Thiers (leader of the opposition), and finally Odilon Barrot as sops to the rebellious crowd gathered

[6] Charles Morazé, *Les Bourgeois conquérants: XIX* siècle (Paris, 1957).

around the Tuileries, shows how little he had gauged the public mood. Having tried in vain to rouse the National Guard to his rescue, Louis-Philippe abdicated on 24 February in favour of his grandson, the comte de Paris, and immediately left Paris for his exile abroad. His action once prompted D. W. Brogan to quip that at least Charles X had had the dignity to depart surrounded by his guards, whereas he—Louis-Philippe—took flight in a cab.[7] This, in the end, may even have seemed a fitting fate for a king whom the more brazen cartoonists of the July Monarchy had so irreverently caricatured as a plump pear. His abdication and departure left France, in effect, with a political vacuum. All the familiar constitutional structures finally collapsed on the same fateful day of 24 February, when the Chamber of Deputies, which had just proclaimed the comte de Paris king and his mother regent, was stormed and dispersed by the crowd. A Provisional Government was immediately formed, and it proceeded at once to proclaim the Republic.

At this point, we need to consider one factor in those events of 22–4 February, because it was probably the most crucial of all in bringing the monarchy down. I refer to the conduct of the Parisian National Guard, whose influence then was more decisive than that of any other section of the bourgeoisie. By choosing to desert Louis-Philippe and join the revolution at a critical moment on 23 February, the Guard ensured the immediate outcome at any rate. A number of earlier writers have observed that, by this particular intervention, it was acting *un*typically. It had rallied, after all, to the defence of the July Monarchy several times during the preceding eighteen years, and some might well have expected it to do so again. Its participation in the February Revolution was therefore unusually important, especially as the units of the regular army with which Marshal Bugeaud had tried so ineffectually to destroy the barricades were quickly withdrawn after the fatal shootings on the 23rd. Its support, in the short term at any rate, gave the revolutionaries the physical power they needed to act in the vacuum left by the king's abdication.

The Provisional Government had, then, assumed office through physical power and a presumptive popular mandate in Paris, rather than by any clearly expressed electoral wish in France as a whole.

[7] D. W. Brogan, *The French Nation from Napoleon to Pétain 1814–1940*, new edn. (London, 1961), 92.

In those heady days of late February 1848, however, few knew what its reform programme would be. Ironically perhaps, the earliest signs of the trouble ahead may be found in the composition of the Provisional Government itself. It was from the start an uneasy coalition of disparate parliamentary deputies and journalists. Of its eleven members chosen by popular acclaim on or shortly after 24 February, only four were committed radical socialists; the other seven were less extreme republicans. Thus, in the former camp there were Louis Blanc, Ferdinand Flocon, Alexandre Ledru-Rollin, and Albert (alias Alexandre Martin), who liked to call himself 'the worker'—all closely associated with *La Réforme*. Albert alone was of genuine working-class origin, the only member who conceivably matched the old prototype of a revolutionary sans-culotte. In the other camp were Lamartine, François Arago, Isaac Crémieux, Dupont de l'Eure, Pierre Marie, Garnier-Pagès, and Armand Marrast. The political roots of most of these latter lay in the liberal press, more particularly in *Le National*, and it would not be unfair to say that some (Arago, Crémieux, Garnier-Pagès, Marie, and Marrast) had discovered their republican credentials by circumstantial logic rather than through long-standing conviction. All were of respectable bourgeois stock, conscious of their duty to secure the principles of the Great Revolution, but also to ensure that existing property rights were not indiscriminately violated. Lamartine, indeed, the new minister for foreign affairs, gained an important symbolical victory on 25 February when he argued successfully for the retention of the tricolour as the national flag, rather than the Red Flag, which his socialist colleagues would have preferred—though in a token concession to the champions of *La Réforme* the Provisional Government did allow a red rosette to be attached to the tricolour standard.

It should also be stressed that such differing visions of reform among the men of the Provisional Government had been conceived in political opposition. None of them had any direct experience of governmental office; yet now they had to act as legislators at the very centre of French politics, and take public responsibility for their actions. As Pamela Pilbeam has recently reminded us, the Second Republic marked 'the first occasion in the world when socialists intervened in national politics . . . [It] offered the first opportunity for socialists peacefully to influence public affairs.'[8] Undaunted

[8] Pilbeam, *Socialism in France*, 3, 9.

by its lack of a prepared or coherent legislative programme, the Provisional Government nevertheless immediately proceeded to issue a series of decrees which, potentially at least, would have enormous social consequences. It seemed determined, if I might borrow a topical phrase, to 'hit the ground running'. One reason for its sense of urgency was the belief, shared by all its members, that 1830 had been 'une révolution escamotée', a revolution smuggled away from them by reactionary forces, as if by malign sleight-of-hand, and that any such trickery must not be allowed to happen again.

The government therefore acted quickly in proclaiming the principles of 'the right to work' and of 'the organization of work' on 25 February, thus anticipating the creation of the National Workshops (*ateliers nationaux*) which it decreed on the following day. On the 26th, again, in formally announcing its own appointment to the public, it roundly declared that 'in the name of the French people, Monarchy, under every form, is abolished without possibility of return'.[9] On 28 February it set up the Luxembourg Commission under the presidency of Louis Blanc, assisted by Albert, with a wide-ranging brief over all aspects of labour relations. On 2 March the Commission duly reduced the working day from eleven to ten hours in Paris, and from twelve to eleven hours in the provinces. In the event, it had neither the authority nor the resources to enforce such measures effectively, but at least its short life as one of the busiest and most interfering 'quangos' in western European history had started in earnest. On 2 March also the Provisional Government fulfilled the demand of the earlier 'banquet campaign' by decreeing universal manhood suffrage for all aged 21 years and above, which at a stroke increased the potential electorate to around eight million. Moreover, during its first month in power it proceeded to abolish subcontracting (*marchandage*), so widely resented by artisans, especially when such work was put out to cheap female labour. It also proclaimed the full freedom of the press and of political association, and abolished the death penalty for alleged political offences.

For all of these early acts, the Provisional Government could count on the support of the artisan militants, and it was also encouraged by the great proliferation of socialist and radical clubs and societies around that time. According to Roger Price, for example,

[9] As cited in Lord Elton, *The Revolutionary Idea in France 1789–1871* (London, 1959), 137–8.

the political clubs in Paris had some 100,000 members at their peak, and workers' associations around 40,000.[10] Blanqui's Société Républicaine Centrale and Armand Barbès's Club de la Révolution were among the most prominent, and also the most extreme; but on 20 March 1848 delegates from some sixty clubs in Paris agreed to found an umbrella Club des Clubs which, it is claimed, was eventually able to send from 300 to 500 organizers out into the provinces. At the same time, major demonstrations in Paris, like that of 17 March, could raise crowds of between 150,000 and 200,000 strong, and the later ones of 16 April and 15 May were to be on much the same scale.[11] In the face of such popular pressure on the Provisional Government to prosecute a policy of radical social reform, what could the propertied élites do? In the early weeks, at any rate, they sensibly chose the course of resigned circumspection. Some of their more prominent and affluent members, fearful for their possessions and perhaps even for their lives, apparently went even further in their prudential gestures of sympathy for the new government. Alexis de Tocqueville, one celebrated observer of those events, writing his *Souvenirs* in 1850–1 with the benefit of both hindsight and irony, recalled that earlier phase of the revolution in the following terms:

A very general effort [was made] to placate the new master. Great landowners liked to recall that they had always been hostile to the bourgeois class and favourable to the people: and the bourgeois themselves remembered with a certain pride how their fathers had been workmen, and when, owing to the inevitable obscurity of genealogies, they could not trace themselves back to a workman who had actually worked with his hands, they would at least attempt to descend from a ne'er-do-well who had made his fortune for himself. In fact the desire for the publicity of such details was as great as a little while ago it would have been for their concealment. . . . Just now everyone did his best to make what he could out of any black sheep the family possessed. Any cousin or brother or son one might be lucky enough to own who had ruined himself by his excesses was well on the way to succeed; while if he had contrived to win notoriety by some extravagant theory or other there was no height to which he might not aspire. The majority of the commissaries and sub-commissaries of the government were persons of this sort.[12]

[10] Roger Price, *The Revolutions of 1848* (Basingstoke and London, 1988), 46.

[11] Ibid. 54.

[12] *Souvenirs de Alexis de Tocqueville publiés par le comte de Tocqueville* (Paris, 1893), 115–16; translation as cited in Elton, *Revolutionary Idea in France*, 138–9.

Even if allowance is made for Tocqueville's lavish dose of exaggeration here, such a situation could not last, especially when the Provisional Government was called upon to devise a financial policy to pay for its social programme, and some two years into a major economic depression at that. The Paris Bourse had closed at the start of the reform demonstrations on 22 February, in an attempt to arrest the sudden fall in the value of stocks, which for a time paralysed all business. The gold reserves of the Bank of France sank so sharply that, on 1 March, all dealings in paper money had to be suspended.[13] It is, then, hardly surprising that when the Bourse reopened on 7 March, business confidence remained decidedly shaky. It was not helped by a decree of 15 March which declared the enforced nominal value (*cours forcé*) of notes issued by the Bank, as well as the issue of new notes in smaller denominations. Soon afterwards, the Provisional Government acted still more provocatively, first by decreeing an additional direct tax of 45 centimes on 16 March, to help meet its burgeoning costs, and then by placing two private railway companies under state sequestration on 4 April. The reaction among those of the propertied classes brave enough to show it was predictably hostile, and they were barely appeased by a further series of measures in April which abolished or reduced several of the old and unpopular indirect taxes. Many among the peasantry, for their part, saw the spectre of a new socialist agrarian law looming before them, and openly denounced the so-called *partageux*—those who advocated a wholesale redistribution of the land in France. They could see only a sinister motive behind the cull of former prefects, subprefects, and a good many mayors, which the commissaries of the Provisional Government were carrying out with some vigour.

In spite of all these bold measures, nothing could alter the fact that the life of the Provisional Government was, after all, intended to be *provisional*, pending elections to a new National Constituent Assembly. Yet here, too, it acted provocatively. On 17 March it summarily announced that the elections, initially decreed for 9 April, would be postponed for a fortnight to the 23rd of that month. Albert it was who argued most strongly for the postponement, backed by workers' demonstrations, as well as by Blanqui and other spokesmen of the Parisian clubs, on the official pretext that the registers would not otherwise be ready in time. In truth, they were more

[13] J. P. T. Bury, *France 1814–1940* (London, 1978), 72.

concerned about the slowness of republican principles to pene-
trate the mass of the electorate, and more especially the newly enfranchised peasant voters, notwithstanding the education drive of
Ledru-Rollin, minister of the interior. Just how that shortcoming
could be made good in a mere two weeks is one of the mysteries of
their reasoning at the time. When the elections *were* finally held, the
results (even in Paris) were a bitter disappointment to the socialist
leaders. Some 84 per cent of the enlarged electorate had actually
voted, the vast majority of them for the first time. Of the 876 members then returned, only about one hundred can be identified as
extreme radicals or socialists. Most of the others were moderate republicans, at best, and they included a sizeable majority of former
Orleanists, Legitimists, and other conservatives, all more reminis-
cent of the *notables* who had served under the July Monarchy, and
who were plainly opposed to any prospect of a socialist Republic.[14]

The first meeting of the Constituent Assembly, thus composed,
took place on 4 May, when it proceeded to an official proclamation
of the Republic. Soon afterwards (9–10 May) it elected an Executive Commission of five, which conspicuously excluded Blanc and
Albert, and which quickly exercised its power to nominate new
ministers, so bringing the Provisional Government officially to an
end. The appointment of General Cavaignac as war minister on
17 May was particularly portentous, and it was no doubt immediately influenced by the violent events of the 15th, when Blanqui, Albert, Barbès, and François Raspail had led a large popular
demonstration to the Assembly, briefly invading it in their attempt
to seize control of power and proclaim a Socialist Provisional Government. The insurgents were dispersed, significantly by the National Guard, assisted on this occasion by the new *gardes mobiles*
raised under an earlier decree of 26 February. The leaders named
above were among those arrested and prosecuted, as the Guard
proceeded easily enough to reoccupy the Hôtel de Ville. In other
ways, too, that particular *journée* proved a serious reverse for the
radical diehards. It marked the eruption of much more widespread
and violent counter-revolutionary disturbances in Paris and elsewhere during the following days. The mood among most of the
new political leaders had clearly hardened, so that when Duclerc,
the minister of finances, proposed the nationalization of all the railways on 17 May, he found the Assembly circumspect and inclined

[14] Ibid. 77.

to stall. Indeed, during a prolonged debate which began on 20 May, more and more deputies openly questioned the current operations and the future of the National Workshops, the flagship of the Provisional Government's social programme.

This whole issue was, and in some ways still is, a curiously sensitive one, and it has long had a central place in the socialist martyrology of the French Left. With hindsight, it is easy enough to understand why the National Workshops have had such a generally bad press from historians over the past 150 years, and in our turn to condemn them as a misconceived exercise in useless and costly labour. First launched in the immediate euphoria of the February Revolution, and endlessly debated at the meetings of the Luxembourg Commission, the scheme progressed rapidly. Estimates of its numbers have varied enormously over the years, but at its height in May–June 1848 it may have employed up to 100,000 or more Parisian artisans and poorer industrial workers who had been laid off during the depression. The work was menial and humiliating, concentrated mainly on the rather pointless levelling of the Champ de Mars at a rate of two francs per worker per day, later reduced to one franc. Such employment of labour seemed altogether unjustifiable to those whose increased taxes were used to foot the bill. And yet that is not how the workers themselves and their socialist leaders saw things at the time. Their argument that all honest labour has its own dignity, however minimal its eventual production in strictly economic terms, was a profoundly moral one. It owed something to the idealism of Marx's early thought, and something also to the Utopian and humanitarian theories of earlier French socialists like Fourier and Cabet.

Oddly enough, in view of Louis Blanc's central position on the Luxembourg Commission, the National Workshops did not in practice closely resemble the 'social workshops' (*ateliers sociaux*) he had advocated in his *Organisation du travail*. He was not himself directly involved in their practical organization, which fell mainly to Pierre Marie and Émile Thomas. The major difficulty, however, was that the National Workshops were not self-financing. Since their costs were met wholly from public funds, they could not be construed as an honourable variant of the producers' co-operatives advocated by earlier socialists. They were, in effect, a larger version of the *ateliers de charité* or *chantiers de charité* already quite familiar in France in times of economic hardship,[15] and a number of prominent figures at the time indeed argued the case for them in terms of public utility. Far better, it was said, that 100,000 unemployed labourers should be taken on by the state to do honest work than be left idle to endanger the public peace. Even Lamartine defended this argument for social control by such means, provided the National Workshops were treated as a temporary expedient to relieve unemployment, rather than as an institutionalized form of state interventionism, i.e. a therapeutic instrument for social betterment, in a more fundamental sense. In his self-justificatory history of the 1848 revolution, published in the following year, he referred to 'this temporary army of national workshops' as 'a sacred and indispensable alms-giving [*aumône*] of the State, whose honour lay in the semblance of work', and as 'only a short-term expedient, terrible but necessary'.[16] Marie, for his part, apparently saw the whole scheme as a kind of public insurance against more extreme socialist demands, one that would actually undermine the position of Ledru-Rollin and other radicals, and boost business confidence![17]

What is not in doubt is that the Assembly's decree of 21 June to wind up the National Workshops, offering younger recruits the alternative option of enlistment in the army, and the others that of employment in the provinces, immediately provoked an extremely hostile workers' demonstration on the following day. This in turn led directly to the ferocious street fighting and bloodshed of the 23rd to the 26th, the notorious 'June Days', in which an estimated total of between 40,000 and 50,000 insurgents may have been involved on the barricades.[18] Some 1,500 combatants on both sides died in the fighting, and another 3,000 captured insurgents were summarily shot. A further 12,000 were arrested, of whom 4,500 were eventually deported, mostly to Algeria.[19] According to Tocqueville's later account of the tragic episode, this was

not the work of a group of conspirators, but the rising of one part of the population against the other. Women took part in it as much as men. . . . [T]hey hoped for victory to ease the lot of their husbands, and help to

---

[15] Thomas R. Christofferson, 'The French National Workshops of 1848: The View from the Provinces', *French Historical Studies*, 11 (1980), 505–20 at 505.
[16] A. de Lamartine, *Histoire de la révolution de 1848* (2 vols.; Paris, 1849), ii. 121–3.
[17] Ibid. ii. 120.   [18] Price, *Revolutions of 1848*, 59.
[19] Sperber, *European Revolutions*, 199.

bring up their children. . . . It was not a political struggle . . . but class war, a kind of slave-war.[20]

Karl Marx, for very different reasons, writing at the time in his *Neue Rheinische Zeitung* of Cologne, and again later in two celebrated tracts, construed the conflict as an incipient 'class struggle' between the exploited industrial proletariat and the capitalist bourgeoisie, along with all its minions.[21] The June Days, he claimed, amounted to nothing less than '*civil war*, civil war in its most terrible form, the war between labour and capital', which marked the victory (if only provisional) of '*bourgeois terrorism*'.[22] Returning to the subject a few years later, he described the June insurrection as 'the most significant event in the history of European civil wars'.[23]

We need to be wary here. More recent studies clearly indicate that the social origins of the combatants of the June Days do not fit any neat 'class model'. In reality, worker fought worker, republican fought republican, and all believed that they had right on their side. Modern studies also confirm that the insurgents were not in any sense an assorted rabble of rootless malcontents. Roger Price, for instance, in a detailed analysis of some 11,600 of those arrested, and whose professions can be identified, shows that the majority were skilled workers, and that they came mainly from the small-scale artisanal trades, most notably building, metalwork, clothing and shoes, and furniture.[24] They had some support from the poorer elements of the National Guard, chiefly in the eastern *quartiers* of Paris, but the essential spontaneity of their uprising had left no time for co-ordinated leadership or mass organization. Most of the better-off National Guardsmen fought with Cavaignac's regular army of some 25,000, as did the 15,000 *gardes mobiles*, in the latter case because (as Price suggests) their younger members still depended on the state for their pay, and had not yet been inte-

[20] *Souvenirs de Tocqueville*, 208–9; translation as cited in Bury, *France 1814–1940*, 79.
[21] Karl Marx, *The Class Struggles in France: 1848 to 1850* (1850), and *The Eighteenth Brumaire of Louis Bonaparte* (1852).
[22] Marx, *Class Struggles in France*, quoting his own immediate commentary in *Neue Rheinische Zeitung* (29 June 1848); translation as cited in Eugene Kamenka (ed.), *The Portable Karl Marx* (Harmondsworth, 1983), 283, 285.
[23] Marx, *Eighteenth Brumaire*; translation as cited in Kamenka, *Portable Karl Marx*, 295.
[24] Roger Price, *The French Second Republic: A Social History* (London, 1972), 165; reproduced in his *Revolutions of 1848*, 60.

grated into craft and neighbourhood communities.[25] The ranks of the counter-revolutionaries were swelled by large numbers of Parisian bourgeois, now willing to be counted on the streets, as they had not been in February. Equally significant, as eyewitness accounts testify, thousands of landowners from provincial France (apparently including peasants of only modest wealth) poured into the capital by train to play their part in what they saw as the defence of the propertied order, while massive reinforcements of troops and National Guards from the provinces were transported to Paris by the same means. It was the first occasion in French history on which the railways, a service relatively new to the general public, was used on such a scale for overtly military purposes.

The immediate political sequel to those troubles had been anticipated, in a sense, at their onset. The Executive Commission of the Constituent Assembly had resigned on 24 June, thus enabling General Cavaignac, now acting in his capacity as chief of the executive power, to apply his chosen physical remedy without any direct governmental or wider parliamentary restraint. His reward was to be named as President of the Council on 28 June, and he promptly formed a new ministry. Later that day his government officially suppressed the National Workshops and also withdrew the earlier proposal for the nationalization of the railways. On 28 July a decree was issued to restrict the activities of the clubs, and, logically enough, similar decrees affecting the freedom of the press followed on 9–11 August. At the end of that month Louis Blanc, with all his favourite projects now scuppered, and no doubt fearing for his own freedom as the hammer of the Assembly's special commission of inquiry began to fall, decided on exile. He took refuge in that universal haven of fallen French kings and ministers, an Austrian chancellor, a Prussian heir apparent, and dangerous socialist revolutionaries: England. The Luxembourg Commission had been disbanded some three months earlier, following the *journée* of 15 May, and after several days of debate the Assembly proceeded on 9 September to restore the twelve-hour working day.

---

[25] Id., *Revolutions of 1848*, 61. The estimated figures for the regular army and the *gardes mobiles* are from Frederick A. de Luna, 'June Days', in Edgar Leon Newman and Robert Lawrence Simpson (eds.), *Historical Dictionary of France from the 1815 Restoration to the Second Empire* (Westport, Conn., 1987), 545–8 at 546.

It was Louis Napoleon Bonaparte who was ultimately to be the main beneficiary of the politics of reaction which followed the June Days. In October 1838, between the failure of his madcap coups of 1836 and 1840, he too had taken refuge in the universal haven across the Channel, where his polemical tract, *Des idées napoléoniennes*, was first published the following year. It was a curious hybrid of authoritarian platitudes and populist rhetoric. As an apology for popular Bonapartism, it has always seemed to me a rather simplistic document, and of course it was to have no discernible influence on the February Revolution. Indeed, returning once again to England in May 1846 after escaping from the fortress of Ham in Picardy, to which he had been condemned for life by the Chamber of Peers following his abortive conspiracy nearly six years earlier, Louis Napoleon had been crying like a voice in the wilderness. A very brief attempt to return to France at the end of February 1848 had ended rather ignominiously, when the revolutionary leaders asked him to leave the country forthwith. Back in England, he had kept his hand in at some deft police work, and in April that year had served as a special constable at the Chartist demonstrations in Trafalgar Square. Then, however, his fortunes had taken a turn for the better. On 4 June he successfully contested a seat in the complementary elections to the Constituent Assembly, when (incidentally) Proudhon, Thiers, and Victor Hugo were also returned. Having decided not to take up his seat, perhaps chiefly because of his earlier rebuff, he could disclaim any personal involvement in the horrors of the June Days. And so, in due course, he was able to answer his critics in the most convincing way possible. On 17 September he topped the poll in by-elections to the Constituent Assembly, and later that month made a dramatic return to Paris, presenting himself in due course as a presidential candidate.

The Assembly's long-running debate on the new Constitution had begun on 4 September. It was briefly interrupted on 15 October, when a recast government, the so-called 'Ministry of Order', was formed. Its first task was to oversee the last phase of the debate on the Constitution, which was finally voted by the Assembly on 4 November. Under the new provisions, the Republic was to have a president, elected by universal manhood suffrage for a single and maximum term of four years, whose functions were intended to strengthen the executive arm of the state, for instance through his power to appoint and dismiss ministers. There was also to be a unicameral Legislative Assembly of 750 members, similarly elected by universal manhood suffrage. After the formal promulgation of the Constitution on 21 November, the presidential elections were duly held (10 December) and proved a resounding triumph for Louis Napoleon. He was returned with more than 5.4 million votes (nearly 75 per cent of the total poll), easily eclipsing his nearest rival, Cavaignac, whose 1.4 million votes (a little over 19 per cent of the poll) came as a great surprise to many who had considered him the likely winner. Of the other four candidates, Ledru-Rollin, representing his new democratic-socialist alliance formed in November, known officially as Solidarité Républicaine, and informally as the neo-Jacobin 'Mountain', did best with rather fewer than 400,000 votes. He was therefore well ahead of Raspail, also standing for the radical Left, who had 37,000 votes; but Lamartine, now presenting himself as a liberal republican, could manage no more than 8,000, and Changarnier even fewer. Detailed modern analyses of these results show that Louis Napoleon had found support across the whole country, and in particular had more or less engrossed the peasant vote, which was in large part also a Catholic vote.[26] His well-targeted propaganda, which emphasized the need for national unity through strong government, had also won over a large number of voters among the conservative 'Party of Order' and urban workers alike.

In sum, then, the year which had begun with the overthrow of the monarchy ended with a Republic headed by a populist president, and a Bonaparte at that. None of the members of the former Provisional Government was allowed to serve in his new administration, and none of their radical social reforms survived into the new year. All that really remained of the great expectations of the February revolutionaries was the Republic itself, which in all essentials was no longer their republic, and universal manhood suffrage, which had largely rejected them in April, and had done so again even more massively in December. Was this, then, another 'révolution escamotée'? For many of the frustrated socialist revolutionaries, that is precisely what it was. Proudhon, for instance, lamenting the outcome some two years later in his *Confessions*, acknowledged: 'Yes, we have been beaten and humiliated. We have

---

[26] A. J. Tudesq, *L'Élection présidentielle de Louis Napoléon Bonaparte, 10 décembre 1848* (Paris, 1965), 252; Maurice Agulhon, *1848 ou l'apprentissage de la république 1848–1852* (Paris, 1973), 85–7.

all been scattered, imprisoned, disarmed and gagged. The fate of European democracy has slipped from our hands—from the hands of the people—into those of the Praetorian Guard.'[27]

This is not the place to recount the subsequent history of the Second Republic in France. But I should, just briefly, note two developments which have an obvious bearing on what has gone before. The first point is that the presidential elections did not altogether snuff out the political ambitions and activities of the French Left during the years which immediately followed. In the elections of May 1849 to the new Legislative Assembly, while the conservative candidates (Bonapartists, Orleanists, and Legitimists) were again returned with a substantial majority, those who now threw in their lot with Solidarité Républicaine did surprisingly well. They practically doubled the number of seats gained by their predecessors in April 1848. Then, secondly, as tougher new laws were introduced to ban their political associations, especially after the street demonstrations of 13 June 1849 against Louis Napoleon's military intervention to put down the short-lived Roman Republic, they shifted their main attention from Paris to the provinces. There, most commonly in the form of secret societies, they aimed to broaden their appeal to artisans and rural smallholders. The revolutionary rhetoric of these *démocrates-socialistes*, or *démoc-socs* as they came to be known, was thus effectively targeted, and they made particular headway in villages and small towns of central and south-eastern France. *They* were to mobilize the last resurgence of the mid-century revolution against Louis Napoleon's *coup d'état* of 2 December 1851, in contrast to the rather muted response that month in Paris and the other large cities of France, where the president's military presence was then much more intrusive. Although they were again defeated, and resoundingly so, in the longer term their legacy to French socialism allowed it to live on and fight another day.[28]

---

[27] P.-J. Proudhon, *Les Confessions d'un révolutionnaire pour servir à l'histoire de la révolution de février* (Paris, 1850), 1–2; translation as cited in François Fejtö, 'Conclusion', in id. (ed.), *The Opening of an Era: 1848. An Historical Symposium* (London, 1948), 414–27 at 414.

[28] Sperber, *European Revolutions*, 237–8; John M. Merriman, *The Agony of the Republic: The Repression of the Left in Revolutionary France 1848–1851* (New Haven, 1978); Ted W. Margadant, *French Peasants in Revolt: The Insurrection of 1851* (Princeton, 1979).

What, in conclusion, were the general themes running through events during 1848–9 in France, and how may they be related to the other European revolutions and counter-revolutions of those years? I began by alluding to the contrasting '*Germinal*' and 'virus' or 'contagion' theses of that whole episode, so familiar in the old and even in some of the more recent textbooks. One connotation here is the notion that the French then played the role of an 'exemplary' people, that they were somehow a 'model' for other peoples to follow, as they had purportedly been in 1789 and 1830—*la Grande Nation*, whose political conflicts had a habit of spilling out over all the surrounding nations. And yet, my own perception of the 1848 revolution in France, like those of 1789 and 1830, stresses rather more its essential *Frenchness*. If one thinks of the most familiar generic terms which have traditionally subsumed the main political and social movements in Europe around that time—nationalism, internationalism, Romanticism, liberalism, republicanism, reformism, democracy, secularism, socialism, and even Communism—it soon becomes clear that France was not a singular model for other states; nor did her own experience of those movements match any other general stereotype. There was no 'Identikit' revolution anywhere in 1848 to serve as a blueprint for all Europe to emulate.

In France, for example, nationalism was hardly an issue at all that year. The country had evolved to the status of a nation-state, with sovereign institutions (whether monarchical, republican, or imperial) at least from the time of the Great Revolution. The ideological warriors of the First Republic had naturalized a brave new concept of *la Patrie*, a classic universalist version of *la Grande Nation*, and even offered it for export during the 1790s; but much of Europe had not willingly espoused it during the Revolutionary and Napoleonic wars. In fact, those wars are often seen as an early training ground for nationalist resistance in other states. French nationalism after 1815 lived on, in a sense, in the fanciful and often sentimental recollection of *la gloire* and *la grandeur* of the imperial past, most notably in the Napoleonic legend, and this was certainly a factor in explaining Louis Napoleon's popular appeal in December 1848. Even then, for what it was, the legend tended to look back, not ahead. It contributed its part to the nostalgic embellishments of European Romanticism, especially after the publication of the *Mémorial de Sainte-Hélène* by Count de Las Cases in 1823, but it never provided more than a partial definition of French national identity.

French dynasticism, again, was more or less a dead issue in 1848. Even in its attenuated form of legitimism, it had almost nothing to do with the defence of the 'Metternich system' in Continental Europe. Louis Napoleon could lay even less claim to dynastic legitimacy than Louis-Philippe might have done, which is why he chose to play the trump card of his popular mandate instead. None of this even remotely compared with the ultimately successful re-establishment of Hohenzollern dynastic authority in Prussia (which, as far as I know, faced very little formal challenge there in any case), of Habsburg authority over the Austrian Empire, or of Bourbon authority over Naples and Sicily. The old nobility had lost their traditional preponderance in the officer corps of the French army during the Great Revolution and under Napoleon I; and, in the event, the *émigré* commanders had enjoyed only a temporary return to favour during the Bourbon Restoration of 1815–30. General Cavaignac, for instance, the strong man of the June Days, was the son of an old Jacobin family, a commoner and a republican through and through. His intervention on behalf of the propertied classes was a military, political, and social act, not a dynastic one. It marked the defence of the social order which had emerged from the Great Revolution, in other words of the 'new regime' in France, against the threat of what might be called a 'new, new regime'. In that respect at least, it was not politically analogous to the military action of, say, General Windischgrätz (a prince) in Prague (June 1848) and Vienna (October 1848), or of General Radetzky (a count) in the recapture of Milan (August 1848), or of the Russian General Paskevich (a prince) at the capitulation of the Hungarian revolutionaries at Világos (August 1849).

What, next, of the liberal movement? Here, too, we need to see the major differences between those French liberals who (like Thiers) had been prepared to work within a reformed and moderate monarchical framework and others who (like Lamartine) were republicans at heart. The latter may well have had something in common with the leaders of the radical republican movements in Italy; but how different they were from the liberals of the Frankfurt Parliament, to cite just one comparison. Whereas their German counterparts, who never actually held real political power, are usually seen as great humanitarian idealists, anxious to effect their visions of reform within existing dynastic structures, whether on a *kleindeutsch* or *großdeutsch* basis, the French liberal republicans of 1848 found their humanitarian ideals quickly evaporating under the sheer pressures of political office. Those ideals, conceived in opposition during the Restoration and the July Monarchy, left them stranded after only a few months of power. The liberal republicans lacked the ability to control the reform engine they had launched, and, in the eyes of the popular movement, they were overtaken by the more radical socialist leaders, who accused them of ideological betrayal.

Ironically, the threat of a 'new, new regime' turned Lamartine and his like-minded colleagues in the Provisional Government into 'trimmers' of a sort, political chameleons who went far enough in one direction to alarm the reconstituted conservative alliance, but not far enough to keep the radical socialists on their side. Their dismal showing in the presidential elections was a popular judgement on their principles, as well as on themselves. Tocqueville used the word 'tergiversations' to describe Lamartine's political conduct at the height of his fame, and added that he had 'never known a less sincere spirit, nor one which had a more complete scorn for the truth'.[29] For almost the exactly opposite reasons, Alexander Herzen, the *émigré* Russian radical, who was a personal witness to the events of 1848 in Paris and lamented the ultimate debacle of the revolution, soon afterwards expressed his more general contempt for the liberal leaders in the following terms:

They want freedom and even a republic provided that it is confined to their own cultivated circle. Beyond the limits of their moderate circle they become conservatives. . . . And it is in this world of logomachy, discord, irreconcilable contradictions, that these futile men wished, without changing it, to achieve their *pia desideria* of liberty, equality and fraternity.[30]

The future of the French liberals was to lie in more pragmatic 'trimming' and, eventually, when republican forms at last took deeper root, in the revolving ministries of 'Opportunist' politics during the last two decades of the century.

As for the much-vaunted internationalism of the 1848 revolutionaries, of the camaraderie of shared assumptions and common goals which transcended state frontiers, very little ultimately came of it. The popular clubs in Paris at the height of their agitation fol-

---

[29] *Souvenirs de Tocqueville*, 162, 164, 171.
[30] Alexander Herzen, *From the Other Shore* (Eng. trans.; London, 1956), 59, 61.

lowing the February Revolution liked to think of themselves as the central source of a greater European and even of a wider world conscience. They passed a good many resolutions expressing support for the revolutionary or reform movements in other states. The official pretext for Blanqui's invasion of the Constituent Assembly on 15 May 1848, for example, was to protest against the suppression of the Polish rebels by the Prussian army in the Grand Duchy of Posen that same month. Such declarations of international fraternity were reinforced by a new flowering of women's clubs in France, albeit on a smaller scale, in which the principles of revolutionary sorority were also expressed in universalist terms. The enthusiasm of the brothers and sisters waned soon enough, however, and after the June Days it carried even less conviction. The net result was that the February revolutionaries did not make much physical contribution to the revolutions elsewhere, while their 'moral' influence declined noticeably after their own defeat in France. The general European war which so many in 1848–9 believed was inevitable did *not* actually occur.

Revolutionary socialism, finally: how important was its immediate impact in France, and how significant was its legacy for the future? We can immediately dismiss the old canard that the French socialists of 1848 were consumed by a wholly secular—even atheistic—ideology. They were not, for the most part, conspicuously irreligious, antireligious, or indeed even anticlerical. Their policies included nothing which might be compared with the so-called 'de-Christianization' campaign at the height of the Terror in 1793–4. Even the leaders of their extreme wing, as represented by the standard-bearers of Marx and Engels, and of the well-timed *Communist Manifesto*, did not advocate the destruction of churches or the slaughter of priests. What the *Manifesto* did give French socialists was a new language of 'class war', also internationalist, which exhorted working men of all countries to unite, since they had nothing to lose but their chains, and a world to win.

Such rhetoric quickly gained currency in the popular clubs, but the strong reaction it provoked had a very much wider support among the general public. Revolutionary socialism soon became too closely identified with political subversion and with dangerous threats to the propertied order. It could not survive the carnage of the June Days intact. It was to revive, of course, in the extraordinary episode of the Paris Commune of 1871, in a metropolitan hothouse atmosphere highly charged by French military defeat; but on that occasion its hold on power lasted no longer. The Commune, too, was cut down by home military forces, with many more casualties than in June 1848. Once again the brutal lesson was learnt that Paris would not be allowed to dictate a socialist future for the rest of France, nor indeed to secede from the nation in pursuit of that cause for itself.

One final observation. Major historical events like the revolutions of 1848–9 are often regarded as instructive by those who later mark their centenaries, bicentenaries, or other similar anniversaries. On such occasions each generation tends in its turn to extract a historical significance relevant to its own age. 'Lessons for our time': the genre is a familiar one. I think in particular of the important gatherings fifty years ago which marked the centenary of 1848, when our present subject was so often paraded as an exemplary analogy in the tendentious didacticism of cold-war politics. Much more recently still, that same analogy seemed no less portentous to those who published commentaries on the great wave of revolutions and liberation movements which spread across eastern Europe in 1989. If such comparisons were often ingenious, they were also just as often anachronistic, as Robert Gildea shows later in the present collection. That caveat must preface my own particular contribution to the genre, which now follows.

Is there, then, any 'lesson' to be drawn from the experience of 1848 in France which could possibly have relevance today? I think I see one. The Second Republic lasted for a little under five years, if we include the 'unconstitutional' year that elapsed between Louis Napoleon's *coup d'état* and the official proclamation on 2 December 1852 of the Second Empire, which itself lasted for nearly eighteen years. There followed a Third Republic; but in its early years only a few understood what sort of republic it was going to be. Adolphe Thiers, its first named 'president', by the grace of the National Assembly, was one of them. 'The Republic will be conservative or there will be no republic', he said in a speech to the Assembly in November 1872—'la République sera conservatrice ou elle ne sera pas'.[31] That Republic was to last for seventy years, to date the

---

[31] Adolphe Thiers, speech to the National Assembly (13 Nov. 1872), *Journal Officiel de la République Française* (14 Nov. 1872), 6981–2. I should like to thank my colleague Robert Gildea for helping me to locate the original source of this quotation. He has published a fuller translation of the speech, along with a brief

longest-serving constitutional regime in France since the Great Revolution of 1789. Between 1870 and 1914 alone there were no fewer than sixty different ministries, yet somehow the fundamental social order over which they governed remained intact. Indeed, perhaps only a fundamentally stable social order could have withstood so many changes of government, and so many scandals and crises.

Thiers, at least, had learnt the lessons of 1848, when that same social order, in part the product of the land settlement of the Great Revolution, as consolidated under Napoleon I, and in part the product of mid-nineteenth-century industrialization, went on the offensive to defend itself against the perceived threat to property. Having weathered the shock of 1870–1, it has survived into the twentieth century, notwithstanding the greater shocks of two World Wars. Important elements of its past still flourish in the Fifth Republic today, whatever the ideological persuasion of any particular government.

FURTHER READING

Most of the standard histories of the European revolutions of 1848–51 offer detailed coverage of France, but two in particular stand out: Roger Price, *The Revolutions of 1848* (Basingstoke and London, 1988; repr. 1989), is a concise and reliable introduction by a leading specialist of the French aspect of the subject; while Jonathan Sperber, *The European Revolutions, 1848–1851* (already noted in Chapter 1) provides an excellent comparative context for the French case. Both of these textbooks also have useful bibliographies on France. Of the general studies of the revolution in France itself, two similarly complement each other well: Roger Price, *The French Second Republic: A Social History* (London, 1972); and Maurice Agulhon, *The Republican Experiment, 1848–1852* (Eng. trans.; Cambridge, 1983), which also includes a detailed chronology. Among the works dealing with more specialized topics, Peter H. Amman, *Revolution and Mass Democracy: The Paris Club Movement in 1848* (Princeton, 1975), and Mark Traugott, *Armies of the Poor: Determinants of Working-class Participation in the Parisian Insurrection of June 1848* (Princeton, 1985), cover the popular aspects of the subject well. Conversely, on the 'high politics' of the revolution and the reaction it provoked, the studies of William Fortescue, *Alphonse de Lamartine: A Political Biography* (London, 1983), and Fred-

discussion of its political context, in his *France 1870–1914*, 2nd edn. (London and New York, 1996), 6, 88–9 (document 3).

erick A. de Luna, *The French Republic under Cavaignac, 1848* (Princeton, 1969), can be recommended. The most authoritative analysis of the presidential election of 1848 is André-Jean Tudesq, *L'Élection présidentielle de Louis-Napoléon Bonaparte, 10 décembre 1848* (Paris, 1965), which unfortunately has not been translated. The best of the regional studies available in English are Maurice Agulhon's classic, *The Republic in the Village: The People of the Var from the French Revolution to the Second Republic* (Eng. trans.; Cambridge, 1982), and Mary Lynn Stewart-McDougall, *The Artisan Republic: Revolution, Reaction, and Resistance in Lyon 1848–1851* (Gloucester, 1984). The persistence of the revolutionary movement in France after 1848 is most extensively examined in major studies by John M. Merriman, *The Agony of the Republic: The Repression of the Left in Revolutionary France 1848–1851* (New Haven, 1978), and by Ted W. Margadant, *French Peasants in Revolt: The Insurrection of 1851* (Princeton, 1979). A valuable collection of essays edited by Roger Price, *Revolution and Reaction: 1848 and the Second French Republic* (London, 1975), publishes the research of twelve specialists on various topical aspects of the revolution in France in the years 1848–52. Roger Price has also edited an interesting collection of *Documents on the French Revolution of 1848* (Basingstoke and London, 1996), a revised version of his original volume *1848 in France* (London, 1975).

Only a few of the more important contemporary writings on the French revolution of 1848 are available in modern English editions. The best-known is the *Souvenirs* of Alexis de Tocqueville, published in several translations, most recently under the title *Recollections: The French Revolution of 1848*, ed. J.-P. Mayer and A. P. Kerr (New Brunswick, NJ, and Oxford, 1987). The two celebrated polemical tracts of Karl Marx, *The Class Struggles in France: 1848 to 1850* (1850) and *The Eighteenth Brumaire of Louis Bonaparte* (1852), have appeared in numerous English editions. Also available is the hard-hitting account of the *émigré* Russian radical Alexander Herzen, *From the Other Shore*, ed. Isaiah Berlin (Eng. trans.; London, 1956). Alphonse de Lamartine's self-justificatory *History of the French Revolution of 1848* can be read in the old edition published in Bohn's Standard Library (London, 1898). But Pierre-Joseph Proudhon's *Confessions d'un révolutionnaire pour servir à l'histoire de la révolution de février* (Paris, 1850) still awaits an integral English translation.

4

The Revolutions of
1848–1849 in Italy

DENIS MACK SMITH

THE revolutionary year opened in an Italy that was divided into independent states. Apart from the minuscule principalities of San Marino and Monaco, there were three kingdoms, three sovereign duchies, and the extensive temporal possessions of the papacy. In each of these an autocratic government encountered a revolutionary challenge during 1848, and such revolutions could later be seen as having been hesitant steps along the path towards Italian national unification. Their original objectives, however, were often quite other than patriotic and their results greatly disappointed patriotic Italians. The word *quarantotto* ('forty-eight') entered the language and is still current to describe anything turbulent, chaotic, and unserious.

Why the revolutions began and why they failed are questions partly explained by differing local circumstances. They were not well co-ordinated and had different objectives. Diversity was to be expected in an Italy that contained no metropolitan city as dominant as Paris, London, or Vienna. Even a common language was lacking. Upper-class Piedmontese spoke French, while the rulers of Lombardy and Venice spoke German, and ordinary Italians used one of a dozen local dialects that were unintelligible outside each several region. Giuseppe Mazzini, the best-known revolutionary leader, had been agitating for over ten years to create a united Italy, but was living as an exile in England and had few followers. Very different was the view of realistic politicians inside Italy, who could sometimes speak of themselves as belonging to a Piedmontese, Sicilian, or Neapolitan nation. No railway connected any of these

independent territories to each other and it was even said that news
reached Milan more quickly from China than from southern Italy.
Trade was hindered by external and internal tariff barriers and by
different systems of coinage. Inside Naples, the largest Italian state,
more than a thousand different terms for weights and measures dis-
couraged internal as well as inter-state commerce.[1] Even the word
'Italy' can have meant little or nothing to most southerners (or
perhaps to most other Italians).

The economic disadvantages of such local isolation were one reason why some merchants and landowners were beginning to want
radical changes in politics and society. A second reason was irrita-
tion with authoritarian kings and dukes who had absolute power
over their subjects but lacked the requisite intelligence and political
competence. A third reason was antagonism against the Austrians
who dominated most of the Italian peninsula. The Habsburg emperor in Vienna ruled over Lombardy and Venice, the most prosperous and efficiently run regions of Italy; and it was a particular
grievance that the Viennese government derived a disproportionate
amount of revenue from its Italian subjects. Austria furthermore
had a military treaty of alliance with the kingdom of Piedmont-
Sardinia in the north-west, whose king had a Habsburg wife. By
other treaties the Austrian emperor kept military garrisons in the
sovereign duchies of Parma and Modena, which meant that as
well as controlling the Alpine passes into Lombardo-Venetia he
controlled roads through the Apennines leading southwards into
Tuscany. Modena was in any case governed by a minor Austrian
archduke. So was the grand duchy of Tuscany, which in 1847 incorporated the hitherto independent duchy of Lucca. Further south,
Naples and Sicily were ruled by King Ferdinand, who, though belonging to a Spanish Bourbon family, had an Austrian wife and
could traditionally count on Austrian military assistance.

In central Italy the Pope was absolute ruler of a large area stretching across Italy from Bologna and the Adriatic to Rome and the
Tyrrhenian Sea; and in addition claimed an ancient right of inheritance to the duchy of Parma. The temporal sovereignty of the
Pope was not yet seen as an anomaly; nor was the fact that he
also governed Benevento and Pontecorvo, which were isolated regions situated inside the Kingdom of Naples; nor was it particularly

[1] R. Ciasca, *L'origine del 'Programma per l'Opinione Nazionale Italiana' del 1847–
48* (Milan, 1916), 331.

anomalous that the rulers of Tuscany and Modena had to cross each other's frontiers to reach parts of their own territory. Such peculiarities, the product of treaties and dynastic unions from the distant past, indicate how untidy and illogical was the political map of Italy in 1848.

The papal state, uniquely, was ruled by an elected sovereign, and Pius IX after his accession in 1846 was generally accorded a moral primacy by other Italian sovereigns. His theocratic kingdom had been by reputation the worst-governed part of Italy, but without being a political liberal his sensitivity to popular wishes led him to relax the ecclesiastical censorship and allow minor participation by laymen in the administration. In so doing he gave encouragement to advocates of political reform elsewhere in Italy. Equally encouraging to reformers was his denunciation of the Austrians when at the end of 1847 they sent troops to occupy Ferrara, a border town inside papal territory, and he reacted by trying to persuade his fellow Italian rulers to form a loosely organized customs' league under his presidency. This was a novel and, to many, an exciting idea. For a few months the Pope was hailed as an Italian patriot and the distant goal of Italian nationality thereby became acceptable to some conservative Catholics as well as to revolutionary Mazzinians.

The first European insurrection in 1848 took place in Sicily some weeks before the much more substantial revolutions in Paris and Vienna. Sicily was the poorest, most rebellious, most ungovernable region of Italy. Very few Sicilians had much inkling about Italian nationality; yet in 1848 (as again in 1860) it was this peripheral and socially backward region that, perhaps paradoxically, started the most decisive revolutions of the Italian Risorgimento. Here the incentives to rebellion included traditions of vendetta, interfamily rivalries, and the endemic war between 'hats' and 'berets', rich and poor. Above all, and far more important than any wish to unite Italy, was the almost opposite desire among Sicilians to break free from the insensitive and alien rule by Neapolitans— who spoke a different language and who in 1816 had suspended the unique parliamentary constitution that Sicily had formerly enjoyed. In addition this island had a centuries-old tradition of what in retrospect could be called Mafia activity. Not only in the criminal underworld, but also among individual peasants and townsmen, the possession of offensive weapons was regarded as legitimate and necessary—a fact of great importance in a revolution.

What triggered insurrection in January 1848 was an unsigned notice surreptitiously posted on buildings in Palermo by one of Mazzini's adherents. This notice announced, on behalf of a probably non-existent revolutionary committee, that three days later a revolt would commence under cover of festivities for the king's birthday. On the appointed day, 12 January, curious crowds gathered in expectation, but nothing happened for some hours until a minor clash with the police started what on the 13th developed into a full-scale rebellion. Barricades appeared in the streets, water supplies were cut off, prisons forced open, tax collectors and policemen killed by anyone with old or new scores to settle. Property-owners, though not always unsympathetic, at first held back, whether fearful of failure or of anarchy. But powerful support came from squads of peasants in nearby villages led by disreputable individuals later identified as *mafiosi*. Lawless gang leaders such as Scordato and Miceli had already acquired a frightening celebrity in the countryside and quickly joined this urban rioting as a possible chance to make money and increase their already lucrative reputation. Another *capo-popolo* was a ferocious lady known as Testa di Lana, an illiterate trousered goatherd whose cruel vendetta against the police was legendary. Without the driving force and menace exercised by such people, this rising could hardly have succeeded.[2]

The king of Naples kept a garrison of 6,000 troops in Palermo and quickly sent another 5,000 in reinforcement, but such was the popularity and ferocity of this Sicilian revolt that after two weeks the town of Messina alone remained under Neapolitan control. A provisional government was formed by senior citizens in Palermo, who needed to impose some legality and political direction on what was happening. To neutralize the revolutionary squads a national guard was created from which the poor were excluded and which was officered by some of Sicily's innumerable princes, dukes, and lesser aristocrats. Armed clashes occasionally took place between

---

[2] W. Dickinson, 'Diario della Rivoluzione Siciliana', in *Memorie della Rivoluzione Siciliana* (Palermo, 1898), 1–150 at 17, 33; G. La Farina, *Istoria documentata della Rivoluzione Siciliana* (2 vols.; Capolago, 1850–1), i. 31–5, 188–9; *Epistolario di Giuseppe La Farina*, ed. A. Franchi (2 vols.; Milan, 1869), i. 418–22; E. A. Edgcumbe, *Extracts from a Journal Kept during the Revolution at Palermo in the Year 1848* (London, 1850), 33.

proletarian squads and national guardsmen, though usually a tacit accommodation emerged out of their shared opposition to Naples.

Eventually a parliament was elected on a restricted suffrage, though its members, being new to public life, spent more time arguing over a new constitution than creating an army to defend their revolution. The Bourbon dynasty was formally dethroned and sovereignty reclaimed by the 'Sicilian nation'. Debates took place about electing a new king, some people even wanting an Englishman, others preferring the future French emperor Louis Napoleon; and their final choice was a second son of the Piedmontese king, who failed to show much enthusiasm for the offer. Another resolution explained that an independent Sicily hoped to join an Italian confederation, and a token force of a hundred soldiers was sent to northern Italy to resist a possible Austrian counter-revolution.

The news from Sicily had a dramatic effect all over mainland Italy. In the city of Naples citizens poured into the streets shouting 'long live Sicily' and calling for a representative parliament. The Austrian ambassador in Naples thought that the demonstrators were fewer than two thousand in a population of two hundred thousand citizens, but at first, just as in Sicily, many spectators were merely waiting to see who would prevail. Students and underemployed lawyers were prominent among the agitators and there were minor sympathetic strikes by printers, tailors, and construction workers. But a strong military garrison made insurrection difficult. Unlike in Sicily, richer Neapolitan citizens were mostly content with their monopoly of positions in the royal court and administration, while the indigent *lazzaroni* of the slums were traditionally kept loyal by charitable handouts from both ecclesiastical and secular authorities.[3]

It was rather in the vast area of the Neapolitan countryside that multiple grievances and a shortage of policemen made rebellion relatively easy and profitable. Baronial feudalism had been legally abolished forty years earlier, when Naples was ruled by the French, but abolition had helped the rich far more than the poor. By freeing transfers of landed property, the legal cessation of feudal tenure

[3] R. Moscati, *Ferdinando II di Borbone* (Naples, 1947), 117–19; G.Quazza (ed.), *La diplomazia del Regno di Sardegna durante la prima guerra d'indipendenza: Relazioni con il Regno delle Due Sicilie (gennaio 1848–dicembre 1848* (3 vols.; Turin, 1952), iii. 103–4.

had led to the acquisition of communally owned land by enterprising members of the rural middle and upper class, so increasing the number of landless peasants who were deprived of traditional rights over woods and pasture that had been necessary for their livelihood. A single bad harvest was now enough to threaten starvation and drive the disinherited to desperate action, especially at any moment of government weakness. The result in 1848 was a widespread forcible occupation of uncultivated land as well as an epidemic of cattle rustling and a refusal to pay tax.

By the end of January, Ferdinand's army commanders confessed their inability to control a generalized disobedience throughout Calabria, Apulia, and the Basilicata. On 10 February he therefore tried to placate disaffection by conceding a parliamentary constitution, and he hoped that this might also recapture the loyalty of his Sicilian subjects. The decision was greeted in Naples with delight and torchlight processions through streets illuminated in his honour. Placing his hand on a Bible, the king swore to obey the provisions of the constitution, calling on God to witness that it was a spontaneous and irrevocable concession on his part.

The royal prerogatives were nevertheless carefully entrenched in this constitution and Ferdinand had no intention of allowing independent powers to an elected parliament. At the same time he promised that, if Sicily returned to its allegiance, the ancient and separate Sicilian parliament would be reconvened after thirty years in abeyance. But the rebels in Sicily were unimpressed and refused to accept anything that fell short of the last Neapolitan troops leaving Messina. A major fracture was thereby exposed in the Italian revolution, because the liberal reformers in Naples not only welcomed Ferdinand's concessions, but condemned their fellow revolutionaries in Sicily for refusing to accept a restoration of Neapolitan supremacy.[4]

The grant of a constitution in Naples gave immediate encouragement to would-be reformers in central and northern Italy. Even Monaco followed suit and acquired a constitution on 12 February. But the news was far from welcome to the Austrians, who saw their supremacy in Italy undermined by any movement towards representative government. To halt a dangerous chain reaction they warned Leopold, the ruler of Tuscany, that he had no right to make

---

[4] G. Massari, *I casi di Napoli dal 29 gennaio 1848 in poi* (Turin, 1849), 67.

concessions to liberalism since he was an archduke of Austria and held Tuscany as a usufruct that might one day revert to inclusion in the Austrian Empire.[5] Leopold was a moderately benevolent despot eager for popular support and had already backed the Pope in advocating a customs union in Italy. On 15 February, after witnessing the enthusiastic reaction in Florence to events in Sicily and Naples, he conceded a constitution out of fear that otherwise his dynasty might be deposed by force. Although careful to retain the executive power in his own hand, he agreed to give some legislative powers to a representative parliament, and as well as proclaiming the equality of all citizens before the law, he specifically granted freedom for Protestants and Jews to practise their own religions.

Religious freedom, though it later became a major achievement of the Risorgimento, was something that the Pope could not permit. Yet Pius had no difficulty in modifying the reactionary political behaviour of his predecessors. He also agreed that Sicilians had a right to demand the restoration of their ancient constitution and spoke in private against the 'absurdity' of Austria's dominant position in northern Italy. Though Italians were in his view unfitted for self-government, he feared that failure to make minor political concessions would play into the hands of Mazzini and the patriotic revolutionaries.[6] He was ready to remove the walls of the Jewish ghetto in Rome even if he would never allow full civic rights to non-Catholics. He could not contemplate abolishing the secretive ecclesiastical tribunals or the Holy Inquisition, but in March went so far as to permit the election of a parliament with very limited powers. In practice his government still remained essentially a theocracy governed by himself and the College of Cardinals.

Another Italian kingdom which tried and then failed to immunize itself against constitutionalism was Piedmont-Sardinia, a frontier state that straddled the Alps and extended from Sassari and Genoa to Turin and Chambéry in Savoy. King Charles Albert, though he followed the example of other Italian sovereigns in conceding some administrative reforms, had solemnly sworn that he would never surrender the prerogatives of absolute monarchy. It was events in

---

[5] N. Bianchi, *Storia documentata della diplomazia europea in Italia dall'anno 1814 all'anno 1861* (8 vols.; Turin, 1865–72), v. 91–2.

[6] F. Curato (ed.), *Gran Bretagna e Italia nei documenti della missione Minto* (2 vols.; Rome, 1960), i. 193, 309; C. Baudi di Vesme (ed.), *La diplomazia del Regno di Sardegna durante la prima guerra d'indipendenza: Relazioni con lo Stato Pontificio, marzo 1848–luglio 1849* (Turin, 1951), 118.

Sicily and Naples that persuaded him to ask the bishops for permission to break this oath. He liked to think of himself as the premier secular sovereign in Italy and resented that his rival Ferdinand of Naples was winning popularity by concessions to representative government. Even some of his more conservative ministers warned him to follow Ferdinand's example before an insurrection compelled him to give way, and the same warning was reinforced in an urgent message to him from Lord Palmerston in England. On 4 March he therefore granted a constitution to his subjects. That *statuto*, though conceded under some pressure, was the only Italian parliamentary constitution which survived intact through the wars and revolutions of this dramatic year.

So far, except in Sicily, reforms had been won more or less peacefully; but two weeks later the Austrian viceroy in Milan had to contend with a violent popular uprising. Already in January the news from Sicily had created great excitement. This had been accompanied in Milan by a boycott of the state lottery and the tobacco monopoly, two important sources of government revenue— the idea of a boycott having been deliberately copied from the famous Boston Tea Party in America. Demonstrations of protest also took place in Venice after several prominent citizens were imprisoned. In Lombardy Mazzini's followers had already been preparing for a possible insurrection, and during February the Milanese gunshops ran out of stock as private citizens began to hoard arms.[7] Such was the state of alarm that, despite the seventy thousand soldiers in the Austrian army of occupation, the British minister in Turin predicted on 8 March that the viceroy might soon be overwhelmed by the force of popular disaffection.[8]

What precipitated violence was another revolution far away in Vienna, where on 13 March the Austrian emperor was forced to replace his minister Prince Metternich and promise political reforms to the states of his composite empire. Reports of this Viennese insurrection reached Venice on 16 March and Milan on the 17th. The city fathers in Milan, notably the Italian mayor Count Casati,

---

[7] L. Ambrosoli (ed.), *La insurrezione milanese del marzo 1848: Memorie di Cesare Correnti e Pietro Maestri* (Milan, 1969), 70–1; A. Monti, *Il 1848 e le Cinque Giornate di Milano: Dalle memorie inedite dei combattenti sulle barricate* (Milan, 1948), 39–42, 57.

[8] F. Curato (ed.), *Le relazioni diplomatiche fra la Gran Bretagna e il Regno di Sardegna, 1848–1860*, i (Rome, 1961), 103.

who was an Austrian appointee, were anxious to avoid any violent response, but small groups of revolutionaries incited the crowds to provoke the Austrian troops, and minor clashes developed within hours into an uncontrollable uprising.

The famous 'five days of Milan' were one of the more extraordinary episodes of this revolutionary year in Europe. The Austrian commander Marshal Radetzky found his artillery of little use for house-to-house fighting inside the thickly populated central area of the city. Nor were his soldiers trained to deal with urban guerrillas who could quickly disappear into surrounding buildings. Narrow streets were ideal for constructing barricades out of paving stones, household furniture, even pianos and church pews. Such obstacles were very effective for interrupting troop movements, severing communications, and cutting off ammunition supplies: observers estimated that more than 1,500 street barricades were erected in a matter of hours.[9]

The rebels were fortunate to find courageous leaders among civilians who had no experience of fighting or mainstream politics. The most notable was the schoolmaster-journalist Carlo Cattaneo, who, though at first he assumed that rebellion could not succeed, was emboldened by popular support and helped to give direction to a disorganized resistance. As soon as the rising showed signs of success, the mayor Casati was persuaded to put himself at the head of a revolutionary government—'to prevent anarchy', he wrote[10]—and Radetzky in the night of 22–3 March prudently began to withdraw his troops to Peschiera, Mantua, and other fortress towns near the border between Lombardy and Venetia.

A further problem for the Austrians was that the citizens of Venice were independently in revolt, led by another patriotic civilian, the lawyer Daniele Manin. Venice was the headquarters of the small Austrian navy, a fleet mostly manned by Italians, whose allegiance was doubtful. On 22 March insurgents captured the naval arsenal and killed its commander. When the city governor capitulated, Manin proclaimed that Venice, as well as intending to become part of a future Italian confederation, would be an independent republic as it had been for many centuries until the Napoleonic

[9] G. de Willisen, *La campagna d'Italia del 1848* (Turin, 1851), 61; L.Torelli, *Ricordi intorno alle Cinque Giornate di Milano* (Milan, 1976), 191–2.
[10] *Carteggio Casati-Castagnetto, 19 marzo–14 ottobre 1848*, ed. V. Ferrari (Milan, 1909), 13.

conquest in 1797. Here, as in Sicily, there were proud memories of a glorious past history, and it was to such memories that the revolutionaries appealed.

The triumph of successive popular insurrections had an immediate impact in Turin, which was the Piedmontese capital. Here King Charles Albert had sometimes nourished a vague ambition to annex Lombardy from the Austrians, though by his own confession he had an equally dangerous enemy in the democratic republicanism of the Italian patriots Mazzini, Cattaneo, and Manin.[11] There was enormous enthusiasm in Turin for sending troops to help the Milanese, and according to the prime minister, Cesare Balbo, a failure to help would make not only Milan but also Genoa 'and most probably Turin' desert monarchy by accepting Mazzini's republicanism.[12] An unforeseen opportunity to act was provided by the revolution in Vienna followed by Radetzky's retreat from Milan. In addition, there were further local revolutions against the dukes of Parma and Modena. On 23 March, therefore, Charles Albert decided to fight, his dual objective being to extend his kingdom into the fertile plain of Lombardy and stop the diffusion of republican sentiment throughout northern Italy. The possible drawbacks were limited because his existing frontier along the River Ticino was in effect under international guarantee, and this placed him in the position of having little to lose from defeat except money and prestige.

Unfortunately the king had never prepared for more than a defensive war, and until the last moment his preferred enemy had been republican France rather than imperial Austria. Forces therefore had now to be quickly switched from west to east and only on 29 March did he cross the Ticino into Lombardy, so giving ample time for the Austrian army to regroup. Nor did he use these few days to organize a general staff or a plausible plan of campaign. The Piedmontese even lacked maps of Lombardy, though this territory had been one of the most fought-over regions in world history: an offer by Cattaneo to supply this deficiency was treated with disdain

---

[11] Ibid. 59; R. Bonfadini, *Mezzo secolo di patriotismo: Saggi storici* (Milan, 1886), 290; P. Pirri, 'La missione di Mons. Corboli Bussi in Lombardia', *Rivista di storia della Chiesa in Italia*, 1 (Rome, Jan. 1947), 38–84 at 74; F. Curato (ed.), *Le relazioni diplomatiche fra il Regno di Sardegna e la Gran Bretagna* (Rome, 1955), 81–2.

[12] N. W. Senior, *Journals Kept in France and Italy from 1848 to 1852*, ed. M. C. M. Simpson (2 vols.; London, 1871), i. 295.

and only later were Austrian military maps procured.[13] Another weakness was that the senior officers were mostly aristocrats with a snobbish disregard for technical competence and no experience of serious fighting; moreover, according to Charles Albert, his generals had no enthusiasm for liberal ideas or Italian nationality.[14]

Among his ministers, too, there was a supposition that the war would be easy and short with no need for a general mobilization of reservists. Neither did Charles Albert's generals move fast enough to harry the retreating Radetzky, nor was any attempt made to block the Alpine passes and prevent Austrian reinforcements from arriving. Worst of all, the king insisted on acting as commander-in-chief, though he was an amateur with no previous history of generalship in combat. His senior officers tried to persuade him to appoint a battle-trained Frenchman instead, but Charles Albert said he would rather abdicate than surrender his God-given right to command and win the credit for victory.[15]

This decision and the initial delay gave the worst possible start to the first war of Italian liberation, and matters were not improved by an unwillingness to co-ordinate objectives with other Italian states. The king's secret intention was to annex Lombardy, despite the objections of many proud Milanese, who had just defeated Radetzky without his help.[16] Milan was larger and more economically developed than Turin. It had been the capital city of Napoleon's Italian kingdom in 1805–14 and many Lombards hoped it would become the capital of a liberated northern Italy. But Charles Albert led people to think that he was motivated less by desire for Italian independence than by a dynastic ambition to enlarge Piedmont. The first of his generals to arrive in Milan was alarmed to find an overwhelming desire to follow Venice in becoming an independent republic, while only the patrician class of *signori* wanted annexation by Piedmont. The English consul agreed that only the 'high aristocratical party' in Lombardy wanted annexation, while

[13] C. Cattaneo, *Tutte le opere*, ed. L. Ambrosoli [vols iii–iv only] (Milan, 1967), iv. 593–5; M. Avetta and T. Buttini (eds.), *I rapporti fra governo sardo e governo provvisorio di Lombardia durante la guerra del 1848* (Rome, 1938), 149.

[14] F. Patetta (ed.), 'Lettere di Carlo Alberto scritte durante la campagna del 1848 al Conte Federigo Sclopis', in *Atti della Reale Accademia delle Scienze di Torino*, 56 (1920–1), 211–85 at 279.

[15] L. Chiala, *La vita e i tempi del Generale Giuseppe Dabormida 1848–49* (Turin, 1896), 428; G. di Revel, *Miei ricordi dal 1847 al 1855* (Milan, 1891), ii, 33.

[16] Avetta and Buttini (eds.), *Rapporti*, 52–3.

'the commercial and literary people together with all the promising youth are for a republic'.[17]

But the *signori* were influential in Milan and had the additional advantage that the republicans were divided. Giuseppe Ferrari and Cattaneo, for instance, both believed that the war would require French armed support, whereas Mazzini, who reached Milan early in April, feared that Italian nationality would be demeaned or invalidated if achieved through foreign help. Cattaneo looked on Charles Albert as a bigoted and perjured reactionary whose government was likely to be more oppressive than that of Austria, whereas Mazzini was prepared to put his own republican opinions aside in the hope that the king would head a common front to defeat the Austrians and create a unified Italian nation.[18] What historians tried subsequently to conceal was that the republican Mazzini wanted above all a united Italy even if it was a kingdom, whereas Charles Albert saw the preservation of kingship as far more important and considered national unification to be a Utopian dream.

Further controversies arose between Charles Albert and other Italian rulers who briefly became his allies against Austria. A week before hostilities began, Tuscany and Piedmont competed with each other by both occupying territory belonging to Modena and Parma. There were even minor clashes between Piedmontese units and the small volunteer army of Tuscany.[19] Charles Albert assumed that because he had a large army the rest of Italy would accept his authority and objectives without question; yet previous history did not encourage confidence in him as a genuine patriot or as a trustworthy constitutional monarch. Tuscans and Neapolitans were sometimes antagonized by his manifest determination to make his subalpine kingdom the dominant power throughout Italy. What added to this suspicion was his lack of enthusiasm for the Pope's proposal to create a league of Italian states: this papal project for a

---

[17] Ibid. 8–9; Patetta (ed.), 'Lettere', 269; *Correspondence respecting the Affairs of Italy, from January to June 1848, Presented to Parliament* (2 pts.; London, 1849), ii. 294–5.

[18] *Scritti editi ed inediti di Giuseppe Mazzini*, ed. M. Menghini (94 vols.; Imola, 1906–43), xxxv. 114–15; A. Monti, *Un dramma fra gli esuli* (Milan, 1921), 78–85.

[19] C. Pischedda (ed.), *La diplomazia del Regno di Sardegna durante la prima guerra d'indipendenza: Relazioni con il Granducato di Toscana, marzo 1848–aprile 1849*, i (Turin, 1949), 6, 25, 31–3, 116, 131; E. Costa (ed.), *Il Regno di Sardegna nel 1848–1849 nei carteggi di Domenico Buffa* (Rome, 1966), 228–9, 252, 274–5.

customs union was supported by Naples and Tuscany but would have had its headquarters in Rome, outside Charles Albert's control.[20] Italian politicians were soon accusing each other of putting private ambition before mutual assistance. When a small unit of Tuscan volunteers was defeated by the Austrians, the nearby Piedmontese army refused a request for help and gave the excuse of lacking orders.

Relations between Turin and the papacy were less fraught. Pope Pius was in his own way an Italian patriot. War to expel the Austrians would, in his view, be a just war as well as inevitable, and he briefly looked upon Austria's defeat as part of God's providence.[21] Since he was the best-known and most admired person in the whole country, his moral support was widely welcomed, and soon was more than merely moral. After inviting a Piedmontese general, Giovanni Durando, to command the papal troops, Pius gave this man equivocal orders to guard the northern papal frontier against an Austrian invasion but also to lend unspecified assistance to the Piedmontese army. He must have known that a Pope should never make war except in self-defence, especially not against another Catholic power; but he also knew that Durando might easily become more actively involved, and this did not worry him unduly. Possibly he was expecting a quick defeat of Austria, for which he could then disclaim any personal responsibility.[22]

The risks involved in such an order were exposed when Durando publicly referred to the war as a religious crusade. Pius was already worried by the spread of Mazzini's republican opinions in Rome and now envisaged the danger of a schism in the Church as people assumed he must be leading a holy war against the leading Catholic sovereign in Europe. In a formal allocution of 29 April he therefore explained that he had been misunderstood and must return to a strict neutrality. He neither condemned the war nor repudiated

[20] L. G. Glueckert, *Between Two Amnesties: Former Political Prisoners and Exiles in the Roman Revolution of 1848* (New York, 1991), 52; Baudi, *Diplomazia*, 5–6, 107, 196; *L'opinione religiosa e conservatrice in Italia dal 1830 al 1850: corrispondenze di Mons. Giovanni Corboli Bussi*, ed. A. Manno (Turin 1910), 295.

[21] G. Montanelli, *Memorie sull'Italia e specialmente sulla Toscana dal 1814 al 1850* (Turin, 1855), ii.59; *Pio IX da vescovo a pontefice: lettere di Cardinale L. Amat*, ed. G. Maioli (Modena, 1949), 117; *Opinione religiosa*, 281; G. Martina, 'Nuovi documenti sull'allocuzione del 29 Aprile 1848', *Rassegna storica del Risorgimento*, 53 (1966), 527–82 at 527.

[22] Baudi di Vesme (ed.), *Diplomazia*, 98–9; *Opinione religiosa*, 223.

Italian nationality, but in practice his allocution greatly damaged the patriotic movement that he had previously helped to popularize.

From now onwards there was small chance that the Pope could preside over an Italian confederation. On the contrary, the temporal power of the papacy would ultimately be seen as incompatible with the political unification of Italy, just as its spiritual authority was incompatible with heterodox ideas about personal, political, and religious liberty. Pius soon learnt that he could never be a constitutional monarch, because his authority derived from God and not from a popular vote. His pronouncement on 29 April was a first step along a different road where in the end he would be forced to anathematize political liberalism and instruct Catholics not to vote in parliamentary elections. Ten years later he issued a collective excommunication against the patriotic leaders, after which the Risorgimento was effectively left to the anticlericals; and for the next century liberal Catholicism could exert only a marginal influence on politics.

The Pope's withdrawal from the war was bound to influence King Ferdinand of Naples, who had unenthusiastically accepted advice from his ministers to join the fighting. Ferdinand had the largest army and navy of any Italian state, which together might well have turned the scales against Austria. But his private conversation shows him as being less anxious to help than to counteract what he called the excessive power of Charles Albert and the annexation of Lombardo-Venetia by a rival claimant to the leadership of Italy.[23] His immediate worry was that the Neapolitan parliament was due to assemble on 15 May and he knew that it would demand a greater say in affairs than he was willing to permit. Many elected deputies refused even to swear an oath of allegiance to him until they had more information about government policy. Some of them were eager to follow the revolutionary example of Palermo and Milan, and in the hours leading up to the opening of parliament there were acts of sabotage and disobedience which the royal Swiss guard forcibly suppressed. Foreign ships in the Bay of Naples were witness to terrible scenes of brutality on the city streets, with hundreds of casualties on both sides. Parliament was at once dissolved before it could be formally constituted, and the king summoned his

[23] Di Revel, *Miei ricordi*, 28; G. La Cecilia, *Memorie storico-politiche*, ed. R. Moscati (Naples, 1946), 459; G. Sforza, *La costituzione napoletana del 1848* (Turin, 1921), 588; N. Rodolico, *Carlo Alberto negli anni 1843–1849* (Florence, 1943), 356.

army back from Lombardy because it was needed to restore royal authority in Naples and reconquer Sicily.

The defection by Rome and Naples left Charles Albert in difficulty, especially since the Lombards could support him with only untrained recruits and Italian deserters from the Austrian army, who lacked their former *esprit de corps*. In newly liberated Milan he could rely on only an improvised civic administration and an extempore hand-to-mouth collection of tax revenue. Though at first his invading army scored minor military successes and in May even occupied Peschiera, its advance was slow and indecisive. Though sometimes on horseback from morning till night, the monarch had been seriously ill before the war began and remained an invalid, often in great pain. His courage was not in doubt, but his military skills were negligible and his temperamental vacillation was a crippling disadvantage in a war that required speed and determination. For well over a month his army remained almost stationary along the River Mincio, and the lack of any preconceived strategic plan became abundantly clear. Instead of cutting off Radetzky's reinforcements from Austria, the king blundered into an ineffective assault on the heavily fortified town of Mantua, where the surrounding swamps led to a quarter of his troops being hospitalized with malaria. This was a summertime hazard well known to the Austrian garrison, but for which the Piedmontese forces seem to have been quite unprepared, and it made matters worse that their ambulance services were ill-equipped and understaffed.

Charles Albert also had difficulties with the Milanese, who were disconcerted when their defeat of the Austrian forces was compromised by his apparent dawdling. At first he tried to convince them that he had no plans to annex Lombardy and they could decide their future by a free vote once the war was won; he even undertook that they could count on Milan replacing Turin as the capital of his kingdom.[24] But his real intentions were quite different. He rejected Mazzini's proposal that monarchists and republicans should agree to postpone political decisions until after the war. On the contrary, he was determined to suppress what he derisively referred to

[24] Carlo Alberto, *Memorie inedite del 1848*, ed. A. Lumbroso (Milan 1935), 201; *Carteggio Casati-Castagnetto*, 153, 158, 168; Avetta and Buttini (eds.), *Rapporti*, 160; A. Depoli, *I rapporti tra il Regno di Sardegna e Venezia negli anni 1848 e 1849* (2 vols.; Modena, 1969), i. 298.

as Mazzini's 'so-called Italian party', and the Milanese were told that an immediate plebiscite must be held to sanction annexation to Piedmont, otherwise he would go home.[25] This ultimatum left no room for discussion. Cattaneo and Mazzini objected that a representative plebiscite could not conceivably be organized in the middle of a war, apart from the fact that an immediate vote would allow no time for debate on what was involved. But the *signori* feared, quite rightly, that a protracted electoral campaign would be divisive. They believed that only a speedy surrender to this demand from Turin would save them from an Austrian counter-attack and from having to compromise with democratic and social reformers such as Cattaneo and Mazzini.

On 12 May the provisional government of Lombardy therefore ordered the holding of a plebiscite in two weeks' time. To appease any critics it was also decreed that a favourable vote would be followed by holding a constituent assembly to discuss minor changes in the Piedmontese constitution—which annoyed many loyal monarchists. There was no time to draw up a roll of electors and it did not matter that in some areas the published results showed that the favourable votes outnumbered the total resident population.[26] The important fact was that Lombardy should register an overwhelming majority for fusion with the Piedmontese monarchy. Parma and Modena also voted in favour of fusion. On 4 July an elected assembly in Venice did the same despite doubts expressed by Manin. So ended the hundred days of a revived Venetian republic and the whole of northern Italy was nominally and briefly a united kingdom.

Already before this the Austrians had put out tentative feelers for a political settlement. In mid-June they offered to sign an armistice based on ceding Lombardy outright to Piedmont and allowing a semi-autonomous administration to Venice.[27] The English government, when asked to mediate, thought that a durable peace would require the surrender of Venice as well, and this opinion was strongly supported by the provisional government of Milan on the grounds that to leave Venice in Austrian hands would be a betrayal of Italian patriotism. Charles Albert, however, had other ideas, and

[25] *Lettere di Carlo Alberto a Ottavio Thaon di Revel*, ed. G. Gentile (Milan, 1931), 78–9; *Carteggio Casati-Castagnetto*, 59.

[26] Cattaneo, *Tutte le opere*, iv. 571–3, 576.

[27] *Correspondence respecting the Affairs of Italy*, ii. 596, 609.

though he later sent royal commissioners to take control of Venice, his secret intention was to hand it back in return for an Austrian agreement to his annexation of Parma, Modena, and Lombardy.[28] Despite being by now a constitutional monarch, he did not bother to consult or inform his ministers on such a crucial point of policy, but assumed that it would be generally admired as the most notable success in many centuries of Piedmontese history.

Leaving Venice inside the Habsburg Empire would, as he knew, upset the 'so-called Italian party'. But the war was costing too much, and Charles Albert also feared that only a quick settlement would prevent the German Confederation from sending troops to help central Europe retain its commercial outlet into the Mediterranean. Another serious worry for him was the prospect of an equally undesirable intervention on his side by the French, who might see this as an ideal opportunity to increase their influence in Italy. Already the provisional government of Milan, in defiance of the king's wishes, had appealed for Switzerland and France to send military help, and on 8 July Casati told the Piedmontese that without such outside assistance they now had little chance of victory. But Charles Albert demurred because he feared that French assistance against Austria would make his kingdom into a satellite of France.[29] Another powerful objection was that France was a republic and her intervention was advocated by Italian republicans such as Manin and Ferrari.

Charles Albert had set his heart on winning the prestige of victory for himself. For this reason he had made little effort to encourage joint action with Tuscany or Naples. He had shown no warmth towards Manin in Venice and was strongly against accepting help from France or from Mazzini's followers. When Giuseppe Garibaldi arrived at royal headquarters to offer his services the offer was rejected. Garibaldi's military victories in South America made him far more widely known and admired than any of the king's generals, but the monarch explained that the employment of

[28] Carlo Alberto, *Scritti e lettere*, ed. N. Bianchi (Turin, 1859), 62–3; A. Omodeo, *La leggenda di Carlo Alberto nella recente storiografia* (Milan, 1957), 113.

[29] *Carteggio Casati-Castagnetto*, 181–2; P. S. Leopardi, *Narrazioni storiche con molti documenti inediti relativi alla guerra dell'indipendenza d'Italia* (Turin, 1856), 318; A. Monti (ed.), *Carteggio del governo provvisorio di Lombardia con i suoi rappresentanti al quartier generale di Carlo Alberto* (Milan, 1923), 205–6.

such an outsider would 'dishonour' the regular army.[30] Garibaldi was a patriot, but politically unsound; and he was also despised as a plebeian who had learnt his trade not in any military academy, but in years of fighting for suspect causes of national liberation.

In rejecting such allies the king naïvely assumed that his main objectives in the war were on the point of being achieved without help from others—and before a single major battle had been fought. But the Austrian commanders had reason to be even more confident. Already in June, Radetzky disobeyed instructions from Vienna that he should sign an armistice, because he had discovered that his Italian enemies were divided, badly led, and bereft of any coherent strategy.[31] By mid-July the regrouped Austrian forces were ready to counter-attack, and on 25 July at Custoza they forced the king's army to retreat in complete disorder. The Piedmontese lost only 212 solders in this celebrated if very minor engagement,[32] fewer than the civilian casualties when the Milanese citizens had defeated Radetzky in March; but the king's failure to prepare a second line of defence turned a small-scale setback into a rout. His generals blamed the Lombard commissariat for failing to keep the troops adequately supplied and, much less honourably, blamed their own soldiers for cowardice; but the real explanation was that the lines of command were impossibly confused. The chaotic retreat that ensued was caused by elementary failures in kingship and generalship.

What happened next was even more serious. The generals collectively advised that the only sensible strategy was to fall back on Piacenza, but the king overruled them and ordered a retreat further north to Milan. This fatal mistake must have been made for political and not military reasons. It allowed people to suspect that his main intention was to prevent Cattaneo and the Milanese republicans from winning further renown by another heroic defence of their city. Against the wishes of royal representatives, an improvised committee in Milan was already supervising the construction of another labyrinth of barricades and placing mines under bridges

[30] C. Spellanzon, *Storia del Risorgimento e dell'unità d'Italia* (5 vols.; Milan, 1933–50) iv. 521–2.

[31] A. Filipuzzi (ed.), *Le relazioni diplomatiche fra l'Austria e il Regno di Sardegna e la guerra del 1848–1849* (2 vols.; Rome, 1961), i. 162, 205–6.

[32] P. Pieri, *Storia militare del Risorgimento: Guerre e insurrezioni* (Turin, 1962), 124.

round the city, but when the king arrived there on 4 August he took steps to discourage a spontaneous movement of popular resistance.[33] Accusations that he was deceitful may possibly be excessive; but as his own ministers pointed out, people were bound to suspect that he saw an Austrian reconquest of Milan as preferable to a political victory for the patriotic 'Italian party'.[34]

There followed what Casati called the two most tragic days in Milanese history. Envoys were sent from royal headquarters to ask Radetzky for an armistice, but when the latter's terms were thought too dishonourable the monarch promised the citizens to lead a last-ditch resistance. In all probability this was merely a ruse, or at all events he at once changed his mind. Fighting his way out of the city through a tumult of angry protesters who saw him as a dissembler and betrayer of their trust, he managed with difficulty to extricate himself and hurry back to Piedmont. At long last an appeal was sent to ask for the support of a French army corps, but this was by now far too late and can hardly have been seriously intended. On 6 August Radetzky entered Milan, and on the 9th an armistice was signed in which Charles Albert agreed to withdraw behind his original frontier.

The end of hostilities came as a tremendous shock, not only to the Milanese and not only to Garibaldi and Mazzini, who proceeded to continue a desultory war of their own in the countryside, but also to the king's ministers, who resigned in protest. Casati, now his prime minister, together with two future Piedmontese prime ministers, issued a public statement in which they called the armistice unconstitutional, since the king's cabinet had not been consulted. In their eyes it was dishonourable as well as illegal and invalid. In private, ministers went further and talked of having been deceived, even of treason, blaming what they called the retrograde 'court party' for its feeble direction of policy and lack of interest in Italian liberation or nationality. The king's personal advisers, so Casati said, were mainly intent on defeating republicanism, whereas in practice the abject surrender of Milan would be a gratuitous boon to republican propaganda. The resigning ministers also demanded an official inquiry into the competence of the army commanders,

[33] F. Restelli and P. Maestri, *Gli ultimi tristissimi fatti di Milano narrati dal Comitato di Pubblica Difesa* (Milan, 16 Aug. 1848), 25, 42, 52.
[34] L. Marchetti (ed.), *Il secondo ministero costituzionale di Carlo Alberto* (Milan, 1948), 124.

an inquiry that could hardly have avoided criticizing the sovereign who had insisted, against ministerial advice, on taking responsibility as commander-in-chief.[35]

Charles Albert reacted by vetoing any public investigation because it might leave him no alternative but to abdicate, and one minister thought that abdication might in any case be unavoidable.[36] Though the generals were asked to draw up a private report, its text was not made public until 1910, when, somewhat belatedly, it was said to be an indispensable document from which lessons should be learnt for the future.[37] Nevertheless, the general drift of these lessons was known immediately when one corps commander, General Bava, infuriated the authorities by privately publishing his own critical recollection of recent events.[38]

Although officialdom prevented the allegations from being too closely scrutinized in parliament, some of the criticisms were soon privately in circulation. A foreign newspaper correspondent with the Piedmontese army reported that the rank and file 'had never failed to do their duty under the most discouraging circumstances', but all officers above the rank of colonel had shown 'a total ignorance of the practices of war' and were the laughing-stock of their subordinates.[39] Staff officers preferred instead to blame the disobedience and panic of their enlisted men. The king's eldest son implicitly criticized his father by ascribing the defeat to bad leadership, and made the revealing admission that a war against Austria was not what the generals had either wanted or were trained to expect.[40] Several people in Turin reported that the returned soldiers were anxious to continue fighting, but against the Lombards and not against Austria.[41] Such individual comments, though of limited

[35] *Lettere di Carlo Alberto a Ottavio Thaon di Revel*, 127–33; *Carteggio Casati-Castagnetto*, 237–8, 243.

[36] A. Neri, 'Alcuni documenti riguardanti il Ministero Casati', *Rassegna storica del Risorgimento*, 11 (1924), 144–9.

[37] Col. Cavaciocchi (ed.), *Relazioni e rapporti finali sulla campagna del 1848 nell'Alta Italia* (2 vols.; Rome, 1910), vol. i, p. i.

[38] Generale Bava, *Relazione delle operazioni militari* (Turin, 1848), 116, 133.

[39] M. B. Honan, *The Personal Adventures of 'Our Own Correspondent'* (2 vols.; London, 1852), i. 98–9, 267, ii. 156.

[40] Cavaciocchi, *Relazioni e rapporti*, i. 276–8; Filipuzzi, *Relazioni diplomatiche*, 428–31; Costa di Beauregard, *Les Dernières Années du roi Charles-Albert* (Paris, 1895), 364–5.

[41] A. Macfarlane, *A Glance at Revolutionized Italy* (2 vols.; London, 1849), ii. 243; C. d'Azeglio, *Souvenirs historiques de la Marquise Constance d'Azeglio* (Turin, 1884), 331.

historical value, are not irrelevant to an analysis of what had gone wrong.

Military defeat dealt a severe blow to morale and confidence. Italian independence remained a distant prospect. The Austrian army proceeded to occupy Parma and Modena. In Lombardy the civilian authoritarianism of Metternich was for the next ten years replaced by the harsher military dictatorship of Marshal Radetzky. Nor is there much doubt that, especially among the peasantry, many accepted or even welcomed the return of Austrian military rule as a safeguard against the perils of further war and revolution.

Piedmont remained independent, and the survival of its parliamentary constitution was of the greatest importance for Italy's future. Charles Albert was compelled to pay an indemnity to Austria and had no territorial acquisitions to compensate for a vast expenditure of money and effort. One indisputable gain was to have shown that this region alone might possibly possess the strength and the will to renew the struggle at some point in the future; yet the Piedmontese monarchy had aroused animosities in the rest of Italy that would take time to dissipate, and its commitment to the patriotic cause was still dubious. Among successive prime ministers in Turin, Cesare Balbo publicly referred to Mazzini's objective of Italian unification as being puerile; Massimo d'Azeglio called it dangerous and chimerical; while Vincenzo Gioberti had to agree that patriotic sentiment was weaker in Turin than elsewhere in Italy. These three Piedmontese politicians were now condemned outright by the excessively critical Cattaneo as impediments to Italian freedom and nationality.[42]

Knowledgeable observers in the rest of Italy mostly agreed in blaming Charles Albert's incapacity as a leader. In Tuscany and Venice prominent citizens such as Giuseppe Montanelli, Gino Capponi, and Niccolò Tommaseo stigmatized this provincial sovereign for disregarding the wishes of other Italian states.[43] Cattaneo in Milan thought that a smaller Piedmontese army would have done

---

[42] C. Spadolini, *Il '48: Realtà e leggenda di una rivoluzione* (Florence, 1948), 20; C. Balbo, *Delle speranze d'Italia* (Capolago, 1844), 18–21; V. Gioberti, *Del rinnovamento civile d'Italia*, ed. F. Nicolini (3 vols.; Bari, 1911–12), i. 232; Cattaneo, *Tutte le opere*, iv. 710, 767; Senior, *Journals*, i. 265 (in conversation with Gioberti).

[43] Montanelli, *Memorie*, ii. 308; N. Tommaseo and G. Capponi, *Carteggio inedito dal 1833 al 1874*, ed. J. Del Lungo and P. Prunas (5 vols.; Bologna, 1911–32) ii. 672, 691, 703.

far better if not commanded by a clique of amateurish royal appointees, and much the same was said by some conservatives in Turin.[44] Monsignor Corboli Bussi, who attended the king as the Pope's representative, thought that the prime factor in defeat had been the divisive attempt by royalists to impose a premature fusion on Lombardy and Venice.[45] This was also the view of the moderate and level-headed Manin, who concluded that Charles Albert's mistake was to have 'made a selfish war for the aggrandisement of Piedmont'. According to Manin, the rest of Italy lost its enthusiasm when the king was seen to be using a war of national liberation as the pretext for a quite different war of ambition and conquest; and though the Piedmontese 'may perhaps be able to forgive the mischief he has done, the rest of Italy cannot'.[46]

Early in August the king's representatives made a brief appearance in Venice, only to abandon it a week later, leaving a disillusioned Manin to govern an independent but isolated city-state which courageously held out for another twelve months against Austrian attacks. Further south the Pope, after his prime minister Pellegrino Rossi was murdered, fled to take refuge in the Kingdom of Naples. Since Pius left no one to govern in his absence, his ministers tried at first to persuade him to return; only when this failed did they seek an alternative system of government. An elected assembly then voted to make Rome an independent republic. Under the inspired leadership of Mazzini and Garibaldi, this Roman republic survived until July 1849 against armies sent from France, Spain, and Naples to destroy it.

By that time Sicily, too, had been overrun by the Neapolitan army. Princes, churchmen, and even the *mafiosi* Miceli and Scordato were among influential Sicilians who found reasons for welcoming back the Bourbon army and the *ancien régime*. Similarly in Tuscany, though a revolutionary government took power after the grand duke fled from Florence early in 1849, this experience persuaded Baron Bettino Ricasoli and other Tuscan gentry to welcome Leopold's return with Austrian troops as a defence against further subversion. In Rome a French army, after forcing Mazzini and Garibaldi

[44] Cattaneo, *Tutte le opere*, iv. 706; M. Minghetti, *Miei ricordi* (3 vols.; Turin, 1888–90), ii. 426; Pischedda, *Diplomazia*, i. 277–9.

[45] *Opinione religiosa*, 293, 296.

[46] N. W. Senior, *Conversations with M. Thiers, M. Guizot and Other Distinguished Persons during the Second Empire*, ed. M. C. M. Simpson (2 vols.; London, 1878), i. 406.

into exile, allowed the Pope to recover his throne, and French soldiers remained in Rome for the next twenty years to defend papal autocracy from another patriotic rebellion. One result of the 1848 revolutions was that foreign occupation of Italy became more serious and extensive than before.

In retrospect the failure of these revolutions had been chiefly due to the divergent interests of different regions, towns, and social classes. Neapolitans and Sicilians fought against each other, and this prevented the southern half of Italy from contributing very much to the crusade against Austria. In the north there was bickering between Turin and Milan, between monarchists and republicans, between centralizers and federalists. Many thousands of Italians had remained in Radetzky's army, where they were recorded as fighting against the Piedmontese with dedication and apparent enthusiasm. Among Tuscans there was resentment against Charles Albert's annexation of neighbouring Modena and his failure to support them in the minor battles of Curtatone and Montanara. Even within Tuscany the common cause was weakened by political differences between Florence, Livorno, Pisa, and Siena—which, according to one Tuscan minister, 'all hate one another even more than they hate Austria'.[47] In Venetia the provincial towns Padua, Vicenza, and Treviso were sometimes strongly critical of the city of Venice where Manin inherited an historic clash of interests with the surrounding terra firma. Also inside Charles Albert's kingdom there was resentment and sometimes almost civil war between monarchist Turin and the citizens of Genoa, who remembered centuries of honourable republican independence. Fortunately it was not generally known that the Piedmontese monarch offered in 1849 to help in defeating Garibaldi's volunteer army in Rome.

As well as political disagreements, social differences complicated and sometimes frustrated the political revolution: the poor against the rich; professional middle classes against a landed aristocracy; rural farmers against urban citizens who wanted cheap food; settled agricultural labourers against wandering herdsmen who damaged the crops of both rich and poor. Each of these conflicts had some influence on the course of events. Property owners, even those who wanted liberal reforms, were bound to fear that political revolution might develop into social revolution, or at least that these two move-

[47] Bonarotti in conversation with Nassau Senior, *Journals*, i. 341.

ments might be mutually inhibiting. In Lombardy the wealthy and enlightened reformer Stefano Jacini came to believe that a victory for the Austrians was probably the lesser evil.[48] In Venice even the liberal Manin was worried by 'the tendency among the lower classes to liberate themselves from subjection'.[49] Nor did ideas of parliamentary government mean much to the great majority. In Florence, when the crowd shouted applause for the grand duke's constitution, some people assumed that this mysterious word 'constitution' must be the name of Montanelli's wife. When some citizens of Turin cried 'Long live Charles Albert and his constitution', others were mistakenly shouting for 'Charles Albert and his uniform'.[50]

Generalizations are always hard to make about people who left no written record of their opinion; but without doubt the urban revolution in Lombardy, as also in Sicily, began with material assistance from peasants who saw this as a chance to free themselves from political and social oppression. Later, however, the rural population was more often alienated by requisitioning, compulsory billeting, and the damage done to agriculture by the passage of contending armies in a cause that was barely understood. One Piedmontese general recalled how he had to threaten the incineration of Lombard villages when their inhabitants, in self-defence against his invading army, flooded the fields by opening dikes which regulated the complex irrigation system of the Po valley.[51] Another misfortune for farm labourers was to find that the revolution merely transferred political power from the Austrian viceroy to their own employers, who were often hostile partisans in a parallel class war. In August 1848 cries of 'Long live Radetzky' were heard in the countryside, and the returning Austrians were careful to support the poor against their landlords.[52]

Only in course of time could the gains and losses of this revolutionary year be assessed. One result, whether gain or loss, was that

[48] *La Lombardia nel Risorgimento italiano* (Milan, 1930), 83.

[49] V. Marchesi, *Storia documentata della rivoluzione e della difesa di Venezia negli anni 1848–49 tratta da fonti italiane ed austriache* (Venice, 1913), 178.

[50] A. d'Ancona, *Ricordi storici del Risorgimento italiano* (Florence, 1914), 255–6; A. Balleydier, *Turin et Charles-Albert* (Turin, 1848), 243.

[51] E. della Rocca, *Autobiografia di un veterano* (2 vols.; Bologna, 1897–8), i. 167.

[52] F. della Peruta, *Democrazia e socialismo nel Risorgimento* (Rome, 1965), 99–103; C. Casati, *Nuove rivelazioni su i fatti di Milano nel 1847–1849* (2 vols.; Milan, 1885), ii. 336; *Correspondence respecting the Affairs of Italy*, iii. 121; Filipuzzi (ed.), *Relazioni diplomatiche*, i. 210–11.

Gioberti's 'neo-Guelph' idea of an Italian federation under the Pope was unviable. Equally remote from reality seemed Charles Albert's confidence in *fare da se*, namely the belief that Italians could deliver themselves from Austrian occupation without foreign assistance. Among positive results, an awareness was growing that there was an alternative to passively accepting subjection under foreign autocratic government. Everywhere in Italy the *ancien régime* had suffered a reverse, and some individuals acquired a novel experience of politics after being hitherto excluded from public life. Everywhere it was becoming more evident that concessions to self-determination and nationality might be required in order to prevent further wars or revolutions; and this is why it can now be seen that the events of 1848 were a necessary stage in the development of national consciousness.

None the less, the turbulent episodes of *quarantotto* were properly seen as Italian defeats, all the more distressing in that the Austrian Empire had been at its very weakest. The rulers of each Italian state briefly accepted constitutional government, but always reluctantly and only under the threat of revolution. There had been talk about forming a customs union like the German Zollverein, but nothing was decided because each state had prior vested interests. The year's end therefore found Italy's more perceptive monarchist politicians pessimistic. The Tuscan Ricasoli concluded that internal discord was the most prominent feature of Italian society.[53] Marco Minghetti from Bologna, a future prime minister like Ricasoli, remarked that Italians, except a few in the better-educated classes, preferred a quiet life under foreign domination.[54] Others agreed that Italians were not sufficiently mature for liberty.[55] According to Massimo d'Azeglio, Italy had been given her best chance in seven centuries of achieving independence, but had fluffed it because her rulers and the great majority of Italians had no feeling for nationality and not enough for freedom from foreign occupation.[56]

Mazzini, too, was deeply disappointed, but more than others had cause for some satisfaction, because at last ordinary citizens were

[53] *Carteggi di Bettino Ricasoli*, ed. M. Nobili and S. Camerani (Rome, 1939–), iii. 209–10.   [54] Minghetti, *Miei ricordi*, ii. 112, 474.
[55] A. Codignola, *Dagli albori della libertà al proclama di Moncalieri* (Turin, 1931), 502, 594–5; Senior, *Journals*, i. 301–2.
[56] M. d'Azeglio, *Scritti e discorsi politici*, ed. M. de Rubris (3 vols.; Florence, 1931–8), ii. 9–10, 57.

tentatively beginning to raise their voices. In Palermo, Livorno, Milan, Venice, and elsewhere the common people had contributed much of the initiative and momentum to the events of 1848, sometimes sacrificing their lives to make reluctant politicians support a revolution. At a later stage, when the regular armies of Piedmont and Naples withdrew from the war disillusioned and empty-handed, individual republican revolutionaries again took power and organized scratch armies of volunteers to continue fighting for another year in Venice and Rome. This gave comfort to Mazzini in his conviction that national liberty should and could come by means of self-determination, not as a gift bestowed by Italian princes or the machinations of foreign diplomacy.

Count Cavour learnt another very different lesson in 1848: that Italy was so fragmentary and disjointed that self-determination or *fare da se* was an illusion. Cavour was the hero of a later stage in the Risorgimento, a realist and diplomatist who was convinced by the events of this year that success would be impossible without foreign assistance; and over the next decade he painstakingly plotted to provoke another major European war in which a foreign army could be persuaded to intervene and bear the brunt of expelling the Austrians from Italy. Cavour and Mazzini were political enemies who each thought of the other as wicked, inexpedient, even potentially disastrous for his country. But the lessons they now learnt, though contradictory in appearance, were both necessary for the formation of a united Italian nation.

FURTHER READING

Books in English on the Italian revolution include the best study on Daniele Manin in any language, Paul Ginsborg's *Daniele Manin and the Venetian Revolution of 1848–49* (Cambridge, 1979). Sympathetic accounts of the Neapolitan Bourbons and Pope Pius IX are to be found in Sir Harold Acton's *The Last Bourbons of Naples 1825–1860* (London, 1961) and E. E. Y. Hales's *Pio Nono: A Study in European Politics and Religion in the 19th Century* (London, 1956). The Tuscan revolution is treated *en passant* in Sir Keith Hancock's *Ricasoli and the Risorgimento in Tuscany* (London, 1926). The diplomatic context of the revolution was the subject of A. J. P. Taylor's very first book, *The Italian Problem in European Diplomacy, 1847–1849* (Manchester, 1934), and more recently an interesting study of the Austrians in northern Italy is Alan Sked's *The Survival of the Habsburg Empire: Radetzky, the Imperial Army and the Class War, 1848* (London,

1979). Military history was the chief interest of G. F. H. Berkeley and J. Berkeley, *Italy in the Making: January 1st 1848 to November 16th 1848* (Cambridge, 1940). For general background on the radical leaders there is G. M. Trevelyan's *Garibaldi's Defence of the Roman Republic* (London, 1907), Clara Lovett's *Carlo Cattaneo and the Politics of the Risorgimento, 1820–1860* (The Hague, 1972), and Roland Sarti's *Mazzini: A Life for the Religion of Politics* (Westport, Conn., 1997).

5

Britain's Reaction
to the Revolutions

LESLIE MITCHELL

THE revolutionary experiences of 1848, not for the first or last time, emphasized the British sense of separateness from the Continent. Very few people had anticipated trouble. Some were made fearful, if only for a moment. Most sank back restfully on the calm belief that such things could never happen here. British history had created conditions in which revolution was inappropriate: 1848 showed the middling sorts rallying to the defence of the constitution. In Europe matters were quite different. In London Chartists were confronted, not with soldiers—who were sensibly confined to barracks for the most part—but by a pantomime farce of special constables, wearing armbands and carrying batons. The contrast with Paris or Vienna could hardly be more striking.

Nothing changed in Britain, because large numbers of people acted to preserve the status quo. Elsewhere, those who should have been interested in the preservation of order did nothing while regimes were pulled down, or actively joined in the process of demolition. Within the British Isles anything threatening was certainly un-English, and probably un-Welsh and un-Scottish. There was great concern about the Irish as usual. Events in Dublin were closely monitored, and the Irish involvement in Chartism noted. Equally, the behaviour of foreign residents in London came under fierce scrutiny. But the doubtful intentions of Irishmen and refugees of one sort or another merely emphasized how extraneous all this upheaval was to the central body politic. Most of Queen Victoria's subjects had nothing to fear. Thackeray believed that his family was 'as safe at Kensington D.V. as in any corner of this habitable globe'.¹ On 10 April, the day of the great Chartist demonstration, Thomas Carlyle thought that if revolution was at hand, he should witness it. The weather was inclement; so, 'all buttoned up', he set out. As he reached the Burlington Arcade, intermittent rain had become a downpour. Having omitted to bring an umbrella, he decided that the revolution would have to take place without him, and he clambered aboard an omnibus heading for Chelsea. Returning home, he assured his wife that, 'there is *no* revolution, nor any like to be for some months or years yet'.²

The revolutions of 1848 took the English unawares. Charles Greville admitted that until trouble actually broke out in France, 'no human being dreamt of a revolution'.³ To the Queen of the Belgians it was all 'an *unbelievable* clap of thunder'.⁴ On 23 February Lord John Russell assured Queen Victoria that the French monarchy was in no serious danger of embarrassment,⁵ and *The Times*, a day later, while reporting disturbances in Paris, was confident that 'no serious popular insurrection is even probable'.⁶ Prices on the Bourse were steady. A gun-shop near the Châtelet had been broken into and a few of the lamp-posts along the Champs Élysées had suffered indignities, but what struck *The Times* correspondent most was 'the best possible temper' that 'had been displayed on both sides'.⁷ Within a week of these comments, the July Monarchy would be at an end. There was good reason for this sense of shock. Virtually no British diplomat had prepared London to expect anything untoward. Despatches are astonishingly innocent of any remark that might have led Palmerston and his colleagues to take stock. Lord Westmorland's reports from Berlin gave no hint

¹ W. M. Thackeray to Mrs Carmichael Smith (10 Mar. 1848), in *The Letters and Private Papers of William Makepeace Thackeray*, ed. G. N. Ray (4 vols.; Oxford, 1945–6), ii. 357.
² T. Carlyle to Jane Welsh Carlyle (10 Apr. 1848), in *The Collected Letters of Thomas and Jane Welsh Carlyle*, ed. K. J. Fielding (25 vols.; London, 1970–97), xxiii. 10–11.
³ Journal of C. Greville (28 Feb. 1848), in *Journal of the Reigns of George IV, William IV, and Queen Victoria*, ed. H. Reeve (8 vols.; London, 1888), vi. 136. Victoria herself shared this sense of shock: 'So much, and such extraordinary things have been happening these days, in France, that I hardly know what to write' (Queen Victoria's Journal, 24 Feb. 1848, Royal Archives, Windsor). I am most grateful to Her Majesty the Queen for permission to use this source.
⁴ Queen Louise of the Belgians to Queen Victoria (27 Feb. 1848), in *The Letters of Queen Victoria*, ed. A. C. Benson and Lord Esher (3 vols.; London, 1908), ii. 150.
⁵ Lord John Russell to Queen Victoria (23 Feb. 1848), ibid. ii. 149.
⁶ *The Times* (24 Feb. 1848). ⁷ Ibid.

that Friedrich Wilhelm IV's government would soon be challenged until 23 March.[8] The British ambassador in Vienna reported the student disturbances on 12 March, but was of the opinion that the imperial authorities would take no notice of them.[9] It is true that Sir Ralph Abercromby, in Turin, thought that Europe was heading for trouble: but not because Austria was to be weakened by revolution; rather because she was strong enough to launch a major campaign in the Italian peninsula.[10]

Oddest of all were Lord Normanby's despatches from Paris. He follows the deepening crisis of January and February very closely. He is clear about the deficiencies in Louis-Philippe's government. Some changes were indeed to be recommended, if only to scotch comparisons being made to the situation in 1830, and 'to prevent ebullitions of popular feeling'.[11] But, basically, the situation could be contained. On 17 February he announced that he did not 'participate' in any 'alarm'.[12] On the 19th he insisted that he would be 'rather surprised' if the Banquet Campaign failed to pass off quietly.[13] On the 21st he wrote two despatches. In the first, he again described Paris as excited but peaceable. In the second, composed after having a conversation with the Préfet de la Seine, he expresses a note of cautious concern.[14] Given reporting such as this, it is little wonder that a Foreign Office circular of 4 March should have described Europe as 'the scene of events of the greatest importance, unparalleled in the rapidity with which they have taken place and . . . little to be foreseen by the most sagacious observer'.[15]

London learnt about the harsh realities of Europe not from diplomats, but from refugees. English workmen expelled from France, discomposed tourists, and political dissidents were crossing the Channel in such numbers that the Brighton and Continental Steamship Company was putting on extra sailings, in spite of weather which made conditions at sea distinctly choppy. On 28 February the duc de Nemours and the duchess of Saxe-Coburg

[8] Public Record Office, FO 64/285, despatches from Lord Westmorland, Jan.–Mar. 1848. For this and other references in the Foreign Office archives I am deeply indebted to Dr A. I. M. Duncan.
[9] Lord Ponsonby to Palmerston (12 Mar. 1848), ibid. 7/347, fo. 28.
[10] Sir R. Abercromby to Lord John Russell (2 Mar. 1848), ibid. 30/22.78, fos. 11–12.
[11] Lord Normanby to Palmerston (7 Feb. 1848), ibid. 27/803, fo. 47.
[12] (17 Feb. 1848), ibid., fo. 116.   [13] (19 Feb. 1848), ibid., fo. 131.
[14] (21 Feb. 1848), ibid., fos. 143, 148–9.
[15] Foreign Office Circular (4 Mar. 1848), ibid. 7/343.

arrived at London Bridge, courtesy of the South-Eastern Railway. On 3 March Louis-Philippe himself landed at Newhaven. He had left France disguised as an Englishman, 'his whiskers shaved off, a casquette on his head, a coarse overcoat, and immense goggles over his eyes'.[16] The imaginative British consul at Le Havre had supplied him with a passport in the name of 'Mr Smith'. Palmerston hugely enjoyed the whole story, and compared it to 'one of Sir Walter Scott's best tales'.[17] English surnames were at a premium in the spring of 1848. Princess Lieven escaped from France as 'Mrs Roberts', with her jewellery sewn into her clothes.[18] The Guizots were in Bryanston Square, the duke of Montebello was in Chesham Place, and the prince of Prussia in Carlton Terrace. London suddenly swallowed a heavy dose of Europe.

The reception of these unfortunates was instructive. Victoria and Albert were distressed to find 'our relations looking indeed dreadfully overwhelmed'.[19] They were deeply concerned that their 'many German friends are in shocking difficulties'.[20] But sympathy had its limits. A lady-in-waiting observed that the junior members of the Orléans family, though exciting compassion for their situation, were also 'naughty, riotous, disobedient and unmanageable'. She tried to intimidate them with the story that Buckingham Palace had a sinister room 'pour enfermer méchants enfants', but this was greeted with Gallic scepticism. An endless provision of raspberry jam tarts was the only way of keeping them under control.[21] The English authorities mingled expressions of concern with sharp reminders that foreign dynasties had brought much on themselves by being autocratic, inflexible, and negligent of sensible advice coming from London. Victoria thought that Louis-Philippe 'had been blind to the facts'.[22] The reception of refugees should not be allowed to compromise future relations with the new regime in Paris. Interviews were to be given infrequently

[16] Mr Featherstonehaugh to Lord Palmerston (3 Mar. 1848), in *Letters of Queen Victoria*, ii. 157.
[17] Lord Palmerston to Queen Victoria (5 Mar. 1848), ibid. 163.
[18] C. Greville, *Journal*, ed. Reeve, vi. 141.
[19] Queen Victoria's Journal (28 Feb. 1848).
[20] Lady Lyttelton to Hon. C. Lyttelton (16 Apr. 1848), in *The Correspondence of Sarah, Lady Lyttelton*, ed. Mrs H. Wyndham (London, 1912), 380.
[21] Lady Lyttelton to Hon. Mrs H. Glynne (1 Mar. 1848), ibid. 374.
[22] Queen Victoria's Journal (28 Feb. 1848).

and as unobtrusively as possible.[23] Guizot was blackballed at the Athenaeum. Louis-Philippe and his family were moved out to the relative obscurity of Claremont House as quickly as possible.[24] This 'unhealthy and gloomy' house had not been occupied since the death of Princess Charlotte. Within weeks three members of the Orléans entourage had been killed by drinking the house's polluted water. Louis-Philippe and the duc de Nemours drank only beer and so remained in good health. As the comtesse de Boigne observed, all of this made 'an impression'.[25] It seemed that the English wished to keep anything European, even the refugee, at arm's length.

These reactions exactly capture the mood of 1848. England, if not Britain, was different, separate, distinct in culture and history. The *Edinburgh Review* stated the obvious in referring to 'revolutions, which have threatened to subvert the constitution and the relations of almost every state, except our own'.[26] Fundamentally, the English were already in possession of what foreigners were demanding. A privileged history had created a chosen people. Eighteenth-century historians, including radical ones like Catherine Macaulay, had written of an Anglo-Saxon world in which parliamentarianism, if not outright democracy, had been firmly established. If the French planted Trees of Liberty in 1789 or 1848, Saxon England knew of them centuries before. Jacobin France, when sporting a *bonnet rouge*, was merely borrowing the headgear of robust Saxon democrats. Even the iconography of liberty was claimed and patented by the English. It was true that tyranny had been imported into England by the Conquest, but, after all, they believed William I to be French, and therefore delinquent. Defiantly, the English fought back. Magna Carta and a hundred other splendid achievements restored the distinctive privileges of the English. What Europeans were just beginning to discover had been unearthed by the English centuries before. Saxonist theories

---

[23] Ibid. (28 Mar. 1848); the prince of Prussia visited Victoria in Buckingham Palace, 'but it was not to be known, or *appear* as a *real* audience'.

[24] Ibid. (7 Mar. 1848): 'Uncle Leopold and the Belgian Government were very anxious for the sake of Belgium, that the King should not make a permanent stay at Claremont. This is a painful thing to say, but the stay must be limited and the King be made aware that he must look for another place.' For Guizot's embarrassment see R. W. Emerson, *English Traits* (Boston, 1856), 124.

[25] C. Nicoullard, *Recollections of a Great Lady* (London, 1912), 303–4.

[26] *Edinburgh Review*, 178 (Oct. 1848), 514.

are reinvoked in the literature of 1848 to underpin a thousand-year experience of parliamentarianism.[27]

Undivided by occupation, defeat, undue religious intolerance or any of the other dislocations of politics that led Europeans to loathe one another, the English had long been accustomed to debate about their differences, to put checks on any single focal point of power, and to abide by majorities. For a century before 1848 all of this thinking, and a great deal more, had been subsumed in the phrase 'the Liberties of Englishmen'. *The Times* rehearsed old themes for its readers:

> If we ask why this country has scarcely felt the shock under which all Europe now reels, it is not from a selfish security or a premature pride. . . . The first and most obvious answer, is that this nation is already reaping the fruits of a harvest which continental Europe is only beginning to sow. We possess those things which other nations are everywhere demanding at the gates of the Palace or the door of the Legislature!—free press, legislature, etc. . . . The State becomes a society for the common good, giving to all its members a rateable share in the common benefit and stock. . . . The British Empire is a great friendly society.[28]

Consensual politics over decades and easy relationships between classes won the admiration of Ralph Waldo Emerson, who had inadvertently chosen the spring of 1848 for a lecture tour of England and France: 'Magna-charta, jury-trial, Habeas Corpus, Star Chamber, ship money, Popery, Plymouth-colony, American Revolution, are all questions involving a yeoman's right to his dinner.'[29]

This wonderful inheritance had recently been confirmed by a generation of reform and innovation. The Reform Bill had been 'our principal breakwater'.[30] The repeal of the Corn Laws, reform of the municipalities, factory acts, mines acts, pressure groups pushing for amelioration high and low, all suggested to *The Times* that the ruling élite had 'thrown themselves into the arms of the people'.[31] No European society could match this. Few European rulers seemed inclined to do so. The result was internecine violence,

---

[27] *Quarterly Review*, 165 (June 1848), 232. The reviewer talked of the British constitution as being 'the growth of ages; taking its rise in the rude but not lawless days of the Saxon, adopted by the Norman conquerors, who had the wisdom to amalgamate their subjects' constitution with their own'.

[28] *The Times* (21 Mar. 1848).

[29] Emerson, *English Traits*, 92. See also *Quarterly Review*, 165 (June 1848), 267.

[30] Lord Cockburn, *The Journal of Henry Cockburn* (2 vols.; Edinburgh, 1874), ii. 212–13 (22 Mar. 1848).   [31] *The Times* (26 Feb. 1848).

a lack of common purpose, and the absurd belief that liberties could be established in a week of barricades, when they could only be founded securely on decades of mutual trust. The Italians suffered from 'a total want of common interest',[32] the Germans were accused of trying 'to *construct* a state',[33] while the various classes in France saw politics as a chance of 'annihilating' their opponents.[34] Such a spectacle allowed the English to be 'great lovers of themselves and of everything belonging to them: they think there are no other men but themselves, and no other world but England'.[35] An English-woman, visiting the Rhineland, bridled at being called a foreigner. 'No', she retorted, '`tis you that are foreigners; we are English.'[36]

Separateness made the English interested observers of events in Europe. A position of superiority allowed them to exercise options. Many tried to be helpful. On 3 April Prince Albert sent a draft con-stitution for Germany to Frankfurt. In doing so, he was not the first person sitting in the security of London to attempt to tutor foreign-ers, who usually showed astonishing levels of ingratitude.[37] Palmer-ston told the British ambassador in Turin to 'represent' to the king of Sardinia that major reform was essential, and that, if it were de-layed, he would richly deserve the fate which had recently overtaken the king of the Two Sicilies.[38] Lord Minto had wrestled with the limited intelligence of this latter individual, but complained that he had been quite unable 'to induce the King to see the daily increasing danger of his position'.[39] All over the Continent British officials lec-tured rulers on what they needed to do, and their efforts were echoed

---

[32] *Quarterly Review*, 165 (June 1848), 229. Another reviewer thought that 'no men have less political sagacity than the modern Italians': ibid. 167 (Dec. 1848), 224.

[33] Ibid. 167 (Dec. 1848), 220–1.

[34] Guizot, as quoted in the *Edinburgh Review*, 180 (Apr. 1849), 557. See also H. L. Bulwer to Palmerston (16 Mar. 1848), Royal Archives, i.49.

[35] *The Journals and Miscellaneous Notebooks of Ralph Waldo Emerson*, ed. M. M. Sealts (16 vols.; Cambridge, Mass., 1960–82), x. 197–8.

[36] Ibid. 214. For the racial and cultural distinction of the English see Archibald Alison in *Blackwood's Magazine*, 64 (Oct. 1848). There were, of course, dissenting voices. Both George Eliot and Matthew Arnold were of opinion that the English lower orders were so intellectually inferior to their European counterparts that they could not rise to the possibility of a revolution, or comprehend the ideas it might provoke: Eliot to J. Sibree ([8 Mar. 1848]), in *The George Eliot Letters*, ed. G. S. Haight (9 vols.; London, 1954–78), i. 254; and Arnold to Mrs Foster (10 Mar. 1848), in *The Letters of Matthew Arnold*, ed. G. W. E. Russell (2 vols.; London, 1895), i. 5–6.

[37] Queen Victoria's Journal (3 Apr. 1848).

[38] Palmerston to Sir R. Abercromby (2 Feb. 1848), Public Record Office, FO, 67/148, fo. 9.

[39] Lord Minto to Sir C. Napier (9 Dec. 1847), ibid. 70/215, fo. 227.

in articles in the leading London reviews.[40] No one much doubted that it was their right and duty to take the Europeans in hand.

Governments were to be patted on the back or slapped on the wrist according to their willingness to make changes, preferably taking England as a model. The grand duke of Hesse-Darmstadt and the king of Sardinia were formally congratulated when they apparently joined the party of movement.[41] By contrast, most regimes seemed afflicted by what Lord Normanby in Paris called 'obstinate blindness'.[42] For them, there was no quarter. Victoria agreed with her prime minister that Louis-Philippe had brought disaster upon himself by his 'ill-fated return to *a Bourbon policy*'.[43] With regard to Germany, she thought that Metternich was 'the cause of half the misfortune'. He had given advice which had inhibited rulers from making concessions with a good grace and in good time.[44] Foreigners were simply not being sensible. They either could not read the signs of the times, or chose wilfully to ignore them. Sympathy for them should therefore be kept within bounds. As John Stuart Mill bluntly told the readership of the *Westminster Review*: 'No government can now expect to be permanent, unless it guarantees progress as well as order; nor can it continue really to secure order, unless it promotes progress.'[45] Oddly enough, the views of Mill and the queen had quite a lot in common. England, in 1848, was a model for Europe, a refuge for Europeans, and an inspiration for reformers. All of this gave it the right to pass judgement on its neighbours.

Not all England's neighbours saw this as self-evident, however. Frenchmen and Germans pointed out that England too had reason to fear violent change. The great Chartist demonstrations of March and April were impressive in their potential to intimidate. To some extent, this reading of events has plausibility. Violent rhetoric was not limited to the columns of the *Northern Star*, and direct compar-

[40] For example, *Blackwood's Magazine*, 63 (May 1848), and the *Quarterly Review*, 163 (Dec. 1847).
[41] F. Orme to Palmerston (7 Mar. and 5 Mar. 1848): Public Record Office FO, 30/104, fos. 89, 72. FO memorandum to Lord Westmorland (22 Feb. 1848), ibid. 64/282, fo. 60.
[42] Lord Normanby to Palmerston (23 Feb. 1848), ibid. 27/803, fos. 172–3.
[43] Victoria to King Leopold of Belgium (16 Apr. 1848), *Letters of Queen Victoria*, ii. 172. See also *The Times* (25 Feb. 1848), which accused Louis-Philippe of following the path of 'infatuation and ruin'.
[44] Victoria to Lord John Russell (16 Apr. 1848), *Letters of Queen Victoria*, ii. 170–1.
[45] *Westminster Review*, 51 (Apr. 1849), 7.

isons were commonly made between what had happened in France and what might happen in England: 'As France has secured for herself her beloved Republic, so Ireland must have her Parliament restored and England her idolized Charter.'[46] The duke of Wellington turned London into an armed camp, even though soldiers were tactfully hidden rather than provocatively paraded. A prime minister suffering badly from influenza recommended a heavily pregnant Victoria to leave London for the security of Osborne. He also asked the archbishop of Canterbury to compose a special prayer for use in 'the present time of Trouble and Disquiet'.[47] There was apprehension of trouble as well as confidence in the good sense of the English. But on the other hand the stock market, on 10 and 11 April, registered neither gains nor losses, and visitors to London admired its orderliness, not its confusion. Princess Lieven thought that 'les laches Français devraient mourir de honte de voir la différence entre les deux pays'.[48] Baron Bunsen described London, on 10 April, as 'a beautiful sight . . . like a large ship cleared for action, everything so quiet, everybody in their place all anxious and ready to do their duty'.[49]

At the time, and certainly in retrospect, the great Chartist demonstration of 10 April proved not that England was threatened by the same violence that disturbed Europe, but precisely the opposite. On that day, both the forces of order and those who challenged the forces of order behaved completely differently from their European equivalents. On the ground, the Chartists were opposed not by professional troops but by an impromptu army of special constables. Estimates of their number vary as widely as do estimates of Chartist sympathizers. Both Emerson and Lady Palmerston thought that there might be as many as 200,000. That is certainly too high a figure, but everyone agreed that they outnumbered the Chartists and made the latter look 'ridiculous'.[50] Even if some workmen were virtually press-ganged into service, it was proudly recorded that volunteers came from all classes and occupations. The specials were all 'higgledy piggledy Peers and Commoners, servants, workmen,

---

[46] M. Hovell, *The Chartist Movement* (Manchester, 1918), 287–8.

[47] Lord John Russell to Victoria (13 Apr. 1848), Royal Archives, c. 56 38.

[48] Lord Palmerston to Mrs Huskisson ([14 Apr. 1848]), in *The Letters of Lady Palmerston*, ed. T. Lever (London, 1957), 299–302.　　　　　　　　　　　[49] Ibid.

[50] Emerson, *Journals*, 263; Lady Palmerston to Mrs Huskisson ([14 Apr. 1848]), in *Letters of Lady Palmerston*, 302. Official estimates gave the Chartists 20,000 supporters. This is certainly too low.

and all kinds of people, all hale fellow well met, an example of union and loyalty and a determination to stand by our constitution which will have a great effect in England, in Ireland, and in Europe'.[51] Col. Sibthorpe, MP, admittedly a man of unnuanced views, rather regretted that the Chartists had not shown more fight, for then they 'would have got the damnedest hiding mortal man ever received'.[52]

Where could a parallel be found in Europe? The National Guard in Paris had not defended the status quo, but had turned its arms against it. English newspapers noted that Metternich dared not arm the middling sorts of Vienna. The social harmony and assimilationist politics that allowed such a tactic simply did not obtain there. The Home Office, by contrast, was not far wrong in thinking that 'there is a good spirit of self-protection among the mass of the shopkeepers & our work people which will give us a very large force of special constables'.[53] A *Punch* cartoon suggested that this force was so large that normal, criminal enterprise was curtailed. Two thieves are shown in conversation:

1st Thief: Talk of interruption of business! Vy, I give yer my vord of honour, that wat with them Specials and the regular Crushers, I aint so much a prigged a single handkercher for a week.
2nd Thief: Oh, it's enuff to make vun turn respectable.[54]

Dickens declined to volunteer on the grounds that 'special constable-ing' had reached 'epidemic' proportions.[55]

In March and April the Chartists, too, showed a marked disposition to behave differently from those seeking change in Europe. Whatever menacing language there was stood in stark contrast to moderate conduct. On 6 March a Chartist demonstration gathered in Trafalgar Square. Described by *The Times* as an assemblage of 'boys and young lads', they broke the windows of the Reform Club and 'occasionally shouted for a Republic, not knowing what it was'.[56] A man called Williams made a speech, in which he expressed a wish, not to murder Louis-Philippe, but to exhibit him

---

[51] Lady Palmerston to Mrs Huskisson (14 Apr. 1848), *Letters of Lady Palmerston*, 302.   [52] *Parliamentary Debates*, 98 (13 Apr. 1848), 293.
[53] Sir G. Grey to Lord Clarendon (2 Apr. 1848), Bodleian Library, Clarendon MSS, dep. Irish., unfol. See also a letter from 'A Working Man' to the editor of *The Times* (7 Apr. 1848).   [54] *Punch* (1848), 14: 166.
[55] C. Dickens to Sir. E. Bulwer Lytton (10 Apr. 1848), in *The Letters of Charles Dickens*, ed. G. Storey and K. J. Fielding (10 vols.; Oxford, 1965–98), v. 274.
[56] *The Times* (7 Mar. 1848).

in 'Woombell's menagerie . . . for six pence per head'.[57] It was true that the carriage of a certain Lady Hogg was stopped by the crowd and its occupant called 'an Aristocrat', but, as the lady's husband had only recently been given a title, she took this as a compliment.[58] It all proved that 'a London mob, though neither heroic, nor poetical, nor patriotic, nor enlightened, nor clean, is a comparatively good-natured body'.[59]

The story was the same on 10 April. O'Connor assured the House of Commons that all would go off quietly: 'If I thought there was any view of endangering the peace, I would not present that petition.'[60] John Arnott and the Organizing Committee for the Chartist demonstration wrote to both *The Times* and the Home Secretary to say the same thing.[61] Chartist posters advertising the event carried the motto 'Peace and Order'. On the day itself, Sir Richard Mayne of the London police famously rode to Kennington to tell O'Connor that no procession would be allowed across any of the London bridges, but that a cab would be provided to carry the petition to the Commons. O'Connor's reception of this news was ecstatic. Calling Mayne his 'best friend', he shook him warmly by the hand before turning to ask the crowd to disperse. Since he had had his pocket picked and his toes much trodden on, popular politics might have lost their immediate allure.[62] If this is to burlesque events, it at least captures the mood of *Punch*. A conversation is held between a 'Mob Orator' and a 'Magistrate':

Mob Orator: Tell me, minion! Is it the intention of your proud masters at all hazards to prevent our demonstration?
Magistrate (blandly): Yes, Sir.
Mob Orator: Then know, o myrmidon of the brutal Whigs, that I shall go home to my tea, and advise my comrades to do the same.[63]

[57] Report by Inspector Haynes on the Trafalgar Square Meeting (6 Mar. 1848), Public Record Office, MEPO 2/64.
[58] Diary of W. M. Thackeray (10 Mar. 1848), in *Letters and Private Papers of Thackeray*, ii. 364.
[59] *The Times* (9 Mar. 1848).
[60] *Parliamentary Debates*, 98 (7 Apr. 1848), 12.
[61] J. Arnott to the Editor of *The Times* (4 Apr. 1848); D. Goodway, *London Chartism, 1838–1848* (Cambridge, 1982), 74.
[62] Col. Phipps to Prince Albert (10 Apr. 1848), Royal Archives, c. 56 21; Lord John Russell, *Recollections and Suggestions* (London, 1875), 288; Queen Victoria's Journal (10 Apr. 1848). Victoria was of opinion that the day had been 'a proud thing for this country, & I trust fervently, will have a beneficial effect in other countries'.
[63] *Punch* (1848), 14: 261.

It all proved that Chartists were Englishmen too.

So all-pervasive was this sense of separateness that those who were afraid in 1848 focused their anxiety on two groups only, the Irish and foreigners resident in London. It was precisely the un-English elements in the situation that carried risks. All else was safe. A British identity may have been available by 1848, but for many it excluded the Irish. Events in Dublin received a coverage in newspapers and official documents far in excess of anything that happened in Scotland or Wales or the north of England. It was noted that much of Chartism was articulated with an Irish accent. Irish names like O'Connor and O'Brien were a little too prominent. Memories of 1798 were rehearsed. At Kennington it was noted that 5,000 Irishman were grouped under a green flag.[64] The foreignness of the Irish was made clear by their willingness to deal with the French.[65] It was rumoured that the new French Republic had promised five thousand volunteers to fight in Ireland,[66] and that useful advice was coming from Paris on how to set up the infrastructure of revolution, in terms of forming clubs and dividing cities into sections.[67] When, in March, Smith O'Brien led an Irish delegation to Paris, the lord lieutenant of Ireland believed that he had gone 'to learn how to make barricades & to bring back with them some proficient in that art'.[68] Their visit was closely monitored by the British embassy. When Lamartine made it clear that he had no intention of meddling in Irish affairs, the sigh of relief in London was audible.[69]

Even more worrying than the Irish, because even more foreign, were aliens living in London. Concern about these people and their politics becomes obsessive. The refugee and the long-term resident became objects of suspicion. Was it a coincidence that Chartist leaders like Ernest Jones had been born and educated in Germany,

[64] *The Times* (11 Apr. 1848).
[65] Sir G. Grey to Lord Clarendon (7 Mar. 1848), Bodleian Library, Clarendon MSS, dep. Irish, unfol.
[66] Clarendon to Grey (6 Apr. 1848), ibid., fo. 200.
[67] 2 Apr. 1848 (ibid., fo. 193).   [68] 25 Mar. 1848 (ibid., fo. 177).
[69] Sir G. Grey to Lord Clarendon (24 Mar. 1848), ibid., unfol. Even so, in the last resort the bulk of the Irish population was still thought to be loyal. Everyone followed the trials of John Mitchell and other Young Ireland leaders closely, but concluded with the lord lieutenant that 'the wealth, intelligence and industry of Ireland are loyal', or with Anthony Trollope that 'there is not enough intelligence in Ireland for any body of men at all to conceive the possibility of social improvement': Clarendon to Grey (20 Mar. 1848), ibid., fo. 166, and Trollope to Mrs F. Trollope ([*c*.Mar. 1848]), in *The Letters of Anthony Trollope*, ed. N. J. Hall (2 vols.; Stanford, Calif., 1983), i. 17. See also *The Times* (4 Apr. 1848).

or that Harney was known to be a friend of Engels? Emerson no-
ticed the self-sufficiency of the German community in Whitechapel
and the French in Spitalfields.[70] 'Why', *The Times* asked, 'are they
here?'[71] Lady Charlotte Guest was clear that they had come 'to
promote anarchy'.[72] The Home Office began to receive letters from
patriots claiming that their districts were 'swarming with French
revolutionary propagandists',[73] and in response even the cool head
of Sir George Grey began to be alarmed that London was 'very full
of Frenchmen'.[74] *Punch* gave its readers advice on how to behave
when meeting a foreign revolutionary.[75] In fact, of course, there was
nothing new about the existence of foreign communities in London.
A Society of Fraternal Democrats from all over Europe had been
set up in 1845, for example. What was new was their demonization.

The English shifted any fear or guilt about their own community onto the shoulders of others. It was deeply suspicious that, at
a meeting of the Society of Fraternal Democrats on 24 February
1848 representatives from France, Germany, Italy, Hungary, and
Poland greeted the news of the creation of a republic in Paris 'with
wild enthusiasm'.[76] In his account of the events of 10 April, written
for the instruction of Prince Albert, Colonel Phipps made a point
of saying that 'there were knots of foreigners about, in groups of ten
or twelve, who when I stopped to look at them, evidently shunned
observation. There were other small parties of desperate looking
ruffians evidently ready to take advantage of any accident.'[77] Such
views became the commonplaces of eyewitness accounts. For those
who believed that the English loved their constitution, it was logical that any challenge to it had to be directed by aliens. Patriotism
was fashionable. The in-tray at the Home Office began to fill up
with letters from citizens trying to be helpful. Many were written

---

[70] Emerson, *Journals*, x. 237.

[71] *The Times* (12 Apr. 1848); see also ibid. (6 Apr. 1848).

[72] Diary of Lady Charlotte Guest (8 Apr, 1848), in Lord Bessborough, *Lady Charlotte Guest* (London, 1950), 209.

[73] 'Amicus' to Sir G. Grey (5 Apr. [1848]), Public Record Office, HO 40/59. See also R. Rouse to Grey (13 Mar. 1848), ibid.

[74] Sir G. Grey to Lord Clarendon (31 Mar. 1848), Bodleian Library, Clarendon MSS, dep. Irish, unfol.

[75] *Punch* (1848), 14: 182. Their recommendation was that such people should be deposited in the nearest fountain.

[76] D. Thompson, *The Chartists* (London, 1984), 318–19.

[77] Col. Phipps to Prince Albert (10 Apr. 1848), Royal Archives, c. 56 21. See also Sir B. Hall to Dr Meyer (11 Apr. 1848), ibid., c. 56 32.

anonymously, denouncing individuals or warning the Home Secretary of vague dangers. Anything or anyone foreign had become an object of denunciation. Typical of this kind of evidence is a letter to Sir George Grey from the proprietor of the White Conduit House Tavern in Islington, dated 13 March 1848:

Having the largest premises and accommodation for public meetings of any place in London, and having been repeatedly applied to within the last two or three weeks, for large public meetings to be held at my house for political purposes but under pretence of Dinners Banquets Tea & Supper parties by French men and men of extreme political opinions, I deem it right to inform you . . . that . . . it is my determination not to allow any meetings to be held here under any pretence which may be calculated to lead to any breach of the peace.[78]

More poignantly, long-standing foreign residents in London also wrote in, both to protest that they had no intention of subverting the British constitution and to plead that they should not be deported as part of a general proscription. Clearly, as London became patriotic, being foreign in London was an uncomfortable experience.

Xenophobia quickly took legislative form. On 2 March E. J. Stanley wrote to the Home Office to enquire if that department had sufficiently extensive powers to control the admission of foreigners into England.[79] On 11 April the duke of Beaufort drew the attention of the House of Lords to 'the great number of foreigners that were to be seen on the streets of London', many of whom 'were known to be the worst characters of France'.[80] In reply, Lord Lansdowne announced that the government was immediately bringing in a new bill to allow the deportation of aliens 'whose objects in this country do not warrant their remaining here'.[81] The measure was rushed into law in just over a week. It was emphasized that foreign residents of seven years' standing had nothing to fear, and that it was a precaution taken only against those with 'unlawful purposes'; but the menace was clear.[82] Chartist gallows humour that the first foreigners to be ejected should be Guizot and Prince Albert was

---

[78] R. Rouse to Sir George Grey (13 Mar. 1848), Public Record Office, HO 40/59, fo. 296.
[79] E. J. Stanley to S. M. Phillipps (2 Mar. 1848), ibid. 45/2386.
[80] *Parliamentary Debates*, 98 (11 Apr. 1848), 135.
[81] Ibid.
[82] Sir D. Le Marchant to Mr Boiteux (14 Apr. 1848), Public Record Office, HO 5/21.

small consolation.[83] In moments of tension the English underlined their sense of distinction by active measures of quarantine. By contrast, sensible, or Anglophile, foreigners knew perfectly well that England was a model for their own activities, not something to be attacked. To quote Emerson once more:

> The culture of the day, the thoughts and aims of men, are English thoughts and aims. . . . The Russian in his snows is aiming to be English. The Turk and the Chinese also are making awkward efforts to be English. The practical common-sense of modern society, the utilitarian direction which labor, laws, opinion, religion take, is the natural genius of the British mind.[84]

Leopold of Belgium thought that the whole of European civilization would be endangered by any threat to England.[85] Compliments such as these were accepted with alacrity. The English saw them as just.

In the many accounts of 10 April one story is told over and over again. Its constant repetition clearly gave those in authority great comfort. It had a talismanic quality. The story is as follows. Among the crowds in Trafalgar Square there appeared a Frenchman. According to one account, he berated the English for being too cowardly to fight. According to another, he offered the crowd practical advice on how to build a barricade. Before he could make much progress, a butcher's boy, to the cheers of the crowd, challenged the Frenchman and knocked him down. In retailing the story to Prince Albert, Lord John Russell concluded by saying: 'This is English patriotism.'[86] In the middle of the Chartist agitation *Punch* produced a cartoon that had a considerable resonance. It showed the British lion lying languidly along the top of the white cliffs of Dover. Its head is resting on an upraised paw. Gazing across the Channel at a Continent on fire, it raises its left eyebrow in puzzled detachment. Sunning itself by the English seaside, the lion can only wonder at the strange goings-on among its neighbours.

[83] *The Times* (13 Apr. 1848).   [84] Emerson, *English Traits*, 41–2.
[85] Leopold I to Victoria (8 Apr. 1848), Royal Archives, Y93 63019.
[86] Lord John Russell to Prince Albert (11 Apr. 1848), ibid., c. 56 28. See also Sir B. Hall to Dr Meyer (11 Apr. 1848), ibid., c. 56 32.

FURTHER READING

For obvious reasons, Britain, unlike most other European countries, has no bibliography that specifically addresses revolutionary potential in 1848. However, in addition to the manuscript sources cited in the text, the following secondary works will prove helpful in assessing British experiences.

1. *Foreign policy*

BOURNE, K., *The Foreign Policy of Victorian England, 1830–1902* (Oxford, 1970).

CHAMBERLAIN, M., *British Foreign Policy in the Age of Palmerston* (London, 1980).

HAYES, P., *Modern British Foreign Policy: The Nineteenth Century 1814–1880* (London 1975).

PREST, J., *Lord John Russell* (London, 1972).

TAYLOR, A. J. P., *The Italian Problem in European Diplomacy, 1847–1849* (Manchester, 1934).

ORR, W. J., 'British Diplomacy and the German Problem, 1848–50', *Albion*, 10 (1978).

TAYLOR, A., 'Palmerston and Radicalism, 1847–1865', *Journal of British Studies*, 33 (1994).

2. *Chartism*

GOODWAY, D., *London Chartism, 1838–1848* (Cambridge, 1982).

HOVELL, M., *The Chartist Movement* (Manchester, 1918).

SAVILLE, J., *1848: The British State and the Chartist Movement* (Cambridge, 1987).

THOMPSON, D., *The Chartists* (London, 1984).

JONES, G. S., 'The Language of Chartism', in J. Epstein and D. Thompson (eds.), *The Chartist Experience*, (London, 1982).

LARGE, D., 'London in the Year of Revolutions, 1848', in J. Stevenson (ed.), *London in the Age of Reform* (Oxford, 1977).

3. *Ireland*

KERR, D. A., *'A Nation of Beggars'? Priests, People and Politics in Famine Ireland, 1846–52* (Oxford, 1994).

KINEALY, C., *The Great Calamity: The Irish Famine, 1845–1852* (Dublin, 1994).

MILLER, K. A., *Emigrants and Exiles: Ireland and the Irish Exodus to North America* (Oxford 1985).

VAUGHAN, W. E., *Ireland under the Union, 1801–1870* (Oxford, 1989).

6

The German Revolutions of 1848–1850 and the *Sonderweg* of Mecklenburg

HARTMUT POGGE VON STRANDMANN

AFTER the war my family and I lived for several years as refugees from Mecklenburg in the small market town of Eutin in Holstein, which up to 1938 had belonged to the grand duchy of Oldenburg. On my way home from school I regularly passed a bookshop which displayed in its window recent publications, of which there were not yet many, and second-hand books. On the hundredth anniversary of the German Revolution of 1848, in the middle of March, the bookshop displayed pictures of the revolution from various books. The shop was concentrating on one main theme of the revolution, the struggle for political freedom. There were pictures of barricades, men in dark suits making speeches, revolutionaries in colourful uniforms with enormous feathers in their hats, and, to my delight, caricatures.

At that time Eutin also had a second bookshop, run by a little old lady called Mrs Grooß. In her shop window there was a display of books with open pages emphasizing the other main theme of the revolution, the struggle for national unity. In 1948 this theme seemed especially poignant, as the division of Germany into eastern and western zones appeared to be becoming more permanent. The revolution was not commemorated in any particular way in the

I would like to thank Dr Klaus Baudis, Dr Peter-Joachim Rakow, and Dr Andreas Röpcke, all three from the Landeshauptarchiv Schwerin, for their help; I am also very grateful to Frank Müller for supplying me with transcripts of British ambassadorial reports about revolutionary events in Mecklenburg.

former grand duchy's state library, housed near the castle, perhaps because the librarian was a Baltic German from Latvia, for whom the Russian revolutions of 1905 and 1917 might have been more relevant than the revolutionary events of 1848 in Frankfurt and Berlin.

Little did I know at the time that the anniversary of 18 March 1848, when over 300 Berliners had died in clashes with the Prussian army, was celebrated as an official holiday in East and West Berlin.[1] Owing to the hardening of the ideological confrontation, the Sozialistische Einheitspartei Deutschlands (SED), the party dominant in East Berlin, disagreed with the celebrations planned in the West and instead had convened a so-called People's Congress, at which the desire for a unified Germany under Communist leadership was voiced.[2] The party authorities in East Berlin also claimed to be the heirs of the radical left of 1848 when they organized, among other events, a demonstrative march to the Friedrichshain, where most of those who died a hundred years earlier were buried. At the memorial the speaker of the all-Berlin assembly, Otto Suhr, told the audience that the German revolution was about freedom and that the struggle for civil rights had started in Berlin in 1848. His moderate speech stood out in the unfolding massive propaganda campaign organized by the Communist authorities. Although the Western representatives in the all-Berlin city parliament were for political reasons unhappy about the SED-inspired propaganda campaign, they joined in the call for a political rally in front of the ruin of the Reichstag, where, under the banner of 'Peace, Freedom, Democracy', Eastern machinations were attacked in various speeches.[3] Afterwards the American commander of Berlin, Lucius Clay, pursued his political agenda when he linked the commemoration of the revolution to the readiness in the Western half of the city to defend democracy and even die for political freedom.[4] Thus, whereas the East emphasized national unity as one of the main themes of 1848, the West regarded freedom as more crucial.

[1] Manfred Hettling, '"Barricade" and "Parliament": Symbols and the Courses of Recollection from 1848 to 1998', unpubl. MS; Laurenz Demps, '18. März 1848: Zum Gedenken an 100 Jahre Märzrevolution in Berlin', in Wolfgang Hardtwig (ed.), *Revolution in Deutschland und Europa 1848–9* (Göttingen, 1998), 11–31.

[2] Edgar Wolfrum, 'Bundesrepublik Deutschland und DDR', in Christof Dipper and Ulrich Speck (eds.), *1848: Revolution in Deutschland* (Frankfurt, 1998), 35–49 at 36–7.   [3] Ibid.

[4] Demps, '18. März 1848', 27.

However, celebrations in Frankfurt, where a few weeks later the beginning of German parliamentarism would be commemorated in the hope that a new German parliament might meet in the reconstructed Paulskirche, were only a pale reflection of what had happened in Berlin, where the memory of the 1848 revolution became a focus of the emerging cold war. Although the rallies in the Friedrichshain continued in subsequent years, neither East nor West developed a commemorative culture of the 1848 revolution as existed in France for 1789 or in the Soviet Union for 1917. One of the reasons for this might be that the revolution of 1848–9 was regarded as a failure—and failures are not normally the stuff of commemorations. Only since the 1970s have historians begun to point to a number of long-term effects which the revolution had on political developments and Germany's political culture.[5]

Back in Eutin, where I caught a glimpse of the hundredth anniversary of the 1848 revolution, I was unaware of the political issues underlying the celebrations in Berlin or Frankfurt. When I enquired at home about the revolution I was told, with a certain family pride, that one of my direct ancestors, Johann Pogge-Roggow (1793–1854), who had been a reformist landowner and politician in Mecklenburg, had in 1848 been a member of the Frankfurt Parliament, and that his name would be displayed again together with those of the other deputies in the rebuilt Paulskirche, the meeting-place of the first all-German parliament. As we had at that time no picture of him, and as no one could tell me any stories about him, my fantasies about him were influenced by the pictures I had seen in the two bookshops.

When I later began to study history I discovered that Pogge had never mounted a barricade, that he had not made a single speech in the Paulskirche, that he did not belong to any political clubs associated with the names of Frankfurt inns and restaurants, and that he was an MP only until the end of October 1848, when he resigned from Frankfurt to take up a seat in the first elected parliament in Mecklenburg.[6] More recently I found out

[5] See *Das Parlament: 150 Jahre Parlamentarismus in Deutschland* (16 Jan. 1998); also Badisches Landesmuseum Karlsruhe (Alfred Frei) (ed.), *1848–9: Revolution der Deutschen Demokraten in Baden* (Baden-Baden, 1998), 497–504. However, in the catalogue for an exhibition held in Frankfurt in 1998 Lothar Gall follows a more cautious approach when he refers to the 'obliging tradition' of the revolution: L. Gall (ed.), *1848: Aufbruch zur Freiheit* (Frankfurt, 1998), 22.

[6] H. Pogge von Strandmann, 'Die Revolution von 1848 in Mecklenburg: Die

in the Mecklenburg Archives in Schwerin that he addressed his
voters through several lengthy letters published in the *Mecklenburgische Zeitung*, and that in the Paulskirche he belonged to the centre
left. Moreover, a Mecklenburg newspaper observed in September 1848 that he sat with the Right and often voted with the
Left.[7]

What Pogge's letters from Frankfurt reveal is that he had become
much more aware of the social problems in other parts of Germany
which had not surfaced to the same extent in Mecklenburg.[8] The
Europe-wide economic and social crisis of the mid-1840s helped
to shape revolutionary events in central Europe in 1848–9 and has
been regarded as the main cause of the German revolution.[9] But
it is safe to assume that without the political reform movement,
economic hardship and social conflicts alone would hardly have
triggered any revolutionary movements in the two grand duchies
of Mecklenburg-Schwerin and Mecklenburg-Strelitz. This is not
to say that existing social and political conditions in the mainly
rural Mecklenburg gave no cause for complaint, but, unlike in other
parts of Germany, in this part of northern Germany the mounting
pressure for political reforms acted as a catalyst for emerging socio-
economic protests.

   Despite the fear which many people in Germany had of an imminent revolution, its outbreak was spontaneous, uncoordinated
and multidimensional. The existing political regimes had done
very little apart from taking suppressive measures to defend themselves. They had relied on repressive Metternich-style methods
which dealt mainly with political issues but could not cope with the
emerging social developments resulting from the process of industrialization and rapid changes in agriculture.[10] As the Metternich

---

liberale Verfassungsbewegung vom Vormärz bis zum 1850 erfolgten "Sieg der
Reaktion"', in Michael Heinrichs and Klaus Lüders (eds.), *Modernisierung und
Freiheit: Beiträge zur Demokratiegeschichte in Mecklenburg-Vorpommern* (Schwerin,
1995),165–85.

   [7] *Das Wiedergeborene Mecklenburg 1848*, 207.

   [8] Johann Pogge-Roggow, in *Mecklenburgische Zeitung* (30 Apr. 1849).

   [9] See, for a recent summary of this view in English, Jonathan Sperber, *The European Revolutions, 1848–51* (Cambridge, 1994), 5–26.

   [10] Wolfgang Hardtwig, *Vormärz: Der monarchische Staat und das Bürgertum*, 4th
edn. (Munich, 1998), 33–50; Thomas Nipperdey, *Germany from Napoleon to Bismarck 1800–1866* (Dublin, 1996), 249–50.

system began to loosen its repressive grip, expectations for political reforms began to grow.[11] Yet the underlying fear of most politically minded people was of a repetition of the Revolution of 1789 as well as the Napoleonic wars.

The concentration on liberal political reforms obviated the need for social reform programmes to be worked out, especially as the peasants, artisans, and craftsmen, as well as the rural and industrial workers, pursued contradictory aims. With few exceptions these groups did not favour a revolution to achieve their goals. Their protests, demonstrations, and disturbances developed into a revolution only where there existed political groups working for political reforms and therefore willing to lead the social protest movements. Whereas the prospect of a revolution was dreaded by most members of the liberal bourgeoisie in Germany, its outbreak equipped them paradoxically with the means of putting pressure on the *anciens régimes* which the continuation of reform activities simply could not have achieved. Political reformers had as much need for social protests to further their cause as those backing social protests depended upon the reformers to articulate their demands. For this interdependence to become effective a major event was needed, and this event was the February revolution in Paris.[12]

In 1847 and early 1848 contemporary observers believed that a revolution, whose causes were social unrest, poverty, and the economic problems of the mid-1840s, could break out in Britain or Belgium. In fact the sequence of revolutionary events started in Switzerland, then moved to Italy, and finally reached France, from where the revolutions in Germany and in the Habsburg Empire were triggered.

The outbreak of the first French Revolution in 1789 had had a great political impact on various social groups in Germany, but did not lead to any major imitations. This situation had changed at the time of the July revolution in 1830, when a number of revolts occurred in Germany, most noticeably in Brunswick, where the duke was deposed and his castle destroyed. Similar violent events

[11] Peter Wende, '1848—Reform or Revolution in Germany and Great Britain', unpubl. MS.

[12] Maurice Agulhon, *1848 ou l'apprentissage de la République, 1848–52* (Paris, 1992); Jean-Claude Caron, *La France de 1815 à 1848* (Paris, 1993). See also Pierre Lévêque, 'Die revolutionäre Krise von 1848–51 in Frankreich: Ursprünge und Ablauf', in Dieter Dowe *et al.* (eds.), *Europa 1848: Revolution und Reform* (Bonn, 1998), 85–123.

took place in Hesse, Saxony, and Hanover, and as a result all four states ended up with a constitution. These actions had not been co-ordinated and national demands were not strong. Yet evidence of a change in attitude was most noticeable at the Hambach Festival of 1832, which 'was so indisputably nationalist as well as liberal-democratic'.[13] It then became clear that these two currents were strongly interlinked.

Metternich's relatively oppressive police system sharpened and increased an oppositional political culture in Germany. By this means the bourgeoisie was able to emphasize its demands for constitutional reforms and national unification. This movement found expression in a series of song festivals, legal and German-language congresses, athletic conventions, building projects which became national symbols, plays, social banquets, and nationwide meetings of artists. Thus considerable sectors of the German bourgeoisie were able to develop some dynamism when putting forward demands for political reform by writing, discussing, singing, eating, drinking, and dancing, even though the prospect of revolution horrified most members of the *Bürgertum*. All these activities were accompanied by political rhetoric in which the term 'freedom' figured prominently. So in 1844 the first words of Schiller's Ode 'An die Freude' were changed from 'Freude . . .' into '*Freiheit* schöner Götterfunken'.[14]

Yet the revolution was no accident. The unprecedented accumulation of social, economic, and political problems was the cause; the events in Paris at the end of February 1848 became the trigger. Of course, professional revolutionaries like Marx and Engels were deterministic in their outlook and encouraged each other in their belief during the last few months of the pre-March period that the real revolution was coming, commenting in their letters on events in England, Switzerland, and finally Palermo and northern Italy.[15]

---

[13] Nipperdey, *Germany*, 269, 327–30.

[14] The rewording of Schiller's poem was done by Adolf Glaßbrenner in 1844. See also Raimund Kemper, 'Ich, Reineke und mein Complot: Zu Adolf Glaßbrenner's "Neuem Reineke Fuchs"', in *Modernisierung und Freiheit*, 358–411.

[15] They welcomed events in Europe as much as they greeted the spreading of the revolution in Germany: *The Marx–Engels Correspondence: The Personal Letters, 1844–7*, ed. Fritz J. Raddatz (London, 1981), 16–17. In one of his newspaper articles Engels pointed out while reviewing events of 1847 that 'all countries were preparing themselves for [forthcoming] gigantic struggles' on an unprecedented scale: 'Die Bewegungen von 1847', *Deutsche Brüsseler Zeitung* (23 Jan. 1848), repr. in Karl Marx/Friedrich Engels, *Werke*, iv (Berlin, 1964), 494–503.

That the revolution, when it came to Germany, did not turn out as they had predicted and hoped for indicated that their reading of events and their estimation of the strength of social forces were, perhaps understandably, over-optimistic. They also neglected the large problems with which the German peasantry were faced, and were therefore surprised when they heard that it was the country-side which saw the first wave of revolution in Germany.

The peasant revolution in south-west Germany, Hesse, the Rhine Province, Thuringia, and Franconia rose against the feudal land-owners and the mediatized princes, against forestry and tax officials, and against Jewish creditors.[16] The unrest was marked by outbursts of violence which extended to rudimentary forms of civil war and reminded observers of the Peasant War of 1525. The violent protest movement was directed mainly against feudal burdens, i.e. fees und duties. Issues of poverty and social conflicts did not figure prominently. The peasant revolts were localized and were mainly suppressed by military means. The newly appointed March ministries in these states were prepared to meet their demands by substantial concessions, but when their implementation took too long many peasants joined the revolutionary struggles of 1849.

The peasant revolution in the south-west and in some other German regions found its equivalent in northern Germany in the unrest and occasional revolt by rural labourers. Rural poverty caused social conflicts in parts of Prussia and in Mecklenburg, Holstein, and Oldenburg. In Silesia the small peasantary rose against the Prussian state authorities. This latter event was of sufficient significance to help persuade the Austrian state to introduce agricultural reforms. A mixture of military suppression and concessions calmed down the countryside for a while, but then the rural labourers started their protest movement. Throughout the revolutionary period they were met by a hostile alliance of peasants and landowners who objected to most of their demands.[17]

Other social groups which responded to the impact of the revo-

[16] Nipperdey, *Germany*, 533–7. See, for a summary of new revisionist research about the peasants in the revolution, Susanne Rouette, 'Die Bürger, der Bauer und die Revolution: Zur Wahrnehmung und Deutung der agrarischen Bewegung 1848–9', in Christian Jansen and Thomas Mergel (eds.), *Die Revolutionen von 1848/49: Erfahrung–Verarbeitung–Deutung* (Göttingen, 1998), 190–7.

[17] Manfred Kossok and W. Loch (eds.), *Bauern und bürgerliche Revolution* (Vaduz, 1985), 199–220. See also Klaus Baudis, 'Bauern- und Tagelöhner-Vereine in Mecklenburg während der Revolution von 1848–9', *Agrargeschichte*, 25. *Geschichte im Spiegel agrarischer, sozialer und regionaler Entwicklungen* (Rostock, 1995), 85–92.

lution were the artisans and urban workers. Factory workers and miners—only 5.3 per cent of the fourth estate in Prussia in 1846—had been relatively peaceful during the pre-March years and during the revolution.[18] The same cannot be said of the large group of casual workers who formed the revolutionary ferment among the working population. Together with groups of artisans, they turned their protest in an anti-modernist way against machines in Mannheim, Mainz, Leipzig, Schmalkalden, and other Thuringian towns. In a similar vein coachmen and boatmen attacked steamship and railway installations.[19] By contrast the Krefeld silk-weavers, acting as a guild, wanted to share out looms rather than to smash them. The majority of artisans were less involved in direct actions in particular regions, preferring instead meetings which would lead to resolutions and petitions.

However, the situation was different in Berlin. Between 1840 and 1847 the population of this growing industrial metropolis had risen by 30 per cent to 400,000. It has been estimated that 85 per cent of that population belonged to the underclass, of whom 60 per cent received poor relief. Over 100,000 inhabitants, that is to say over a quarter of the city's population, 'live[d] below the officially defined poverty line'.[20] Only a tenth of Berliners (40,000) were workers with regular employment, of whom half were apprenticed to various trades. When Borsig, Prussia's largest machine-building firm in Berlin, sacked 400 workers in March 1848, despair became widespread and the potential for social unrest rose steeply, as the head of the city's police had warned. The deterioration of social conditions in Berlin reflected the worsening agricultural and industrial crisis of 1846–7. Although the harvest of 1847, hailed as a jubilee harvest, should have eased the situation, in fact food prices rose by a factor of two or even three. This exacerbated the industrial situation, and because of falling demand production dropped

[18] Nipperdey, *Germany*, 192–216, 535.

[19] Ibid. 534–5.

[20] Hagen Schulze, *The Course of German Nationalism from Frederick the Great to Bismarck, 1763–1867* (Cambridge, 1991), 11–12; Rüdiger Hachtmann, 'Die europäischen Hauptstädte in der Revolution von 1848', in Dowe et al. (eds.), *Europa 1848*, 455–91 at 466–70. See also, for a more detailed breakdown of Berlin's population statistics, id., 'Zwischen konservativer Beharrung und demokratisch-sozialistischer Utopie: Politische Einstellungen und Organisationsverhalten von Bürgertum, Mittelstand und Proletariat während der Berliner Revolution von 1848', *Berlin in Geschichte und Gegenwart: Jahrburch des Landesarchivs Berlin* (1995), 101–29 at 101–9.

even further. It has been estimated that the economic crisis was not over until the autumn of 1849. One indicator of social hardship was German overseas emigration, which rose between 1840 and 1849 to about half a million, mostly leaving from the south-west of the country. Thus, the general economic hardship was the prelude for the first spontaneous revolutionary wave in March and April 1848. This was accompanied by strong aspirations for reform in political institutions at local, regional, and state levels.

During the first revolutionary wave the revolts by peasants, as well as protests by artisans and casual workers, lacked central co-ordination. Only during the second phase of the revolution, when the spontaneous outbursts were overtaken by a drive to create new political institutions, did some sort of co-operation take place. This second phase was largely dominated by various groups of the educated and property-owning bourgeoisie, which gave the revolution more of a constitutionally reformist and nationalist direction. It was only partially supported by the peasants, rural workers, artisans, and day labourers.

One of the important questions of the history of 1848 is how the reformist pressures and expectations in the bourgeoisie of the pre-March period were galvanized into revolutionary action. As the liberal bourgeoisie did not favour any radical solution to political and social problems, it tended to rely on a small group of opponents of the existing situation who articulated political and social aims. This group hoped to bring about a civil society with equal rights and a strong, unified Germany accompanied by political reforms in the individual German states. Although its members had some sympathy for social complaints and wanted to improve conditions generally, it did not favour mass actions or the use of violence. Indeed, such actions, actual or threatened, caused the reform groups to press for constitutional changes which were to be used as a palliative against the potential for radicalization.

It is difficult to decide when the anti-radical stance of reformers became one of the main motives for their demands and actions, but it is clear that their opposition to radical attitudes gained growing support in late 1847 and early 1848. The first of a string of later reformist meetings appears to have been largely free of anti-radical motives. When a group of left-liberal politicians from the south-west German states met at Offenburg on 12 September 1847, it put forward thirteen demands which were approved by 500–600 participants of that public assembly.[21] These demands extended from the rescinding of the repressive Karlsbad Decrees of 1819 to the creation of an institution to represent the German people alongside the existing Bundestag (federal diet) in Frankfurt. This group also asked for the introduction of civil rights, the abolition of all privileges in society, and a progressive income tax. A month later eighteen moderate liberal constitutionalists met at Heppenheim—not far from Offenburg—and discussed a programme for the founding of a unified German federal state, social welfare, and press freedom. Both programmes were to be the beginning of German party history, but neither scheme mentioned anything about reforming the parliaments of the German states.[22] This situation was to change on 12 February 1848, when Friedrich Bassermann called in the Baden parliament for the formation of a national representative body of the various state legislatures.[23] Bassermann's motion did not mean that the reformist initiative was to pass to individual parliaments and their governments. He, like many other Germans, looked for an all-German solution to the political reform efforts.

Declarations like Bassermann's and other speeches were, however, challenged by 'the meeting of people' from below, convened by the republican Gustav von Struve at Mannheim on 27 February.[24] This important meeting put forward four resolutions. It demanded the creation of a German democratic state, absolute press freedom, trial by jury, and the arming of the people. The radical stance of the Mannheim group was what the more moderate liberals had feared all along. To prevent further developments in this direction a conference of fifty-one German liberals and democrats from the south-west, the cradle of the German Revolution, was convened in Heidelberg on 5 March, well before the revolutionary movements had succeeded in any of the individual German states, to work out what common steps should be taken next.[25] This was not an easy task as the meeting was divided between moderate liberals and democrats, the former wanting a constitutional monarchy, the latter, led by Struve and Hecker, preferring a republic. Their

    [21] Hardtwig, *Vormärz*, 196–7. The demands were published in the *Augsburger Allgemeine Zeitung* (19 Sept. 1847).
    [22] Manfred Botzenhart, *Deutscher Parlamentarismus in der Revolutionszeit 1848–1850* (Düsseldorf, 1977), 84–90.   [23] Ibid. 91, 93.
    [24] Badisches Landesmuseum (Frei), *1848–9*, 199–200.
    [25] Botzenhart, *Parlamentarismus*, 115–20.

disagreements were not resolved, but the moderate liberals were determined to act fast and keep the dynamics of revolution moving in their favour. Thus they succeeded in persuading the meeting to ask the German governments to hold all-German elections, and in preparation for this to ask the federal diet to send delegates from their states to Frankfurt to decide on procedural rules for the elections. The old Bundestag accepted this resolution and a Bundestag committee of seventeen was set up to convene what is commonly called the 'Pre-Parliament' (Vorparlament), which was to meet in Frankfurt's Paulskirche between 31 March and 3 April 1848.

The speed of developments between late February and late March was staggering, if one bears in mind the tasks German liberalism had set for itself.[26] By the end of March constitutional demands had been fulfilled in some of the German states and German unity seemed to have become achievable. The double task of bringing about national unity as well as establishing constitutions at national and state levels may have put too heavy a burden on the liberal movement, which it could not carry out successfully when challenged by regrouped conservative and military forces.

Until the end of March the revolutionary movement had not, as in 1830, toppled any monarchs from their thrones, because the liberal majority was not anti-monarchical. But there were two exceptions. In one case the legitimacy of the Danish king was questioned when he invaded the duchy of Schleswig to annex it. This led to an uprising in the two duchies of Schleswig and Holstein and the first national war for the new German state. The other incident involved the king of Bavaria, who found himself in a severe governmental crisis because of the interference in Bavarian politics by his mistress Lola Montez or, as she proudly titled herself, Donna María Dolores de los Montez.[27] She was in fact called Betsy Watson and was born in Scotland. As the king was unwilling to give in to demands for her removal, he abdicated in favour of his son on 8 March and the latter promptly set up a reformist March ministry.

Generally speaking, all these March ministries had been installed by the old order without much violence. This was typical for the

[26] Ibid. 121–30. Dieter Langewiesche, 'Revolution in Deutschland. Verfassungsstaat—Nationalstaat—Gesellschaftsreform ', in Dowe *et al.* (eds.), *Europa 1848*, 167–95 at 170–1. Heinrich Best, 'Strukturen parlamentarischer Repräsentation in den Revolutionen von 1848', ibid. 629–69 at 632–4.

[27] Karl-Joseph Hummel, 'Zonen der politischen Stille', ibid. 535–54 at 539–42. Nipperdey, *Germany*, 311.

states of the so-called Third Germany: Hanover, Saxony, Hesse, Württemberg, Baden, Oldenburg, and Brunswick. The two major states, Austria and Prussia, proceeded differently, probably because they did not have the political institutions which were needed to solve emerging conflicts, as did some of the states of the Third Germany. Therefore it was not surprising to see that peaceful demonstrations in Berlin turned into confrontations between the military and the people in which hundreds of civilians were killed.[28] These civilians were chiefly artisans, earth-moving labourers on work-creation schemes, and some women who had helped those fighting on the barricades. Even at this point there was not much demand for the abdication of the king. In fact it was he who ended the fighting by ordering his troops to withdraw from Berlin and who was then forced to honour the dead, the *Märzgefallenen*.

Both events confirmed the opinion of the mass of revolutionary supporters that a decisive victory had been won. Nothing was further from the truth, however. All the king had done was to gain time and, like his fellow princes in Germany, make concessions so as to keep his throne. Thus even the king of Prussia appointed a March ministry, although rather belatedly compared with some of the other princes. Yet the withdrawal of the army proved to be vital, because the king kept this counter-revolutionary force intact and made use of it when the reaction against the revolution took shape and gained pace in the autumn of 1848.

While the conservative forces began to regroup, the divisions between the constitutionalists and the supporters of democracy and republicanism emerged more clearly during the meeting of the 'Pre-Parliament' in Frankfurt, where 574 members gathered between 31 March and 3 April. There were 141 representatives from Prussia, 17 from the two Mecklenburg duchies, but only 2 from Austria.[29] Their main task was to prepare the elections to a national assembly. However, the liberal majority pursued an additional agenda. By speeding up the electoral process it tried to prevent a radicalization of the revolution. Struve and Hecker's motions to create a democratic republic and abolish all professional armies as well as all indirect taxation, and to let the Pre-Parliament sit until the elected national assembly was convened in Frankfurt,

---

[28] Wolfram Siemann, *Die deutsche Revolution von 1848–9* (Frankfurt, 1985), 67.

[29] C. L. F. Pohle, *Die Beschlüsse des Frankfurter Congresses* [Pre-Parliament] *und unsere Verfassungsreform* (Schwerin, 1848), 3–15.

were defeated by a majority which preferred monarchy based on the people's sovereignty. It was already here that the plan for Prussian leadership was mooted in this new Germany.

After Struve and Hecker's motions had been rejected, these two popular revolutionaries returned to Baden and, for reasons which had little to do with their defeat at the Pre-Parliament, began to fight for a democratic republic.[30] Their uprising was crushed quickly by the still existent Federal Army, with soldiers from Hesse, Nassau, Württemberg, and Baden. Even if the liberal constitutionalists were to triumph, it did not mean the end of democratic efforts. What the moderate liberals had achieved was that they had successfully put themselves at the head of the revolutionary movement and were now able to press for German unity against the power of the individual states. Most constitutional liberals were not supporters of revolutions: they hoped they had channelled revolutionary energies into political reforms; but the conservative forces in conjunction with some particularist governments were to prove stronger than expected. Nevertheless, the aims for constitutional reforms and German unity brought about a temporary community of intrests between moderates and radicals. However, this weakened and fell apart in the following months.

So far some aspects of the pre-March period and the first phase of the revolution in Germany have been sketched out. In tracing the main currents and events of the Pre-March period and the euphoric phase of the revolution, the answer to one of the decisive questions of the German revolution may have become clear. How could the expectations for reform have been transformed into a revolutionary process sweeping along most of the German states and their provinces? It is clear that in the south-west and west of Germany the early reform movement and its subdivision between radicals and constitutionalists set the pace in 1848, but apart from the early peasant riots it was the violence of the revolutionary struggle in Berlin with its bloodshed which marked the first or euphoric phase of the revolution.[31] Yet if not only the western provinces of Prussia were affected by the revolution, but also the very different central

[30] Alfred Georg Frei, 'The Revolution, 1848–9: Baden's Special Way?', unpubl. MS of a paper presented in Oxford, 30 Nov. 1998.

[31] See, for the protest movement in Prussia, Manfred Gailus, *Straße und Brot: Sozialer Protest in den deutschen Staaten unter besonderer Berücksichtigung Preußens, 1847–9* (Göttingen, 1990).

and eastern ones as well, then it may be worth while to look at other north German regions outside the Prussian domain, to complete the picture of an all-German revolution.

Let us now return to the grand duchies of Mecklenburg-Schwerin and Mecklenburg-Strelitz and see how Mecklenburg, not known for its revolutionary tendencies in 1789 or in 1830, was affected by the pre-March period and the first phase of the revolution.[32] The two duchies were governed by a constitutional document known as the *Landesgrundsätzliche Erbvergleich* of 1755, in which the local aristocracy had, together with the towns, triumphed over the dukes' absolutist tendencies.[33] At the regularly held annual meetings of the diet (Landtag) the large landowners were represented by the *Ritterschaft*, in which the non-noble members were in a majority from 1844 onwards, and the municipalities were represented by the so-called *Landschaft*, in fact the mayors of the towns. The *Domanium*, the property of the dukes with their tenant farmers, was not represented in the diet at all. Thus the *Ritterschaft*, the *Landschaft*, and the dukes' governments dominated the political landscape in the two duchies. However imperfect this system was, it did incorporate a constitution based on the powers of the estates whose property rights were guaranteed by the dukes.

This system may have reflected the social and economic conditions of the time, but since the 1830s gradual changes in the social composition of the *Ritterschaft* in the diet, the modernization of the agricultural sector, and the beginning of industrialization all helped to start a wider political discussion despite the practice of rigorous press censorship. Thus in 1846 it was stated in one of the newspapers that 'this system of estates no longer suits the changing conditions of the nineteenth century'.[34] Various reform proposals had been made to the Landtag, supported by the growing number of non-noble landowners, but only seldom did these proposals find the backing of a majority. Although it became increasingly clear that the diet might have outlived its usefulness in solving the growing economic and social conflicts, the setting up of a more representative constitution had not yet been discussed.[35] During

---

[32] For the pre-March period in Mecklenburg see the several contributions to Heinrichs and Lüders (eds.), *Modernisierung und Freiheit*, 165–672.
[33] See, for the latest survey, Wolf Karge *et al.*, *Die Geschichte Mecklenburgs* (Rostock, 1993), 88–94.
[34] Pogge von Strandmann, 'Revolution in Mecklenburg', 168.   [35] Ibid.

the last years before the revolution a minority in the Landtag took up the demands for reform and suggested a catalogue of changes, including amendment of the constitution and the legal as well as the taxation systems, improvement of the social conditions of the day labourers in the countryside, and accession to the Prussian-dominated Zollverein. While these were specific Mecklenburgian issues, the catalogue also included the same liberal demands as in the other German states, such as press freedom, freedom of association, separation of church and state, and free elementary education.

The spokesman for the reform movement in the Landtag was Johann Pogge-Roggow, who, with his motion of November 1847 to introduce some form of representative constitution, provided the relatively weak reform movement with a political agenda.[36] Although his demands were ridiculed in the Landtag and sidelined as his personal opinion, his initiative was taken up in the assembly by the deputy from Schwerin, Mayor Theodor Floerke, who acted on instructions from the capital's magistracy.[37] Outside the diet the first noticeable wave of political petitions in support of Pogge's motion was sent to the government and the Landtag. Overnight he had become a popular man, which probably explains why he was put up as a successful candidate for the Frankfurt Parliament in April 1848. His reputation as a reformer was still strong enough for him to be elected to the first Mecklenburg parliament a few months later, at the end of September 1848.

During the ensuing debate about political reforms, the news from France reached Mecklenburg on 28 February 1848. This was the day on which Grand Duke Friedrich Franz celebrated his twenty-fifth birthday with a performance of Flotow's opera *Martha* at the Schwerin theatre.[38] The Grand Duke was especially concerned for the life of his aunt, who, as the Duchess of Orleans, was Louis-Philippe's daughter-in-law. However, there were no disturbances in Schwerin until 13 March, and the duchies' social problems did not erupt as in other German states. There was no March revolution and no March ministry. Instead a host of political meetings were organized all over the territory, which swamped the govern-

---

[36] Pogge's original proposal (*Diktamen*), in Landeshauptarchiv Schwerin, Landständisches Archiv, Landtag. Chronologische Serie, Landtag zu Sternberg, 27 Nov. 1847; Pogge von Strandmann, 'Revolution in Mecklenburg', 170–6.
[37] Hans Heinrich Leopoldi, *Schwerin im Jahre 1848* (Schwerin, 1948), 3–32.
[38] Ibid. 12.

ment with a second wave of petitions for reform. Initially these petitions were moderate in tone and asked, in reference to Pogge's proposals of November 1847, for some constitutional changes. But gradually the character of the petitions was to change and more radical demands were put forward as well.[39]

Most of the addresses came from the country towns and were signed by artisans, merchants, lawyers, teachers, and occasionally even workers. The first major political meeting took place on 9 March in Mecklenburg's ancient university town, Rostock, strongly backed by a radical faction from the university.[40] No social demands were made, but the government was asked, in seventeen 'propositions', to convene an assembly which should draft a constitution with an elected Landtag. Furthermore this Rostock assembly called for land reforms and the granting of the liberal freedoms of the March movement. Two days later even the university petitioned the Grand Duke with a request to reform the constitution. This was unusual, as most of the other German universities were still passive. The Rostock 'propositions' carried about one thousand signatures, mostly of artisans, merchants, workers, and sailors. Six professors had signed, but four times as many lawyers. It was handed to the Grand Duke by a delegation from Rostock, but Friedrich Franz II was still unwilling to grant any reforms, except by lifting press censorship. The Grand Duke's stubbornness led to further meetings in the duchy, and as a result more letters were addressed to the monarch. Now the hitherto silent *Domanium* also started sending petitions, and this caused some additional concern in Schwerin.

The change of mood in the duchy also affected members of the old Landtag. Thus on 16 March thirty-nine non-noble and two noble deputies met in Güstrow and agreed that they would be willing to relinquish some of their privileges and rights.[41] They also advised the Grand Duke to lift his recently imposed ban on further petitions. It is difficult to decide whether he would eventually have adapted to the rapidly changing mood in the country; but as so often in Mecklenburg's history the final impetus came from outside the

---

[39] Hans Schröder, 'Die Revolution von 1848–9 in Mecklenburg-Schwerin', unpubl. MS (Greifswald, 1961), 103–14.

[40] Elisabeth Schnitzler, 'Die Universität Rostock im Jahre 1848', in Heinrichs and Lüders (eds.), *Modernisierung und Freiheit*, 423–51 at 429–35. See also K. Baudis, 'Die Demokraten im Parteilager der Revolution von 1848/49 in Mecklenburg', ibid. 452–96 at 453–5.

[41] Schröder, 'Revolution', 131. One of the signatories was Johann Pogge.

duchy. In March 1848 the violent days in Berlin and the uprising in Vienna forced the Grand Duke to make a declaration in which he agreed to convene a special meeting of the Landtag in order to discuss constitutional reforms; but he did so only to gain time, like his royal uncle in Berlin, not because of a change of conviction.

While the Grand Duke geared himself up to making more concessions to prevent a repetition of Prussian events in Mecklenburg, those who had backed the petition movement now wanted to co-ordinate their efforts for reform and mobilize wider support. The poet Hoffmann von Fallersleben, author of the *Deutschlandlied*, had a strong influence on the formulation of the 'Twenty Demands of the Mecklenburg People', which was to become the agenda for the first Reform Conference in Güstrow on 2 April 1848.[42] Associations as forerunners of political parties were formed in Saxony and Baden as well, but this movement in Mecklenburg stands as one of the earliest in Germany.[43] The gathering had been called on 23 March by a committee in Rostock which had asked the recently established Reform Associations in the country to send delegates to Güstrow. The aim was to provide the reform movement with an organizational basis. The formation of political opinion was accompanied by two more proclamations by the Grand Duke in which he agreed to the freedom of association and to a reform of ducal landholdings. He even accepted the idea of an all-German representational body, but believed it ought to consist of the German estates. Elections were not yet part of his thinking, but he was being reluctantly pushed along this path.[44]

So far the bourgeoisie and the lower classes in towns and countryside still acted together in Mecklenburg. But this was to change during the first Reform Conference on 2 April. Based on Hoffmann von Fallersleben's catalogue for reforms, the seventeen clauses of the Rostock Committee were passed. They dealt with rural reforms, such as the partitioning of the very large estates, the change of the short-term tenancies into freehold properties, and the abolition of entailed estates. Improvements in poor relief, school education, and

[42] See the published minutes of that assembly, *Protokoll der Versammlung Mecklenburgischer Reformfreunde* (Güstrow, 2 Apr. 1848). This meeting was attended by 173 deputies from 46 townships and 8 districts of the *Domanium*.
[43] Botzenhart, *Parlamentarismus*, 324–38.
[44] Ludwig von Hirschfeld, *Friedrich Franz II., Großherzog von Mecklenburg-Schwerin und seine Vorgänger*, i (Leipzig, 1891), 237–8.

housing followed. Then there were the usual liberal demands being made all over Germany. But the problems of rural and urban workers were not addressed.[45]

Meanwhile the Reform Associations' activities did not remain unopposed. The aristocratic landowners, among them 144 members of the old Landtag, organized a conservative meeting, also at Güstrow, a few days after the meeting of the Reform Conference (14 April).[46] Their rhetoric was strongly anti-reformist, but their position was regarded as weak. No wonder their resolutions were overtaken by the second Reform Conference, also convened at Güstrow a couple of days later. The delegates to that conference found it difficult to agree on procedural rules as to how to put together a list of candidates for the forthcoming elections to the Frankfurt parliament.[47] Speed was, however, important as the elections for the Paulskirche in the duchies were to be among the earliest in Germany. In Mecklenburg they took place between 19 and 22 April, whereas in Prussia they were held between 1 and 8 May. A committee of the conference, consisting of sixteen members, was delegated to meet representatives of the *Domanium* on the following day, also at Güstrow. The *Domanium*'s representatives consisted of peasants, rural artisans, and day labourers. All of them were taking part in the reform process for the first time, and it was probably also the first time that they articulated in public political and social ideas. After a surprisingly short discussion the committee and the *Domanium* agreed to nominate sixteen candidates for the eight constituencies to the Frankfurt Parliament. Among them were only four landowners and one peasant. The remainder consisted of lawyers, judges, and teachers.

Merchants and artisans were missing. Whether they were unwilling to spend the time or had not gained a big enough reputation in the early phase of the revolution is not clear, but it is generally true of the Frankfurt Parliament that businessmen were underrepresented. This phenomenon may have been true of all German parliaments in the nineteenth century, and in all these diets state employees may have formed by far the largest group. But this does

---

[45] See also Baudis, 'Demokraten', 457–9.

[46] *Güstrowsches Wochenblatt* (16 Apr. 1848).

[47] Minutes of the *Verhandlungen der Versammlung von Deputierten der Mecklenburgischen Reformvereine* (Güstrow, 17 Apr. 1848). The meeting had become necessary after the government had published on 12 Apr. the law establishing how the forthcoming elections to the Frankfurt Parliament were to be conducted.

not mean that the entire revolution was primarily a 'revolution of the intellectuals', as Namier would have it.[48] If one defines university professors as intellectuals, then that group only constituted just over 5 per cent of those at Frankfurt. So Namier may have overestimated the numerical strength of that vociferous group in the revolution in general and in the Frankfurt assembly in particular. Perhaps it makes more sense to call the revolution the revolution of idealists rather than intellectuals.

During the elections in Mecklenburg to the first German parliament, some violent outbursts against landowners, merchants, and artisans occurred, but they did not lead to any riots. In the first round of elections a number of day labourers were voted in as electors for the second round of elections. The Reform Associations had tried to influence the election process by handing out voting papers with printed names, but this method seems to have been more successful in the second round of elections than in the first. By that point day labourers as electors tended to vote for widely respected candidates, i.e. notables. Lawyers and teachers were the most successful candidates, followed by one landowner and one civil servant.[49] The elections were a triumph for the Reform Associations, because all their candidates won, including seven potential replacements. The nobility did not manage to win a single seat in the two duchies. No reliable figures exist concerning the turn-out except from a few constituencies, but the estimates vary between 35 and 40 per cent in some parts of northern Germany and up to 75 per cent in some of the southern German states.

After the relatively early elections for the Frankfurt assembly in Mecklenburg, the public debate concentrated on the next move, the franchise of the new Mecklenburg Landtag and its functions. The old Landtag was convened at the end of April and its majority, in the belief that it controlled the countryside, opted for equal direct elections. But the Schwerin government proposed a system of electoral divisions according to which the twenty-three deputies representing the large estates would be elected directly, whereas

[48] Lewis Namier, *1848: The Revolution of the Intellectuals* (London, 1946; repr. 1992), 4.

[49] Pogge von Strandmann, 'Revolution in Mecklenburg', 179–82. The other elected deputies were Kierulff, Haupt, Böcler, Reinhard, Sprengel, Drechsler, and Genzken. See also Schröder, 'Revolution', 199–202; Karl Obermann, *Die Wahlen zur Frankfurter Nationalversammlung im Frühjahr 1848* (Berlin, 1987), 236–45.

other country constituencies and the towns would vote indirectly for twenty-nine and thirty-three deputies respectively.[50]

During these deliberations the duchies were swept by the first wave of riots of day labourers, who turned against detested landowners and employers. The Mecklenburg army had to be called out and it quelled all the riots, but this did not make for an easy climate between the various political factions. During the following weeks the government dithered and did not publish an electoral law until 15 July 1848, which led to a storm of protests from the Reform Associations meeting for their third conference at Güstrow on 21–2 July.[51] The government had insisted on a *Vereinbarungsprinzip* (principle of agreement), but had otherwise included some suggestions of the Reform Associations. The *Vereinbarungsprinzip* meant that the new assembly would be dependent on the Grand Duke's approval of the constitution. Probably he had copied this idea from Prussia, where the king, together with the old estates, had on 18 April passed the new franchise for a Prussian constituent assembly, whose eventual constitution had to be agreed upon by the ruler.

However, the *Vereinbarungsprinzip* in Mecklenburg had not been favoured by the Reform Associations earlier on, and the attempt to reintroduce it now was anathema to them, given their insistence on the principle of people's sovereignty and a constituent assembly which had to be independent from the monarch. The ensuing dispute within the Reform Associations finally led to a division, in which the right-wing liberals split from the moderate liberals and democratic elements and set up their own Constitutional Association in August 1848. Obviously this movement was influenced by the initiative to centralize the efforts of other Constitutional Associations in Berlin at the end of July. But nothing much followed, although some of these associations were larger than the democratic ones. Members of the middle and upper classes predominated in them, while those representing the lower-middle classes kept themselves in the background.[52]

Historians have argued that the emerging division between mod-

[50] Landeshauptarchiv Schwerin, Staatsministerium 392, 22 Apr. 1848; Pogge von Strandmann, 'Revolution in Mecklenburg', 180–1. See also Adolf Werner, *Die politischen Bewegungen in Mecklenburg und der außerordentliche Landtag im Frühjahr 1848* (Berlin, 1907), 87–117.

[51] *Stenographischer Bericht über die Verhandlungen der Deputierten der Mecklenburgischen Reform-Vereinen* (Güstrow, 21–2 July 1848).

[52] Siemann, *Deutsche Revolution*, 104–7.

erate and radical reformers in Mecklenburg between the first Reform Congress in April and the third one in July can be attributed clearly to a polarization between liberals and democrats. As developments in Mecklenburg showed, the difference was not as great as the terms may indicate. A certain consensus in favour of a constitution continued to predominate. What did, however, become clear over the summer was that republicanism had little support in the Schwerin duchy. The main political line of division in this respect ran between liberal and more democratically orientated monarchists, although there was some overlap.

At the end of the third Güstrow meeting a two-party scheme began to emerge. In the rest of Germany, by contrast, the roots of a five-party scheme could be discerned, which would later dominate the party structure of imperial Germany.[53] The majority passed the so-called Güstrow Proclamation, which emphasized its belief in the principle of popular sovereignty. It was also hoped that an elected assembly would draw up a constitution without the Grand Duke's agreement, although not necessarily against him. The reformers also insisted that they were not in favour of revolutionary struggle. Nevertheless, their resolutions were rejected by the governments in Schwerin and Strelitz. So the liberal and democratic associations continued to reject any dictated (*oktroiert*) electoral law. They also demanded a change of government. Expectations that the Frankfurt assembly might provide guidelines for representative institutions in the German states were to be disappointed.

Subsequently in the war of words the Reform Associations changed their tactics and turned to the countryside to mobilize the rural population. But this tactic was not without danger. Thus the associations were able to score their biggest success when a large demonstration of about 1,500 people tried to petition the Grand Duke of Strelitz for a reform of the drafted electoral legislation. The people had gathered on 7 September in front of the palace in Strelitz in order to put pressure on the ruler for reforms, including the appointment of a new ministry. For a short while the demonstration got out of hand: windows were broken and the crowds occupied parts of the palace. In this worsening situation the Grand Duke was prepared to make substantial concessions. A new government was

[53] Dieter Langewiesche, 'Die deutsche Revolution von 1848–9 und die vorrevolutionäre Gesellschaft: Forschungsstand und Forschungsperspektive', *Archiv für Sozialgeschichte* 21 (1981), 458–98 at 470.

to be appointed and the electoral law was to meet the objectives of the Güstrow meeting. A few days later his cousin in Schwerin followed suit, and the two duchies were headed—rather belatedly—by new 'March ministries'.[54] The Strelitz incident caused the British ambassador in Berlin to send his very first report to Palmerston about the revolution in Mecklenburg. He called the Strelitz incident 'unexpected', because the grand dukes had 'expressed their determination to grant the liberties which other German states may enjoy and have already taken the steps which lay within their attributions'.[55]

This short-lived radicalization occurred at the same time as the Danish–Prussian armistice was debated in Frankfurt. The war with Denmark had a great impact on Mecklenburg, and there were many who were keen to bring it to an end as quickly as possible. In this situation the Reform Associations began to prepare for the elections to the new Landtag. This meant mobilizing the people in the countryside by offering rural reforms, including the partitioning of large estates. Otherwise prospective candidates dealt with the economic problems of the artisans and the difficulties of the harvest. The first round of elections took place on 26–7 September 1848, and they turned out to be based on a similar franchise to that of the Paulskirche. The emerging success of the Reform Associations was confirmed in the second round of voting on 3 October, when the actual deputies were elected.

There were altogether 103 members of the new Landtag, of which only 20 represented the countryside, but in 18 constituencies the elections had for various reasons to be repeated on 20 October.[56] Finally the rural population of the duchy of Schwerin was represented by 20 deputies, whereas townspeople had elected 55. The remaining 10 may have represented rural constituencies, but did not have agricultural occupations. The legal profession and the landowners predominated in the Landtag. Each group had 15 deputies in the Schwerin sections. Officials followed with 11, artisans and teachers with 7 each. There were 4 doctors, 3 professors, 3 pastors, 2 merchants, 1 manufacturer, 1 day labourer, 1 book dealer, 1 student, and 1 choir master. Out of 85 deputies of that duchy, 46

---

[54] Schröder, 'Revolution', 396–8.
[55] Public Record Office, London, FO 64/289, Westmoreland to Palmerston (18 Sept. 1848).   [56] Schröder, 'Revolution', 428.

belonged to the Reform Associations and only 7 were conservatives. The remaining 32 either belonged to the Constitutional Associations or were without any clear affiliation. This was to change when the Landtag opened and later on when the Left began to lose its majority.[57]

The elections had been hailed as a victory of the Left, however moderate it may have been, at a time when the Paulskirche began to lose its influence against the increasing strength of the reactionary forces in Berlin and Vienna. In addition there was a mounting challenge to the Frankfurt Parliament, based on social and economic dissatisfaction on the part of artisans, democratically minded professionals, and peasants for whom the promised reforms took too long to be implemented. There were disturbances in Silesia, Saxony, Bavaria, and Baden. In Düsseldorf, Cologne, and Mannheim protests were voiced, and in some towns even the cry for a 'social republic' was heard.[58] In Frankfurt social dissatisfaction was mixed with national enthusiasm when a large crowd assembled outside the city to protest against the Parliament's acceptance of the armistice with Denmark. Riots and street battles took place in which eighty people died and two right-wing deputies who had helped the authorities to quell the first signs of the uprising were murdered. The incidents in Frankfurt were followed by military suppression, the declaration of a state of siege, legislation against revolutionary 'excesses', and other counter-revolutionary measures in Vienna and Berlin. These culminated in the storming of Vienna by the Austrian army under Windischgrätz at the end of October. The execution there of the Frankfurt deputy Robert Blum took place on 9 November and the military occupation of Berlin under Wrangel a day later. The roll-back of the counter-revolution began to gain momentum.

The division between liberal-constitutionalist and democratic sectors of the population was completed when the Prussian king was able to dismiss the Prussian parliament through a *coup d'état* on 5 December and dictate a constitution. This act may have given the impression that the end of the revolutionary period was reached in the power-centres of Paris, Berlin, and Vienna; but in Hungary, Venetia, and Rome the revolutionary struggle continued. In Frank-

[57] Julius Wiggers, *Die Mecklenburgische constituierende Versammlung und die voraufgegangene Reformbewegung: Eine geschichtliche Darstellung* (Rostock, 1850), 55–79.   [58] Siemann, *Deutsche Revolution*, 162.

furt, as well as in Mecklenburg, political strife was not yet over, although the return of military power in the above-mentioned capitals did not bode well for further developments.

During this period of accelerating counter-revolution the all-German Democratic Associations organized a second congress in Berlin, between 26 and 31 October, just as the elected Mecklenburg Landtag met for the first time. The aim of the congress was to centralize democratic efforts, demand new national elections, and restrict the growing power of the reaction. The congress represented 260 associations from all over Germany and had admitted the Reform Associations from Mecklenburg as members.[59] The duchy's delegates formed, with those from Pomerania, Brunswick, and East Prussia, the political right, whereas the political left came from Silesia, Hesse, and the Rhenish Province. The victory of the military in Berlin put an end to the democrats' activities there. The representatives moved to Frankfurt and, together with the factions of the left from the Paulskirche, founded the Central March Association in order to defend the achievements of the March Revolution. By April 1849 about 950 associations with nearly half a million members had established links with the Central March Association, which then made a last-ditch attempt to defend the revolution the following month.

Back in Mecklenburg the newly elected Landtag dealt in its first sessions in November 1848 with rural problems, the economic difficulties of the artisans, the constitution, and the structure of the agenda for debates and resolutions. The government regained some of its support when it stationed troops in the town of Malchow to maintain law and order. The initial euphoria was over. On the whole riots did not have much effect on the political groups. It was the constitutional question which in the end was to weaken the Left. In the relevant committee it was agreed unanimously that all power came from the people. In the plenary session the committee was able to add a bill which was to bring to an end the powers of the old estates. Both blows to the old order were met with the landowners' opposition. They pointed out that only the Grand Duke had assented so far to an agreed constitution. The weakening of the Left in the Landtag led to the formation of the 'General Political Association for Mecklenburg', which was backed by those land-

[59] Ibid. 99–104; Schröder, 'Revolution', 439–40.

owners who had left the Constitutional Association. A number of non-noble landowners joined the new group. This may also have been the consequence of the Constitutional Association's moving closer again to the position of the Reform Associations when faced with the growing power of the reaction.

The opposition in Mecklenburg gained ground when it was made clear to the Grand Duke that he should delay for as long as possible the bill to bring the power of the estates finally to an end, especially because the Grand Duke of Strelitz also objected to this step. That left the new Landtag to some extent in limbo because after the events in Prussia the threat of a dictated constitution loomed large. In spite of this threat, the diet passed with a large majority a resolution demanding that the Grand Duke give the bill his assent. Meanwhile a circular note from Prussia had disputed the constituent power of the Frankfurt Parliament, and it was suggested that the Paulskirche had the task of revising the old federal constitution in conjunction with the particularist German states.[60] The majority of the Mecklenburg Landtag, under the leadership of the senator from Schwerin, Pohle, did not accept the Prussian interpretation and insisted that the constituent power of the German parliaments was the foundation of the independent existence of the National Assembly. The linkage of the fate of the Mecklenburg Landtag to that of the Paulskirche found widespread support.

In this renewed and defiant euphoria the Reform Associations of Rostock and Schwerin decided to celebrate with public banquets on 24 February 1849 the anniversary of the revolution in France.[61] However, the members of the conservative opposition rejected the Landtag's vote on the grounds that it had overstepped its constitutional power. Although they referred here mainly to the national question, they also implied that it was not the Landtag's task to draft a constitution, but to discuss a draft elaborated by the duke's government. This view was shared by the Schwerin Grand Duke, and thus it seems that the confrontation between the Schwerin government and the Landtag's majority had not been resolved, especially as the latter voted on 1 March in favour of a democratic and monarchical constitution. The government delayed any final decision by pointing out that it was constitutionally obliged to come to an agreement with the Strelitz government. Moreover, the Strelitz

Grand Duke proved to be stubborn and unwilling to accept the Landtag's vote.

Despite the special developments in Mecklenburg, the main decisions affecting that state were reached in other parts of Germany. Austrian politics had prevented German unity and had pushed the Frankfurt assembly to resolve the Kaiser question by offering the title to the Prussian king on 28 March, with a vote of 290 in favour and 248 abstentions.[62] The delegation sent to Berlin included one Mecklenburg deputy. However, on 3 April the king rejected the proffered crown.[63] The Grand Duke of Schwerin had pleaded with his uncle to accept it, as he could not see how else a united federal state might come about.[64] His fear was not unjustified. The king's decision went further. He made it clear that he did not recognize the constituent power of the Paulskirche. To his mind the parliament could do no more than produce a constitutional draft the practicability and realization of which could be decided upon only by the sovereign princes of the German federation. The king's rejection led the assembly in Frankfurt to defend the new constitution as a 'sacred institution of the nation'.[65] This stance was backed by nearly all Mecklenburg members of the Frankfurt Parliament, although the radical democrat Reinhard voted against it. In Schwerin the chamber supported the Frankfurt assembly's resolution by a vote of 72 to 9.[66]

In Frankfurt the Mecklenburg envoy, Karsten, under instructions from Schwerin, now convened the envoys of twenty-two German states in his lodgings, where they decided to accept the Paulskirche's resolution to offer the imperial crown to the king of Prussia.[67] It was expected that the king might accept the crown if the offer was backed by the other German states. If he did not accept, then the assembly was to dissolve itself or attempt to work out a compromise with the Prussian government. In the event the Prussian king rejected the crown again and invited those princes to Berlin who had opposed the German constitution passed by the Frankfurt assembly. The king's second rejection was not approved

[62] Siemann, *Deutsche Revolution*, 192–200.   [63] Ibid. 200–4.
[64] Schröder, 'Revolution', 552–4.
[65] Siemann, *Deutsche Revolution*, 204–18. See also Roger Price, '"Der heilige Kampf gegen die Anarchie": Die Entwicklung der Gegenrevolution', in Dowe *et al.* (eds.), *Europa 1848*, 43–81.   [66] Schröder, 'Revolution', 562.
[67] Ibid. 563.

by the other German states, 29 of which had accepted the Frankfurt constitution.[68]

One of the few princes who opposed developments in Frankfurt was the Grand Duke of Mecklenburg-Strelitz, who accepted the king's invitation to come to Berlin together with representatives of Bavaria, Saxony, and Hanover. The king's rejection of the constitution provoked a campaign for its survival in Saxony and the Palatinate, especially after the assembly had voted with the narrowest majority (two votes) to ask governments, assemblies, and 'the entire German people' to defend the German constitution. Now Germany was faced with a third wave of violent revolts und uprisings; the first one had taken place in March and April 1848 and the second in September 1848.

In Mecklenburg a number of petitions were sent to the Landtag asking for the mobilization of the people to defend the achievements of the Frankfurt constitution. It is difficult to ascertain how strong mobilization in the two duchies really was, but it looks as if support for the Frankfurt constitution was widespread. But in any case the pressure from the people did not persuade the Grand Duke to publish the new German constitution. Instead he sent Mecklenburg troops to south-west Germany, ostensibly to protect law and order, but in reality to suppress the campaign for the preservation of the constitution and thus the last remnants of the Paulskirche. He also joined the alliance of the three kings (Prussia, Hanover, and Saxony), who were busy in June annihilating the revolutionary forces in Baden, the Palatinate, and parts of the Rhenish Province.

After the Frankfurt assembly had moved to Stuttgart as a 'rump parliament', the remaining two Mecklenburg deputies, Reinhard and Wöhler, were recalled by their government.[69] They protested, as they doubted the legality of this move; but it had become clear in June that the Schwerin regime had openly joined the reactionary forces, although it was not an anti-liberal government. However, neither the Grand Duke nor his ministers were willing to accept all the Landtag's resolutions. Thus the government was still anti-parliamentarian. Yet by October 1849 the grand duke was prepared to accept the constitution.

By July and August 1849 the revolution was over in most of Germany and even in Hungary, but in Mecklenburg the struggle for

[68] Ibid. 566.   [69] Ibid. 598.

the constitution continued. In the Landtag the majorities backing various proposals were constantly changing, and it is difficult to find a consistent line among the factions. In any case the government in Schwerin proved to be stubborn, although in some instances it was prepared to modify its position. It was, for instance, willing to accept the chamber's proposals about the transfer of the *Domanium* to the state and about the civil list. When the Landtag accepted the government's draft of the electoral law and the grand duke's decision to retain his power to dissolve the diet, three members of the left resigned their seats in protest.[70]

The new electoral procedure was based on electoral divisions as in the first draft in April 1848. In any case the Mecklenburg assembly had agreed that its sucessor should have a general, un-even, direct, and secret franchise. The Grand Duke of Strelitz had suggested the Prussian model of a three-class franchise, but the Schwerin government prevailed with its plan to allow a third of the future deputies to be elected by 'economic interests', i.e. land-owners, merchants, and artisans, a third according to the tax levels (census), with the last third chosen by a free vote. This may have been a far cry from any universal franchise, but it was more demo-cratic than the Prussian electoral law or that of most other German states.

At the end of August the Landtag majority had moved much closer to the government's position, despite its original opposition to the principle of an agreed constitution (*Vereinbarungsprinzip*). After 151 sessions the constituent Landtag completed its work, and although the political left was understandably disappointed, a number of liberal principles were enshrined in the new consti-tution. The 'Basic Law' (*Staatsgrundgesetz*) of 10 October 1849 went beyond the Grand Duke's initial proclamation of 23 March 1848 and, unlike the Prussian constitution, was not dictated from above.[71] It included a civil-rights catalogue, abolished the death penalty, and guaranteed free education. But it did not include a full parliamentary system, which meant that the Landtag was not to elect the government. In contrast to other states, the Landtag was

[70] Ibid. 620.

[71] Hermann Brandt, 'Das Staatsgrundgesetz für das Großherzogtum Mecklen-burg-Schwerin vom 10. Oktober 1849 im Lichte der mecklenburgischen Verfas-sungsbemühungen des 19. Jahrhunderts', in Heinrichs and Lüders (eds.), *Moder-nisierung und Freiheit*, 497–516 at 503–8.

to meet only for a period of at least two months once a year. Both the Grand Duke and the Landtag were able to initiate legislation.

The British ambassador in Berlin, Henry Howard, who in his reports to Palmerston clearly supported the grand dukes, informed the foreign secretary in August that the Mecklenburg Landtag 'has shown great disregard for the spontaneous conceptions so promptly offered by the two Grand Dukes, and has voted a Constitution of so democratic a character that, if adopted in its present form, the consequences will in all probability be most detrimental to the interests of those hitherto peaceable and flourishing Grand Duchies'.[72] He went on to complain about the way the Grand Duke of Strelitz had been treated by the assembly, with the result that he had broken off all negotiations with the chamber. As might be expected, the sentiments of the British ambassador were shared by the General Political Association which represented a number of large landowners. The association tried to delay the publication of the new Basic Law, in order to prevent it from becoming law. The Association also pointed out that if the union between the two grand duchies was broken the Basic Law would become invalid.

Only a group of twenty-four estate owners and members of the old *Ritterschaft*, among them Pogge-Roggow, endorsed the new constitution because they regarded it as a great improvement on the old estates constitution.[73] The majority of the large landowners tried to win over the Grand Duke of Schwerin to their views, but at that stage he refused to receive their address or even to meet them.[74] The landowning nobility was especially concerned about the law abolishing the old estates, about the abolition of the nobility, and about the end of the union with Strelitz. By this stage the Grand Duke in Schwerin was giving the impression that he was determined to go with the time and publish the basic law. This was done on 10 October 1849, after he had indicated on 23 August his intention to do so. In Schwerin the publication was met by cheering crowds, who celebrated the Grand Duke as well as the leading minister.

---

[72] Public Record Office, London, FO 64/302 (21 Aug. 1849).

[73] Landeshauptarchiv Schwerin, Staatsministerium 417, petition to the Grand Duke (17 Sept. 1849). See also Wiggers, *Die Mecklenburgische constituierende Versammlung*, 166–8.

[74] Wiggers, *Die Mecklenburgische constituierende Versammlung*, 69; Schröder, 'Revolution', 625–6.

The dissolved assembly had recommended to the Schwerin government that Schwerin should separate from the union with Strelitz. The Grand Duke of Strelitz found this to be unacceptable and, according to the British ambassador's report, insisted that the question of the constitution and union should be submitted to the former estates. In his view these had been only suspended since April 1848 but not abolished. The Grand Duke's views were supported by the landed interests and the town of Wismar, but not by Rostock as the ambassador had thought. Howard was then able to inform Palmerston that the Grand Duke of Strelitz had taken a further step and turned to the council of the alliance between Prussia, Saxony, and Hanover. His aim was to 'stop the promulgation of the new constitution'.[75] The council referred the Strelitz government to the court of arbitration of the alliance in Erfurt and advised Schwerin to withhold publication. But this was not done and even the *Preußische Staatsanzeiger* published the *Staatsgrundgesetz* on 15 October 1849; a day later it reported the defence of the Schwerin government against the complaints by Strelitz.

While the Mecklenburgers were preparing the forthcoming elections to the new Landtag, which were to be held on 5 February 1850, the Prussian king made a threatening move.[76] He wrote to his nephew, Friedrich Franz, that to his mind the new constitution was not yet legally binding. A similar step followed from the Austrian emperor after delegates of the old estates visited Vienna and complained to him about the *Staatsgrundgesetz*. At the end of December the old estates, together with the Grand Duke of Strelitz, began to sue the Schwerin government at the Federal Central Commission in Frankfurt. The commission turned against the constitutional developments in Mecklenburg and offered at the end of March to settle the matter by a court of arbitration. Friedrich Franz accepted this proposal, but his government resigned.[77] This happened at the same time as the second elected Landtag met for its opening session in Schwerin on 3 April 1850. Minister-president Lützow read out the memorandum of the Federal Central Commission and then announced in public the cabinet's resignation. The Grand Duke took this opportunity to adjourn the Landtag for three months. The political centre and the right accepted Friedrich Franz's decision

[75] Public Record Office, London, FO 64/303 (11 Oct. 1849).
[76] Julius Wiggers, *Aus meinem Leben* (Leipzig, 1901), 138–42.
[77] Ibid. 143.

and left the chamber. The left protested, but without any success because the Landtag had become inquorate.

The reaction of the Left was understandable, as the Landtag elections in February 1850 had turned out surprisingly well for them, although there had been an official reaction against it. Elections and the Left had remained popular despite the fact that the electorate had been called out to vote four times within the last three years—for the Frankfurt parliament, for the first Landtag, for the Prussian-dominated and ill-fated Erfurt parliament of 1850 and for the second Mecklenburg Landtag.[78] As the population had never voted before, and was not to vote again until 1867, it is difficult to judge how far the process of politicization had gone; but a sense of frustration must have prevailed during those seventeen years. The relatively high turn-out figures for the elections to the North German Reichstag in 1867 seem to indicate that Mecklenburg's electoral zeal did not suffer.

In its victorious election campaign the Left had emphasized the need for furthering the democratic development of the *Staatsgrundgesetz*, whereas the Constitutional Associations were so vague in their programme that they attracted a number of landowners back to their ranks. Together they founded the Electoral Associations for Town and Country, but they could not prevent the Left's victory. In parliament the left and the centre were more evenly balanced, but the left made sure that its members would be voted into the presidium. Even this triumph did not make the Landtag an effective forum for new reforms. The threat of intervention from outside hampered its work and undermined the basic law. Thus, during the five weeks of its existence the second elected Landtag did not achieve much. By this time in the rest of Europe the revolution was over, and in Germany the conservative forces had finally triumphed. So Mecklenburg, belatedly as ever, took more time to adapt to the new reactionary climate than any other region.[79]

After Lützow's resignation, Friedrich Franz's new minister-president, Bülow, began to undo the constitutional achievements of the last two years, probably predicting or even knowing in advance what the result of the arbitration might be. Thus liberal

---

[78] For the Erfurt parliament, see Siemann, *Deutsche Revolution*, 218–22; also Christof Dipper, 'Zerfall und Scheitern: Das Ende der Revolution', in Dipper and Speck (eds.), *1848: Revolution in Deutschland*, 401–19 at 416–19.

[79] Wiggers, *Aus meinem Leben*, 144–9.

freedoms were rescinded and the second Landtag was dissolved.
At this stage the Grand Duke let it be known that his proclamation
of 23 March 1848 should now be the guideline for the state's politics until the arbitration was announced at Freiinwalde near Berlin
on 11 September 1850. These moves were a clear indication that
the new government anticipated losing the arbitration case. It may
even have hoped for it. As the case for Schwerin did not look good,
the Grand Duke of Strelitz withdrew his complaint. Now only the
old estates (*Ritterschaften*) disputed the legality of the Grand Duke
of Schwerin's acceptance of the *Staatsgrundgesetz* in October 1849.

In their dispute both sides had agreed for the kings of Prussia and
Hanover to act as arbiters. They had appointed a commission of
lawyers to deal with the case. After some deliberation the commission decided that the publication of the Basic Law and the abolition
of the executive committee of the *Ritterschaften* were invalid. The
commission also asked Friedrich Franz to convene the old Landtag.
The British ambassador felt that

> this decision will free the Grand Duke of Mecklenburg Schwerin from the
> embarrassment in which he was placed by the oath he had taken on the
> new constitution. . . . At the same time . . . it opens out the prospect of
> a satisfactory settlement of Mecklenburg affairs and tends to secure the
> legislative and constitutional Union of the two Grand Duchies which a
> maintenance of the new Constitution would have severed.[80]

He was then happy to report that the Grand Duke of Strelitz was
satisfied with the judgment. He assured Palmerston, should he be
concerned that there might now be no representative institutions in
the duchies, that Mecklenburg had 'possessed them from time im-
memorial'. In Howard's opinion the new constitution would have
destroyed the union between the two duchies, and this would have
been damaging to both of them. So he implied that Mecklenburg
would fare better under the old constitutional arrangements.

The fact that Friedrich Franz lost credibility by joining the reactionary forces was of no concern to the British ambassador in
Berlin. He was in agreement with the majority of the *Ritterschaften*
when they celebrated the abolition of the *Staatsgrundgesetz*, the end
of the elected Landtag, and the reconvocation of the *ancien régime*
Landtag of pre-1848. When that Landtag was convened at Malchin

---

[80] Public Record Office, London, FO 64/320, Howard to Palmerston (16 Sept.
1850).

on 15 February 1851, Johann Pogge-Roggow, who had started the ball of reform rolling in November 1847, assumed again the role of the unofficial leader of the opposition when he gathered fifty members round him and started pressing for the same reforms as he had done between 1845 and 1847.[81]

The judgment of Freiinwalde was a complete victory for the noble landowners and their ally, the Grand Duke of Strelitz. But the Left of the second elected Landtag did not give in easily. Its president, Moritz Wiggers, convened members of the dissolved chamber to a meeting at Schwerin. This planned meeting was even commented upon by the British ambassador in his dispatch to Palmerston.[82] He wrongly believed that the meeting had been prevented from taking place.[83] However, it did take place and the two party groups, even in this hour of need, could not agree on a common programme of action. So in the face of police obstructions the second elected Landtag and the constitutional reforms of the last two years came to an abrupt end.[84] The pendulum had swung back from constitutional modernism to the politics of the pre-March era.

But the new regime in Mecklenburg was not satisfied merely with the defeat of the forces of liberalism. As in other parts of Germany, a period of the darkest reaction was to follow in Mecklenburg as well. All civil and liberal rights were suspended and former political activists were even imprisoned. Yet even in Mecklenburg, as in other German states, some revolutionary achievements survived. These had brought to an end patrimonial jurisdiction and had left intact the new organization of the governmental ministerial structure, the recent introduction of a consistorial councillor (*Oberkirchenrat*) for church and educational affairs, and permission to smoke in the streets. The struggle for reforms could only be taken up again when the two duchies joined the North German Federation after 1866 and the German empire was created in 1871. After 1867 the whole Mecklenburg electorate had the vote for Reichstag elections, but the combined Landtag of the two duchies remained unreformed. Despite several Reichstag resolutions requesting constitutional reforms in Mecklenburg, the *Ritterschaften* held out against the mounting pressure for modernization until the

[81] Pogge von Strandmann, 'Revolution in Mecklenburg', 183–4.
[82] Public Record Office, London, FO 64/320, Howard to Palmerston (19 Sept. 1850).   [83] Ibid. (26 Sept. 1850).
[84] Wiggers, *Aus meinem Leben*, 146–7.

revolution of 1918, although the last grand duke supported the introduction of political reforms there. Only then did Mecklenburg's *Sonderweg* come to an end and its constitutional development fall in line with that of other German states.

FURTHER READING

In the most recent literature about the German revolution of 1848–50, the previously prevailing view that there was only one German revolutionary event has given way to a fragmented picture of several revolutions at the same time. Regional and local studies are no longer mere examples of the central event of the German revolution with its traditional emphasis on liberalism, the nation, and the bourgeoisie. Instead, studies of individual aspects, namely social, economic, political, cultural, and communicative dimensions, have given revolutionary works greater depth. In following these approaches an evaluation of the long-term effects has been added to the former orthodoxy about the failure of the revolution.

An overemphasis on the failure of the revolution, as well as Rudolph Stadelmann's view that the Germans were a 'people without a revolution', may both explain why so few books on the revolution have been made available in English. Stadelmann's pioneering work of 1948 was translated in 1975 unter the title *Social and Political History of the German 1848 Revolution*. Veit Valentin's detailed prewar narrative *Geschichte der deutschen Revolution von 1848–9* (2 vols.; 1930–1, repr. Weinheim and Berlin, 1998), has not yet been translated, perhaps because it does not pursue a particular argument. Whereas Valentin's work attempts a 'history of the people', Frank Eyck's book on *The Frankfurt Parliament of 1848–9* (London, 1968) follows a liberal line by blaming the radicals and the Left for the failure of 1848. But Eyck offers a more penetrating analysis than Theodore Hamerow, who in *Restoration, Revolution, Reaction: Economics and Politics in Germany, 1815–71* (Princeton, 1958) regards the revolution as a precursor to the unification under Bismarck. P. H. Noyes, *Organization and Revolution: Working-class Associations in the German Revolution of 1848–9* (Princeton, 1966), is not as wide-ranging as the title promises. A new approach to regionalism can be found in Jonathan Sperber's *Rhineland Radicals: The Democratic Movement and the Revolution of 1848–9* (Princeton, 1991). However, Sperber's *The European Revolutions, 1848–51* (Cambridge, 1994) does not offer any specific interpretation of the German situation. Obviously this is different in Wolfram Siemann's comprehensive analysis of 1985, which has just appeared in English as *The German Revolution of 1848–9* (London, 1998), since Siemann's book is underpinned by the author's research into various aspects of the German revolutions. Quite a different approach is found in Karl Wegert's study

German Radicals Confront the Common People: Revolutionary Politics and Popular Politics, 1789–1849 (Mainz, 1992), in which he puts the tavern at the centre of an emerging revolutionary culture. Then there are books which deal with the German revolution in long chapters: David Ward, *1848: The Fall of Metternich and the Year of Revolution* (London, 1970); Peter N. Stearns, *The Revolutions of 1848* (London, 1974); and Roger Price, *The Revolutions of 1848* (London, 1988).

As a result of the sesquicentenary a number of new works have been published in Germany which offer an interesting mixture of reinterpretation and new research. At the risk of being unjust to some, I restrict my list to four anthologies which also direct attention to newly published monographs about aspects of the revolution: Wolfgang Hardtwig (ed.), *Revolution in Deutschland und Europa, 1848–9* (Göttingen, 1998); Christian Jansen and Thomas Mergel (eds.), *Die Revolutionen von 1848–9: Erfahrung—Verarbeitung—Deutung* (Göttingen, 1998); Christof Dipper and Ulrich Speck, *1848: Revolution in Deutschland* (Frankfurt and Leipzig, 1998); Dieter Dowe *et al.* (eds.), *Europa 1848: Revolution und Reform* (Bonn, 1998). Although all of these studies emphasize multidimensional aspects of the various revolutions in Germany, they concentrate on the main action zones in Berlin, the Rhineland, south-west Germany, and Saxony. Areas like Mecklenburg, Holstein, Pomerania, or Silesia remain by contrast very much neglected.

During 1998 numerous exhibitions were held in various parts of Germany in order to commemorate the revolution. One of their purposes was to enable people to identify more easily with the revolution as a local and national event. Some of the exhibitions' catalogues cover important aspects in cultural history: Lothar Gall (ed.), *1848: Aufbruch zur Freiheit. Eine Ausstellung des Deutschen Historischen Museums und der Schirn Kunsthalle Frankfurt zum 150jährigen Jubiläum der Revolution von 1848/49* (Berlin, 1998); Badisches Landesmuseum Karlsruhe (Alfred Frei) (ed.), *1848/49: Revolution der Deutschen Demokraten in Baden* (Baden-Baden, 1998); Ottfried Dascher and Everhard Kleinertz (eds.), *Petitionen und Barrikaden: Rheinische Revolutionen 1848/49* (Münster, 1998).

7

A Pyrrhic Victory: The Russian Empire in 1848

DAVID SAUNDERS

SHROVETIDE lasts a week in Russia and can involve extensive bingeing. For St Petersburg aristocrats in 1848 it culminated on Sunday, 5 March, in a day of abandon at the palace of the heir to the throne. Those who intended to dance were bidden for two o'clock in the afternoon, others for nine in the evening. At five, Nicholas I entered the ballroom exclaiming unclearly about a coup in France and the flight of the king. The company followed him into his son's study, where he read out a despatch from his Berlin ambassador to the effect that the French had declared a republic. Grand Duke Konstantin seems to have been alarmed. 'We will not yield!' he declared, and waxed nostalgic about the days before Peter the Great when Russia was 'so remote from Europe, so compliant, and so religious, that an event of this kind would have attracted no notice from us whatever'. The tsar, however, was exultant. 'So,' he said—in French, of course—'the comedy has been played out to the end and the knave has fallen'; the revolution in France was to be applauded for ridding Europe of the usurper Louis-Philippe. 'How desirable it would be', Nicholas went on, 'for the French, in their momentary fury, to move at once on the Rhine.' The Germans would resist them 'out of national pride', and, if the French got matters in hand and brought the Germans to their senses, German 'communists and radicals' might set in train a revolution of their own.[1]

---

[1] This paragraph relies on the eyewitness account of a confidant of the tsar, Baron M. A. Korf: 'Iz zapisok' (I), *Russkaia starina* [hereafter *RS*], 101 (1900), 545–88 at 556–8. On Korf see I. V. Ruzhitskaia, 'M. A. Korf v gosudarstvennoi i kul'turnoi zhizni Rossii', *Otechestvennaia istoriia* (1998), 2: 49–65. On Shrovetide bingeing in

To judge by this account, Nicholas I positively welcomed the prospect of chaos in western and central Europe. Although scholars tend to reject the view that his unclear first words were a call to dancing guards officers to take to their horses and launch a Russian drive on the West,[2] his euphoria was such that they might have been. From the perspective of about 1850, it may seem that Nicholas had been right to be exhilarated in early 1848. Abroad, he had invaded the Danubian principalities in 1848 and Hungary in 1849, and was holding the ring between Austria and Prussia in central Europe. At home, he had exposed the conspiratorial circle which centred on Mikhail Petrashevsky and consigned the young Dostoevsky and others to Siberia. Can the way in which the tsarist regime responded to the European crisis of 1848–9 therefore be accounted a success?

I shall contend in what follows that it cannot: that even the ostensible successes were really failures, because the regime paid prices to achieve them that it could not afford; and that the prices the regime paid were not confined to the military, diplomatic, and ideological spheres to which I have referred. To support these propositions, I shall first look more closely at the regime's conduct of international relations and the way it maintained ideological conformity (to show how these can be made to look less successful than they appear at first sight); and then move on to financial matters, the peasant question, and ethnic relations (the other spheres in which, I believe, the regime paid prices it could not afford). In all these respects, I shall claim, the tsarist regime lost more than it gained as a result of the way in which it responded to the European revolutions of 1848.

There are perhaps four negative points to be made about the ostensible increase in the regime's international authority. First, it was less extensive than the tsar probably hoped it would be. Second, enhancement of the regime's authority *vis-à-vis* Austria and Prussia turned out to be a Greek gift. Third, Nicholas made the mistake of believing that his behaviour in the course of the revolutions of 1848–9 brought him closer to Britain, with the result that he de-

Russia see Robin Milner-Gulland, *The Russians* (Oxford, 1997), 22. To facilitate comparison with the rest of the book I give dates on the Gregorian rather than the Julian calendar.

[2] See e.g. *Mezhdunarodnye otnosheniia na Balkanakh 1830–1856 gg.*, ed. V. N. Vinogradov (Moscow, 1990), 193, and E. A. Chirkova, 'Revoliutsiia 1848–1849 godov i politika Rossii', in O. V. Orlik (ed.), *Istoriia vneshnei politiki Rossii: Pervaia polovina XIX veka* (Moscow, 1995), 346–61 at 346.

ceived himself in the subsequent diplomatic preliminaries to the Crimean War. Fourth, the changes in the central and west European order that survived the revolutions of 1848–9, minor though they were, widened the gap between the ideological premisses on which the Russian empire rested and those on which its competitors rested, with the result that antipathy between St Petersburg and the rest of the Continent became likelier in the future.

With regard to the first of these points, it should be said that whatever the extent of the tsar's pugnacity when he learnt that a republic had been declared in Paris, his troops did not make anything like the mark on Europe in 1848 and 1849 that their predecessors had made in the later stages of the Napoleonic Wars. Even if Nicholas had seriously contemplated substantial military intervention in the affairs of the countries to the west of him, he was sensible enough to give up the idea. A few days after publishing a violently anti-revolutionary tirade on 26 March 1848,[3] he allowed his foreign minister to publish a temperate gloss on it.[4] His invasion of Hungary in 1849 may have made him look determined, but the diplomacy that preceded it had been extremely thorough and the fighting did not involve many risks. 'The tsar and his generals expected an easy campaign marked by heart-warming victories',[5] which was more or less what they got. Nicholas may even have been sincere when he claimed to believe that Poles were running the Hungarian rebellion and that they were threatening to carry disaffection north of the Carpathians.[6] If he was, he was bound to

---

[3] 'Manifest: O sobytiiakh v zapadnoi Evrope', *Polnoe sobranie zakonov rossiiskoi imperii*, 2nd ser. (55 vols.; St Petersburg, 1830–84) [hereafter *PSZ* 2], xxiii/1. 181–2 (No. 22,087).

[4] For the text of the gloss see N. Shil'der, 'Imperator Nikolai I v 1848 i 1849 godakh', *Istoricheskii vestnik*, 78 (1899), 173–93 at 184–6.

[5] Istvan Deak, *The Lawful Revolution: Louis Kossuth and the Hungarians, 1848–1849* (New York, 1979), 291.

[6] According to Eugene Horváth, 'both Austrians and Russians skilfully manœuvred with the assertion that the Hungarian Revolution was not a Hungarian national movement, but a Polish plot against the Russian State': 'Russia and the Hungarian Revolution (1848–9)', *Slavonic Review*, 12 (1933–4), 628–43 at 635. A later expert on the Russian intervention in Hungary feels that 'there can be little doubt that [the tsar] was finally persuaded to act as a result of the Polish involvement': Ian W. Roberts, *Nicholas I and the Russian Intervention in Hungary* (Basingstoke and London, 1991), 102. Korf's memoirs make it clear that Nicholas was indeed troubled by the influence of Hungarian events on his Polish territories at the time he drew up his manifesto on the intervention: 'Iz zapisok' (II), *RS* 102 (1900), 27–50 at 41. The manifesto itself, however, mentioned Poles only in passing: 'Manifest: O dvizhenii armii nashikh dlia sodeistviia Imperatoru Avstriiskomu na

conclude that his vital interests were at stake. The most wanton of his foreign exploits could therefore be said to have been conceived, misguidedly, as an act of self-defence.

Understanding the other three negative points about the ostensible increase in the regime's international authority requires a broader chronological perspective. That both Austrians and Prussians felt irritated rather than pleased by the way in which St Petersburg saved them from one another at the turn of the 1850s (when they seemed to be on the verge of going to war over the question of primacy in Germanic Europe)[7] can perhaps be extrapolated from the fact that they both behaved in ways inimical to the interests of the Russian empire thereafter. Austria, notoriously, intimated at the end of 1855 that she might enter the Crimean War on the side of Britain and France, with the result that Nicholas's successor, Alexander II, had to move more rapidly than he was inclined to do in the direction of abandoning the fray.[8] Prussia undermined the entire central European policy of the Russian empire when she established her predominance in Germany in the years 1864–70. After she defeated the Habsburg empire in 1866, it ceased to be reasonable for St Petersburg to assume that the two great Germanic powers could always be played off against one another. Admittedly, Alexander II welcomed Prussia's forward moves to the extent that they allowed him, in 1870, to proclaim the Russian empire's intention to remilitarize the Black Sea.[9] Other Russians, however, felt that the tsar was being manipulated. A prominent civil servant recalled later that 'our government was never so much at odds with public opinion as it was at the time of the destruction of France by the German hordes

---

potushenie miatezha v Vengrii i Transil'vanii', *PSZ* 2 xxiv/1. 235 (No. 23,200, 8 May 1849).

[7] On Russian involvement in the rivalry between Austria and Prussia at the beginning of the 1850s see W. E. Mosse, *The European Powers and the German Question, 1848–71* (1958; New York, 1981), 25–42.

[8] Paul W. Schroeder, *Austria, Great Britain, and the Crimean War: The Destruction of the European Concert* (Ithaca, NY, and London, 1972), 311–46; David Wetzel, *The Crimean War: A Diplomatic History* (Boulder, Colo., 1985), 174–81.

[9] On the formal conduct of Russo-Prussian relations in the late 1860s and early 1870s see S. S. Tatishchev, *Imperator Aleksandr II: Ego zhizn' i tsarstvovanie* (2 vols.; 1903; repr. St Petersburg, 1996), ii. 65–73, and L. I. Narochnitskaia, *Rossiia i otmena neitralizatsii Chernogo moria 1856–1871 gg.* (Moscow, 1989), 143–206.

[in 1870]'.[10] Mikhail Katkov, the leading Russian journalist of the day, had been 'entirely justified', this civil servant believed, 'in saying that [at that time] we did not have a Russian ministry of foreign affairs but a foreign [i.e. Prussian] ministry of Russian affairs'.[11]

To understand why the diplomacy of the revolutionary period misled St Petersburg in respect of its dealings with the British, one has to go backwards in time as well as forwards. Nicholas had been misinterpreting Britain's attitude towards him since the beginning of the 1840s. It was a fundamental goal of Nicholaevan foreign policy to drive a wedge between Britain and France. Nesselrode, the tsar's foreign minister, believed he had achieved this end in the course of the 'second Mehemet Ali crisis' of 1839–41.[12] The tsar himself came away from a visit to England in 1844 convinced that he had British support for the possibility, in certain circumstances, of partitioning the Ottoman empire.[13] As soon as he learnt of the proclamation of the Second Republic in France in 1848 he started wondering whether Britain would back him in a policy of intervening against unwelcome changes in the European order.[14] Not long afterwards he received British (and, ironically, French) support when he sought to prevent Prussia from relieving Denmark of Schleswig-Holstein.[15] Having received qualified support for his invasion of Hungary from Palmerston in the House of Commons, and having covered some of the costs of the invasion by borrowing from Baring Brothers of London,[16] he probably felt at the end of the revolutionary period that his relations with Britain were continuing to improve. He certainly found it difficult to believe, in the early 1850s, that Britain would take France's side against him in

---

[10] E. Feoktistov, *Za kulisami politiki i literatury, 1848–1896* (1929; repr. Moscow, 1991), 126.   [11] Ibid.

[12] K. R. Nesselrode, 'Vsepoddaneishii otchet za 25 let tsarstvovaniia Imperatora Nikolaia I', *Sbornik imperatorskogo russkogo istoricheskogo obshchestva* [hereafter *SIRIO*], 98 (1896), 287–98 at 292–3.

[13] Vernon John Puryear, *England, Russia, and the Straits Question, 1844–1856* (Berkeley, 1931), 40–63; W. Bruce Lincoln, 'The Emperor Nicholas I in England', *History Today*, 25 (1975), 1: 24–30 at 29–30; Harold N. Ingle, *Nesselrode and the Russian Rapprochement with Britain, 1836–1844* (Berkeley, 1976), 166–71.

[14] Korf, 'Iz zapisok' (I), 557.

[15] W. Carr, *Schleswig-Holstein 1815–48: A Study in National Conflict* (Manchester, 1963), 293.

[16] *Hansard's Parliamentary Debates*, 3rd ser., 107 (1849), 807–15; A. S. Nifontov, *Rossiia v 1848 godu* (Moscow, 1949), 38–9.

the dispute over the holy places in Palestine which turned into the Crimean War. This, however, is what Britain did.

Finally, in the international sphere, it needs to be said that after the revolutions of 1848 the Russian empire's political order looked even more out of kilter with that of central and western Europe than it had before. For Jonathan Sperber, the 'second main consequence' of the European revolutions was 'the introduction of constitutional government in pre-1848 absolutist monarchies'.[17] Nicholas I had told the marquis de Custine in 1839 that although he could see the point of both monarchies and republics, constitutional government ('a representative monarchy') signified 'the rule of lies, fraud and corruption'.[18] If, then, after 1848 he hoped to make sense of the newly constitutional Prussia (the country in Europe with which he felt the strongest natural affinity), he was going to have to learn quickly. France, meanwhile, had instituted adult male suffrage. Although the Habsburg empire had not succumbed to the constitutionalist trend, neither, according to a recent study, had it reverted to type; for its post-1848 ' "neo-absolutist" government was not restorative . . . but innovative'.[19]

To deal with these new regimes, the Russian empire looked likely to need an unaccustomed flexibility. But its constitutional arteries were hardening. Although it had long been an autocracy, and although Nicholas I had long been one of its most interventionist autocrats, the tsar's penchant for working through his personal chancery and *ad hoc* committees rather than through government ministries or the state council seems to have become even more marked in and after 1848 than it had been before.[20] Nor, after 1848, does Nicholas seem to have hunted very hard for imaginative executive officers. The new Moscow governor he appointed in the revolutionary year, Arsenii Zakrevskii, thought even the Moscow Slavophiles were dangerous subversives; a mer-

---

[17] Jonathan Sperber, *The European Revolutions, 1848–1851* (Cambridge, 1994), 251.

[18] Marquis de Custine, *Letters from Russia*, ed. and trans. Robin Buss (Harmondsworth, 1991), 87.

[19] R. J. W. Evans, 'From Confederation to Compromise: The Austrian Experiment, 1849–1867', *Proceedings of the British Academy*, 87 (1995), 135–67 at 137.

[20] On the tsar's administrative practices in general see N. P. Eroshkin, *Krepostnicheskoe samoderzhavie i ego politicheskie instituty (Pervaia polovina XIX veka)* (Moscow, 1981), 137–202. The 'Buturlin Committee', on which see below, may serve as an example of the further growth in the importance of committees in and after the revolutionary year.

chant likened him to an Asiatic khan or a Chinese viceroy.[21] It seems reasonable to say that as a result of the revolutions of 1848 the political chasm that divided the Russian empire from the other European states was widening, not only by virtue of leftward movement in the west, but also by virtue of rightward movement in the east.

Thus it can be argued that the Russian empire's apparently successful military and diplomatic activity at the time of the 1848 revolutions was both less triumphant than it might have been and pregnant with dangerous implications for the future. The same can be said of the way in which the tsar handled ideological matters, for, on the one hand, Nicholas's best efforts could not ultimately prevent news of the central and west European developments of 1848 from entering his domains and, on the other, his many attempts to keep the flow of ideas in check within the empire merely increased the determination of thinking people to take the earliest opportunity of counteracting his obstructionism.[22]

Because Aleksandr Nifontov explained long ago how news and appeals from the west overcame the tsar's attempts to deny them entry into the Russian empire at the time of the European revolutions of 1848,[23] I shall not dwell on the matter here. But it may be worth dwelling for a moment on Nicholas's heavy-handedness within the empire. The regime's attempts to stifle the domestic circulation of ideas were by no means confined to the arrest of Mikhail Petrashevsky and his associates in May 1849.[24] In April 1848 Nicholas set up the 'Buturlin Committee' (named after its first chairman), a sort of super-censorship which remained in being

---

[21] N. M. Druzhinin, 'Moskva v gody krymskoi voiny', in id., *Izbrannye trudy: Vneshniaia politika Rossii, Istoriia Moskvy, Muzeinoe delo* (Moscow, 1988), 143–85 at 143–4. On Zakrevskii see now V. N. Baliazin, *Moskovskie gradonachal'niki* (Moscow, 1997), 311–23.

[22] Parts of this section come from my *Russia in the Age of Reaction and Reform, 1801–1881* (London and New York, 1992), 190–6.

[23] Nifontov, *Rossiia*, 45–101.

[24] Recent literature on the 'Petrashevsky affair' includes B. F. Egorov (ed.), *Pervye russkie sotsialisty: Vospominaniia uchastnikov kruzhkov petrashevtsev v Peterburge,* (Leningrad, 1984); J. H. Seddon, 'The Petrashevtsy: A Reappraisal', *Slavic Review,* 43 (1984), 434–52; id., *The Petrashevtsy: A Study of the Russian Revolutionaries of 1848* (Manchester, 1985); A. F. Voznyi, *Petrashevskii i tsarskaia tainaia politsiia* (Kiev, 1985); *Dostoevsky as Reformer: The Petrashevsky Case*, ed. and trans. Liza Knapp (Ann Arbor, 1987); and B. F. Egorov, *Petrashevtsy* (Leningrad, 1988).

until 1855 and became the coping-stone of his obscurantism.[25] In September 1848 the regime prosecuted Moscow University's Society of Russian History and Antiquities for publishing a translation of Giles Fletcher's *Of the Russe Commonwealth*, a description of Muscovy written in the late sixteenth century. Fletcher's book was so antique that its scholarly translators must have thought themselves safe in making it accessible. But because the work contained a 'devastating description of Russian manners and morals', the relevant issue of the society's journal was recalled, the journal itself was temporarily closed, and the secretary of the society, Professor Bodianskii, was banished to Kazan. Giles Fletcher was not to appear legally in Russian for another fifty-seven years.[26]

In mid-May 1849, eight days after the arrest of the Petrashevtsky, Nicholas reduced student enrolments to 300 per university, a cut of 60 per cent.[27] This undermined the relatively enlightened minister of education, Sergei Uvarov. The minister said of his last years in office that he felt as if he were being pursued by a wild animal and could only throw off his clothes to distract its attention. 'During the reaction of 1849 there was nothing left to throw off, and Uvarov retired.'[28] His successor, Shirinskii-Shikhmatov, shared none of Uvarov's intellectual curiosity. On a visit to Moscow University in 1850 he was appalled by the historian Sergei Solov'ev's observation that it was difficult to establish what exactly the monk Nestor had written in the original version of the medieval chronicle which bore his name. In the minister's opinion Nestor's chronicle ought not to be subjected to academic analysis.[29] Students at the university, meanwhile, were banned from going into cafés to read newspapers and ordered to do up their jackets and wear three-cornered hats and swords.[30]

Severity of this kind turned out to be deeply counter-productive. The punishment of Petrashevsky and his associates, the establishment of the Buturlin Committee, the Fletcher affair, the reduc-

---

[25] On the genesis of this committee see Korf, 'Iz zapisok' (I), 571–4, and Eroshkin, *Krepostnicheskoe samoderzhavie*, 196–9.

[26] Richard Pipes, 'Introduction to Giles Fletcher's *Of the Russe Commonwealth* (1591)', in id., *Russia Observed: Collected Essays on Russian and Soviet History* (Boulder, Colo., 1989), 7–36 at 26 (quotation), 31–2 (consequences of publication).

[27] Cynthia H. Whittaker, *The Origins of Modern Russian Education: An Intellectual Biography of Count Sergei Uvarov, 1786–1855* (DeKalb, 1984), 235.

[28] B. N. Chicherin, *Vospominaniia: Moskva sorokovykh godov* (Moscow, 1929), 28.

[29] S. M. Solov'ev, *Izbrannye trudy; Zapiski* (Moscow, 1983), 325.

[30] Chicherin, *Vospominaniia*, 81.

tion in the number of university students, and the retirement of Uvarov alienated not just potential revolutionaries but supporters of the regime. One of the tsar's right-hand men, Baron Korf, disapproved of the limitation on university enrolments.[31] Aleksandr Nikitenko, an official in the censorship, spoke for many when, in 1852, he privately advised people who thought for themselves 'to completely scorn this stupid nonsense, this contemporary life, while consoling yourself (if you can) with faith in a brighter future'.[32] In the Crimean War even the conservative historian Mikhail Pogodin 'roundly condemned the entire course of Nicholas I's foreign policy' and called upon the government to undertake a series of reforms at home.[33] With friends like these, the tsar did not need enemies. His sharp turn to the right made a turn in the opposite direction all too likely.

The alienation of educated Russians from the state had begun at the end of the eighteenth century, but in and after 1848 it accelerated dramatically. In what is probably the best-known study in English of the Russian empire at the time of the revolutions of 1848, Isaiah Berlin argued that because educated Russians failed to stage a revolution in 1848 they were 'unbroken by the collapse of liberal hopes in Europe in 1849–51' and lived to fight another day.[34] This ought not to be taken to mean that future Russian dissidents were to be liberals. The way in which the tsarist government handled ideological matters in the wake of the 1848 revolutions was much more likely to generate radicalism. The intensity of Nicholas I's insistence on ideological conformity in the last seven years of his reign played a significant part in the genesis of a subsequent and no less intense condemnation of all that tsarism stood for.

Since Nicholas was no fool, he may have been aware that his actions in the ideological sphere were going to cut him off from the educated. He may, indeed, have been deliberately looking for an alternative constituency. It is noteworthy that his violently anti-revolutionary tirade of 26 March 1848 made no mention of 'Ortho-

---

[31] Korf, 'Iz zapisok' (II), 43–5.

[32] Aleksandr Nikitenko, *Diary of a Russian Censor*, ed. and trans. Helen Saltz Jacobson (Amherst, 1975), 130.

[33] I. V. Bestuzhev, 'Krymskaia voina i revoliutsionnaia situatsiia', in M. V. Nechkina *et al.* (eds.), *Revoliutsionnaia situatsiia v Rossii v 1859–1861 gg.* (Moscow, 1963), 189–213 at 204–7 (quotation from 205).

[34] Isaiah Berlin, 'Russia and 1848', in id., *Russian Thinkers*, ed. Henry Hardy and Aileen Kelly (London, 1978), 1–21 at 6.

doxy, Autocracy, and Nationality', the three abstractions with which the tsar had associated himself since Uvarov employed them in a circular of 1833. In alluding to the three concepts, it gave them the more Russian-sounding names 'faith, tsar, and fatherland'.[35] Since it also employed the phrase 'Holy Russia', a term of indubitably popular origin hardly ever found in official proclamations,[36] and since, in this document, the tsar deliberately eschewed the use of the word 'estates' (a recent neologism in Russian, and again unduly abstract),[37] it looks as if Nicholas was trying to strike a demagogic note, to appeal to his subjects at large rather than merely to the privileged. Such an appeal could have been efficacious, however, only if Nicholas had been prepared to go beyond words and liberalize his social policy; and this, as we shall see, was far from his mind. In short, Nicholas maintained ideological order at the time of the 1848 revolutions not only at a price too high for the educated to stomach, but also, in so far as he attempted a sham populism, in a way which ran the risk of arousing hopes among subjects who had not been used to having them.

I move on from international affairs and the maintenance of ideological conformity to three other spheres in which the regime paid prices it could not afford for the sake of attempting to counter the spirit of 1848. First, and most obviously, the financial sphere. Campaigning in the Danubian principalities and Hungary seems to have cost the imperial exchequer just over 9 per cent of its total revenue in 1848 and about 12.5 per cent in 1849.[38] Since, even in time of peace, the armed forces accounted for about two-fifths of Nicholas's total expenditure,[39] it was perhaps not surprising that at the end of 1849 the tsar lacked the courage to confess to the state

---

[35] For the text of the tirade see n. 3 above.

[36] Michael Cherniavsky, '"Holy Russia": A Study in the History of an Idea', *American Historical Review*, 63 (1958), 617–37 at 625.

[37] Korf, 'Iz zapisok' (I), 567, and, for the novelty of the term, Isabel de Madariaga, 'The Russian Nobility in the Seventeenth and Eighteenth Centuries', in H. M. Scott (ed.), *The European Nobilities in the Seventeenth and Eighteenth Centuries* (2 vols.; London and New York, 1995), ii. 231 n.

[38] [A. Z. Khitrovo], 'Obzor deistvii Gosudarstvennogo Kontrolia s 1825 po 1850 god', *SIRIO* 98 (1896), 499–529 at 515 (expenditure on war in 1848 and 1849); Walter McKenzie Pintner, *Russian Economic Policy under Nicholas I* (Ithaca, NY, 1967), 77 ('total ordinary revenues' of the imperial government in 1848 and 1849).

[39] 40.3% in, for example, 1852: Iu. Gagemeister, 'O finansakh Rossii', in A. P. Pogrebinskii, 'Gosudarstvennye finansy Rossii nakanune reformy 1861 goda', *Istoricheskii arkhiv* (1956), 2: 100–25 at 117.

council just how little money he had left for civil purposes and, to cover his confusion, deliberately falsified the budget for the coming year.[40]

But if, as the Prussian ambassador to St Petersburg reported at the end of 1848, Nicholas was troubled in the revolutionary year by his inability to lay his hands on cash,[41] he did not do everything in his power to prevent himself from getting into similar difficulties in future. It could be argued, indeed, that as a result of the 1848 revolutions he actually denied himself one of the best means of increasing the revenue available to him. Soviet historians used to date the beginning of Russia's industrial revolution to the 1830s.[42] If it did begin then, it took a serious knock as a result of the impact on Nicholas of the European revolutions. In 1849 the tsar's new hard-line governor of Moscow, Zakrevskii, proposed preventing the expansion of existing factories in the city and banning the construction of new ones because of the potentially threatening character of the workforce they attracted. The tsar liked the proposal, put it up to the committee of ministers, and enacted it despite resistance from both the minister of internal affairs and the minister of finance.[43] For a time, at least, the effect of the European revolutions of 1848 seems to have been to put a stop to Russian industrialization. It is not much of a surprise to learn that, when the next reign began in the mid-1850s, a frustrated official in the ministry of finance asked his superiors whether the government intended 'long . . . to resist the development of the industrial forces of the people'.[44]

If the actions of the imperial government in the wake of the 1848 revolutions had the effect of impeding Russian industrialization,

[40] A. P. Pogrebinskii, *Ocherki istorii finansov dorevoliutsionnoi Rossii (XIX–XX vv.)* (Moscow, 1954), 20.

[41] Gerkhard Bekker, 'Oppozitsionnoe dvizhenie v Rossii v 1848 g. (Po doneseniiam prusskogo posol'stva v Sankt-Peterburge)', *Novaia i noveishaia istoriia* (1968), 1: 68–75 at 74.

[42] For a brief account of their disagreements on this question see A. M. Solov'eva, *Promyshlennaia revoliutsiia v Rossii v XIX v.* (Moscow, 1990), 9–10.

[43] For the law see *PSZ* 2 xxiv/1. 363–4 (No. 23,358, 10 July 1849). For its origins and enactment see Druzhinin, 'Moskva', 144; Eroshkin, *Krepostnicheskoe samoderzhavie*, 101–2; and especially Iu. Ia. Rybakov, *Promyshlennoe zakonodatel'stvo pervoi poloviny XIX veka* (Moscow, 1986), 47–8.

[44] Gagemeister, 'O finansakh', 115. For a more sanguine view of the tsarist regime's industrial policy in the last years of Nicholas I see Pintner, *Russian Economic Policy*, 235–7.

they put a much more dramatic end to change in the countryside. This may seem an odd thing to say, in view of the fact that Nicholas I's interest in bringing about agrarian change has not always been thought to be very great at the best of times. To judge, however, by the number of secret committees he established on rural matters, it was.[45] Nor were his committees necessarily a way of kicking agrarian affairs into touch, for sometimes the tsar proceeded to legislation. At the beginning of 1838, for example, he established a ministry of state properties under P. D. Kiselev whose principal concern was to initiate far-reaching changes in the lives of peasants who did not live on the estates of private landowners. Since peasants of this kind constituted about half the peasantry as a whole, the significance of the new ministry proved to be far-reaching.[46] In April 1842 the tsar made a rare personal appearance at the state council to justify the promulgation of a 'Law on Obligated Peasants'. While making it clear, on this occasion, that he did not intend to abolish serfdom forthwith, he also committed himself to the view that 'the present state of affairs [in respect of landlord–peasant relations in the countryside] cannot continue for ever', and that it was 'necessary . . . to prepare the way for a gradual transition to a different order of things'.[47]

Just before the revolutions of 1848, Nicholas went further. Russian law described very few circumstances in which peasants could buy their freedom as of right (rather than by agreeing terms with the landowner to whom they were ascribed). It was difficult, moreover, to make use of such loopholes as there were. There cannot have been many cases like that of Nikolai Shipov, for example, a peasant from the province of Nizhnii Novgorod who in 1845 exploited a statute which granted freedom to peasants who escaped

---

[45] On the secret committees see S. V. Malashkina, 'Sekretnye komitety pri Nikolae I', in A. K. Dzhivelegov et al. (eds.), Krepostnoe pravo v Rossii i reforma 19 fevralia (Moscow, 1911), 160–74; V. P. Alekseev, 'Sekretnye komitety pri Nikolae I', in A. K. Dzhivelegov et al. (eds.), Velikaia reforma: Russkoe obshchestvo i krest'ianskii vopros v proshlom i nastoiashchem (6 vols.; Moscow, 1911), ii. 194–208; and S. V. Mironenko, 'Odinnadtsat' sekretnykh komitetov', in id., Stranitsy tainoi istorii samoderzhaviia (Moscow, 1990), 100–95.

[46] See N. M. Druzhinin, Gosudarstvennye krest'iane i reforma P. D. Kiseleva (2 vols.; Moscow, 1946–58); Bruce F. Adams, 'The Reforms of P. D. Kiselev and the History of N. M. Druzhinin', Canadian–American Slavic Studies, 19 (1985), 28–43.

[47] M. A. Korf, 'Imperator Nikolai v soveshchatel' nykh sobraniiakh', SIRIO 98 (1896), 101–283 at 115.

after having been captured by mountain bandits in the Caucasus.[48] At the end of 1847, however, the tsar created what promised to be a much larger rent in the cloth of serfdom when he gave peasants the right to buy themselves out if the estate on which they lived was being sold at auction.[49] Since the indebtedness of mid-nineteenth-century Russian nobles was great and their estates tended to come under the hammer frequently, the new escape clause had potentially far-reaching implications.[50]

Unfortunately, the new escape clause fell victim to the mood engendered in the privileged classes of the Russian empire by the European revolutions of 1848. At the point the revolutions broke out, Nicholas appeared to be trying still harder to improve the lot of the peasantry, for ten days after learning of the fall of Louis-Philippe (and despite some muttering at the state council) he extended to peasants on private estates the right of landownership which peasants on state-owned land had possessed since 1801.[51] Subsequently, however, he began to think again about his auctions edict of late 1847. It had generated considerable excitement in the rural heartland of the empire, where peasants were doing everything they could to interpret it to their own advantage and landowners were finding it ill-advised at a time of pan-European upheaval.[52] Without formally repealing it, a massive law of July 1849 on the description, valuation, and sale of property effectively rendered the auctions edict of 1847 a dead letter.[53]

[48] See the untitled volume of memoirs containing V. N. Karpov's *Vospominaniia* and Shipov's *Istoriia moei zhizni*, ed. P. L. Zhatkin and N. V. Iakovlev (Moscow and Leningrad, 1933), esp. 448, 458, 497.

[49] *PSZ* 2 xxii. 841–2 (No. 21,689, 20 Nov. 1847); on the genesis of this law see Korf, 'Imperator Nikolai', 248–62.

[50] See, however, Evsey D. Domar and Mark J. Machina, 'On the Profitability of Russian Serfdom', *Journal of Economic History*, 44 (1984), 919–55 at 948–9, which claims that mid-19th-cent. Russian nobles were less heavily indebted than they are usually said to have been.

[51] *PSZ* 2 xxiii/1. 157–8 (No. 22,042, 15 Mar. 1848); Korf, 'Iz zapisok' (I), 560–1; V. G. Chernukha, *Krest'ianskii vopros v pravitel'stvennoi politike Rossii (60–70 gody XIX v.)* (Leningrad, 1972), 10.

[52] For the impact of the law in the countryside see V. A. Fedorov, *Krest'ianskoe dvizhenie v tsentral'noi Rossii 1800–1860 (po materialam tsentral'no-promyshlennykh gubernii)* (Moscow, 1980), 97–100; M. A. Rakhmatullin, *Krest'ianskoe dvizhenie v velikorusskikh guberniiakh v 1826–1857 gg.* (Moscow, 1990), 188–200; and David Moon, *Russian Peasants and Tsarist Legislation on the Eve of Reform: Interaction between Peasants and Officialdom, 1825–1855* (Basingstoke and London, 1992), 87–106.

[53] *PSZ* 2 xxiv/1. 552–602 (No 23,405, 31 July 1849). Korf ('Imperator Nikolai',

What the rise and fall of the auctions edict may show is that in 1848 the tsar fell back on a pro-noble policy to which his commitment had been diminishing in the years immediately prior to the revolutionary year.[54] Between 1825 and 1848 Nicholas had been treading a fine line between the long-standing policy of relying on nobles and the new policy of bureaucratization.[55] He had not abandoned a noble orientation altogether—indeed, in 1845 he had given long-established nobles one of the things they most wanted when he raised the level on the Table of Ranks that conferred hereditary nobility from rank eight to rank five—but in taking on vastly more officials and in encouraging, if not obliging, nobles to take a more beneficent view of the 'peasant problem', he had been demonstrating that he did not consider nobles to be quite the mainstay of the monarchy that the Romanovs had held them to be since, say, Catherine the Great had promulgated her 'Charter to the Nobility' of 1785. The Decembrist revolt with which Nicholas's reign had begun in 1825 gave him every justification for mistrusting nobles, for the rising had been led by members of some of the most distinguished families in the empire. Aspects of the tsar's ambitious early attempts at legislation, notably the abortive 'Supplementary Law on Estates' of 1830, give the impression that he was trying, in his first years on the throne, to alter the social foundations on which the monarchy rested. His admittedly tentative, but repeated, attempts at peasant reform may imply that even if Nicholas was too timorous to envisage full-blown emancipation, he saw the need to moderate the worst of the landlords' abuses.

Shortly after the outbreak of the 1848 revolutions, however, whatever courage Nicholas had possessed in the field of social affairs appears to have deserted him. Less than three weeks after granting peasants on private estates the right to own land he addressed the nobles of St Petersburg in terms which made it clear that he

267) makes it clear that paragraph 186 of this law (p. 570) was intended to override the earlier edict.

[54] The best study of the imperial authorities' changing attitude to the nobility in the first half of the 19th cent. is Jerry Lee Floyd, 'State Service, Social Mobility and the Imperial Russian Nobility, 1801–1856' (diss. Yale, 1981), from which some of the information in this paragraph is taken.

[55] On the growth of the bureaucracy between the mid-18th and mid-19th cents. see Walter M. Pintner, 'The Evolution of Civil Officialdom, 1755–1855', in Pintner and Don Karl Rowney (eds.), *Russian Officialdom: The Bureaucratization of Russian Society from the Seventeenth to the Twentieth Century* (Chapel Hill, 1980), 190–226.

was falling back on their support. Insisting, in the face of gossip to the contrary, that he had never contemplated taking any part of the nobles' land away from them, he concluded: 'Gentlemen! I have no police, I do not like them: you are my police . . . If we go forward amicably and act unanimously, we shall be invincible.'[56] Three days later his minister of internal affairs despatched a secret circular to all provincial governors entitled 'On Supporting the Legal Authority of Landowners'.[57] Whatever the extent to which the regime improved the condition of peasants on state-owned land and attempted to modify serfdom in the decades prior to 1848, its principal concern in the crisis of 1848 was not to give nobles cause for dissatisfaction. And since, to quote Jonathan Sperber again, 'by far the most significant and never altered consequence of the [European revolutions of 1848] was the abolition of serfdom and other seigneurial institutions',[58] Nicholas's abandonment of attempts at peasant reform had the effect not merely of failing to close the gap between the social structure of the Russian empire and that of the countries to the west, but of widening it.

So far I have argued, first, that the tsarist regime's losses in the crisis of 1848–9 outweighed its gains in respect of foreign affairs and ideology and, second, that to achieve its ostensible successes it also paid prices it could not afford in respect of its finances and the way it was handling the peasant question. Its handling of ethnic relations suffered too. Although it is remarkable that, broadly speaking, the Russian empire in 1848 was so little affected by the 'springtime of the nations' in central and western Europe—Nicholas's border controls seem to have been proof, on the whole, against infection of the empire on the part of insurgent Poles or nationally inclined Germans or the newly emancipated Ukrainian peasants of Austrian Galicia[59]—ethnic relations within the Russian empire nevertheless suffered in 1848 because the regime was so paranoid about the

[56] V. V. Golubtsov, 'Imperator Nikolai Pavlovich v ego rechi k deputatam s.-peterburgskogo dvorianstva, 21 marta [i.e. 2 Apr.] 1848g.', *RS* 39 (1883), 593–6 at 595–6.
[57] Iu. I. Gerasimova, 'Krest'ianskoe dvizhenie v Rossii v 1844–1849 gg.', *Istorich-eskie zapiski* [hereafter *IZ*], 50 (1955), 224–68 at 261 (circular of 5 Apr. 1848).
[58] Sperber, *The European Revolutions*, 250.
[59] See Nifontov, *Rossiia*, 81–98, for evidence that a few inflammatory documents got through, but also ibid. 98–9 for the author's fairly low estimation of their significance.

mere possibility of infection from central and western Europe that in the south-western part of the empire, where questions of ethnicity were particularly taxing, it significantly modified an ambitious policy whose full implementation might have constituted one of its greatest triumphs.

The 'south-western part of the empire' means the provinces of Kiev, Podolia, and Volhynia, where the gentry were predominantly Polish, the peasantry overwhelmingly Ukrainian, and the officials Russian. Poles under Russian rule tended to be mutinous. To prevent a recurrence of their rebellion of November 1830, Nicholas had installed a viceroy in their 'Congress Kingdom' who ruled it with a rod of iron for nearly a quarter of a century.[60] To undermine Polish authority in what Russian bureaucrats called the 'western provinces' of the empire (the nine provinces due east of the Congress Kingdom), the tsar had closed the greater part of the University of Vil'na, abolished one of the few outposts of the Uniate Church still in existence on the soil of the Russian empire, secularized the land of this and other Roman ecclesiastical organizations, and put an end to the practice of allowing Poles to lease land owned by the government.[61] In April 1844 he went further, making clear that he intended to interfere in the relations between the Poles of the western provinces and the peasants on their estates.

These relations had long been regulated by contracts called 'inventory rules', but until 1844 the rules had not been subject to governmental scrutiny. Now Nicholas ordered that they be collected, compared, and standardized. Dmitrii Bibikov, the governor-general of the three southernmost of the nine western provinces, moved faster than the more northerly governors and issued standardized inventory rules in June 1847. The storm caused by the process of putting the new rules into effect came to a head in 1848. Poles ob-

[60] For Field-Marshal Prince Paskevich's activities in the Congress Kingdom in the years 1832–50 see his 'Raport Namestnika Tsarstva Pol'skogo Ego Imperatorskomu Velichestvu', *SIRIO* 98 (1896), 597–615.

[61] Piotr S. Wandycz, *The Lands of Partitioned Poland, 1795–1918* (Seattle and London, 1974), 125 (closure of the university and campaign against the Uniate Church); *PSZ* 2 xvi/2. 138–9 (No. 15,152, 11 Jan. 1842), and A. L. Zinchenko, 'Reforma gosudarstvennoi derevni i sekuliarizatsiia tserkovnogo zemlevladeniia v zapadnykh guberniiakh rossiiskoi derevni', *IZ* 112 (1985), 98–125 (church lands); *PSZ* 2 xiv/1. 989–1183 (Nos. 13035–6, 9 Jan. 1840: introduction in the western provinces of the empire-wide changes in the administration of state-owned land, which had the effect of abolishing leaseholding). On ecclesiastical matters see also the recent study by S. V. Rimskii, 'Konfessional'naia politika Rossii v Zapadnom krae i Pribaltike XIX stoletiia', *Voprosy istorii* (1998), 3: 25–44.

jected to the reform both on principle (because it seemed to them to be an illicit intervention in affairs they considered to be private) and in practice (because their Ukrainian peasants stood to benefit from it). Peasants took exception to the parts of the new rules which set norms higher than those to which they were accustomed and sought to push the parts that benefited them beyond the point they were supposed to go. Another Polish–Ukrainian bloodbath began to seem a possibility.[62]

The Russian authorities were in what chess-players call *Zugzwang* ('move compulsion', a situation in which a move has to be made but all possible moves render the position worse). At a time when Parisians were invading their parliament to call for war on behalf of Poles,[63] and in a part of the empire adjacent to the Habsburg province of Galicia, where Ukrainian peasants were being emancipated,[64] the tsar had to put an end to the south-western disorder. If he took the side of the Poles, however, he would be contradicting the whole tenor of his policy towards them since 1831; and if he took the side of the Ukrainians, he ran the risk of alarming landowners throughout the empire by signalling that he was prepared, in certain circumstances, to override landlord authority. The minister of internal affairs told Bibikov in early April 1848 that the tsar had begun to fear that 'in the present situation' enacting the inventory reform 'might have damaging consequences, in that it has provoked dissatisfaction and grumbling among both landlords and peasants'.[65] But pointing out the difficulty was one thing; resolving the Polish–Ukrainian conundrum was another.

Broadly speaking, and very remarkably, the Russian authorities turned away from their reform initiative and came down on the side of the Poles. In October 1848 they tried buying them off by halting

[62] For the possibility that a bloodbath like that of 1768 was in the offing see David Moon, 'Memories of the Cossack Era, the Haidamak Movement, and the Koliivshchyna in Right-bank Ukrainian Peasant Unrest in 1848', in Ia. Isaievych and Ia. Hrytsak (eds.), *Druhyi mizhnarodnyi konhres ukrainistiv: Dopovidi i povidomlennia, Istoriia, chastyna I* (L'viv, 1994), 166–71. I am extremely grateful to Dr Moon for commenting on an earlier version of the present chapter and for allowing me to read a longer, unpublished article he has written on peasant unrest in the south-western part of the Russian empire in 1848.

[63] Peter Amann, 'A *Journée* in the Making: May 15, 1848', *Journal of Modern History*, 42 (1970), 42–69.

[64] John-Paul Himka, *Galician Villagers and the Ukrainian National Movement in the Nineteenth Century* (Basingstoke and London, 1988), 26–36.

[65] A. Z. Baraboi, 'Pravoberezhnaia Ukraina v 1848 g.', *IZ* 34 (1950), 86–121 at 114.

all lawsuits which concerned abuses of landlord power in the south-western provinces prior to the introduction of the new rules.[66] In January 1849 they went further and revised the rules. Under the most pro-noble of the revisions, landowners acquired the right to move peasants from one part of an estate to another. As a result, they could oblige them to render poor land fit for cultivation, then take it back into the demesne and oblige the peasants to do the same again somewhere else. Since peasants in the south-western part of the empire tended henceforward always to be working relatively infertile land, the quality of the land they received when serfdom was eventually abolished in the 1860s was usually poor.[67]

According to the greatest historian of the pre-emancipation countryside of the Russian empire, the rules of January 1849 nevertheless remained 'the most energetic measure on behalf of serfs out of everything that was done for them in the epoch of Nicholas I'.[68] It is hard, however, not to feel that the reform would have been much more substantial if the Russian authorities had not been feeling fragile and had had the courage to hold on to the version of the rules they had promulgated in 1847. They might even have had the courage to insist that what Bibikov had done for the south-west be imitated by the governors-general of the other six western provinces.[69] The tsar had been thinking of all nine of his 'western provinces' when he set the inventory reform in train in 1844. He finished up with a botched reform in three of them.[70]

[66] *PSZ* 2 xxiii/1. 646–7 (No. 22,652, 27 Oct. 1848).
[67] V. I. Semevskii, *Krest'ianskii vopros v Rossii v XVIII i pervoi polovine XIX veka* (2 vols.; St Petersburg, 1888), ii. 500–1, 503–4; Baraboi, 'Pravoberezhnaia Ukraina', 117; V. I. Dovzhenok, 'Krest'ianskoe dvizhenie na pravoberezhnoi Ukraine v 40-kh gg. XIXv.', *IZ* 12 (1941), 144–64 at 153.
[68] Semevskii, *Krest'ianskii vopros*, ii. 504. This was also the opinion of I. I. Ignatovich: *Pomeshchich'i krest'iane nakanune osvobozhdeniia*, 2nd edn. (Moscow, 1910), 166.
[69] On the failure of the Russian authorities to breathe life into the inventory reform in the other six provinces see Ignatovich, *Pomeshchich'i krest'iane*, 174–84, and N. N. Ulashchik, *Predposylki krest'ianskoi reformy 1861g. v Litve i Zapadnoi Belorussii* (Moscow, 1965), 452–9.
[70] The inventory reform has occasioned a large literature. Apart from the studies mentioned above, see O. Levitskii, 'O polozhenii krest'ian iugo-zapadnogo kraia vo 2-oi chetverti XIX veka', *Kievskaia starina*, 93 (1906), 1st pagination, 231–74; N. P. Vasilenko, 'Krest'ianskii vopros v iugo-zapadnom i severo-zapadnom krae pri Nikolae I i vvedenie inventarei', in Dzhivelegov *et al.* (eds.), *Velikaia reforma*, iv. 94–109; I. O. Hurzhii, *Borot'ba selian i robitnykiv Ukrainy proty feodal'no-kriposnyts'koho hnitu (z 80-kh rokiv XVIII st. do 1861 r.)* (Kiev, 1958), 105–32; and Daniel Beauvois, *Le Noble, le serf et le révizor: La Noblesse polonaise entre le tsarisme et les masses*

In some of the above I may have implied that, but for the effect on him of the European revolutions of 1848, Nicholas I would have been remembered as a major economic and social reformer and a major innovator in the field of ethnic relations. I must be careful not to claim so much. Although, but for 1848, Zakrevskii would not have become governor of Moscow and industry in the city might have continued to develop relatively freely, and although a few more peasants would have succeeded in gaining their freedom by buying themselves out under the auctions edict and more Ukrainians in the western provinces of the empire would have secured government-backed statements of their obligations and thus a measure of protection from exploitation on the part of Poles, it would have taken many more reforms than these to put the Russian empire in a position to compete effectively with the countries it considered to be its rivals.

Russia in 1848 was a backward place. Demographically speaking, towns were probably in decline.[71] Railway-building had hardly begun.[72] To judge by the length of time it took the news of Louis-Philippe's fall to reach St Petersburg (nine days), communications were not very good. Count Adlerberg launched Russia's postal revolution in 1848, but only after the relevant legislation had been referred back to him to take account of the likelihood that the stamps he was proposing to introduce would be grist to the mill of forgers.[73] Owing to the predominance of wooden buildings, fire was a perennial hazard. In January 1849 Nicholas banned the sale of matches in quantities of less than a thousand to prevent them from falling into the hands of the incautious.[74] Climate and soil fertility were such that agricultural returns were poor. In 1848 the sun

---

ukrainiennes (1831–1863) (Paris and Montreux, 1985), 58–66. Some of the documents on peasant reactions to the reform have been published in A. V. Predtechenskii (ed.), *Krest'ianskoe dvizhenie v Rossii v 1826–1849 gg.* (Moscow, 1961), and M. N. Leshchenko et al. (eds.), *Selians'kyi rukh na Ukraini 1826–1849 rr.* (Kiev, 1985).

[71] B. N. Mironov, *Russkii gorod v 1740–1860-e gody: demograficheskoe, sotsial'noe i ekonomicheskoe razvitie* (Leningrad, 1990), chs. 1–2.

[72] Richard Mowbray Haywood, *The Beginnings of Railway Development in Russia in the Reign of Nicholas I, 1835–1842* (Durham, NC, 1969), esp. 242.

[73] *PSZ* 2 xxiii/1. 67–8 (no. 21,927, 7 Feb. 1848), 276 (No. 22,211, 8 May 1848), 600–2 (No. 22,612, 9 Oct. 1848). See also [Count Adlerberg], 'Otchet Glavnonachal'stvuiushchego nad Pochtovym Departamentom, 1825–1850', *SIRIO* 98 (1896), 464.

[74] *PSZ* 2 xxiii/2. 146 (No. 22,875, 10 Jan. 1849).

scorched the ground and the harvest failed.[75] When agricultural returns were poor, the exchequer suffered because peasants were unable to pay the poll tax. In 1848 it was collected in full in only a fifth of the empire's provinces.[76] Although the reforms initiated by the ministry of state properties in 1838 are usually held to have been relatively successful, and although their principal purpose was to improve the condition of the state's finances, even after they had been under way for fourteen years the shortfall in payments from peasants on state-owned land may have been increasing.[77] Disease, meanwhile, stalked the land. Owing to cholera, more people died in the Russian empire in 1848 than were born.[78] When, at the end of 1848, the *Economist* of London reflected on the revolutionary year, it was right to attribute the Russian empire's freedom from disruption to the fact that 'her population is not yet civilised enough to feel those yearnings after freedom and self-government which have agitated Europe'.[79]

The tsar had not shown many signs that he was aware of the full extent of his difficulties. Prior to the revolutions of 1848, however, he had been addressing himself to a few of them. In and after 1848, by contrast, he took steps which not only marked the abandonment of his tentative reform initiatives, but further depressed the condition of his empire. One might argue, indeed, that his various responses to revolution in Europe were not far behind the effects of the Crimean War in the checklist of short-term reasons for the 'great reforms' on which his son embarked in the second half of the 1850s. This chapter began by floating the possibility that Nicholas I dealt well with the threat of 1848. It went on to argue that, in reality, and even by his own fairly narrow military, diplomatic, and ideological criteria for success, the tsar's actions created more problems

---

[75] A. V. Dulov, 'Prirodnye usloviia i razvitie proizvoditel'nykh sil Rossii v XVIII—seredine XIX veka', *Voprosy istorii* (1979), 1: 38–53 at 44.

[76] Pogrebinskii, *Ocherki*, 31.

[77] Gagemeister, 'O finansakh', 105. The ministry painted a more attractive picture: [P. D. Kiselev], 'Obzor upravleniia Gosudarstvennykh Imushchestv za poslednie 25 let s 20 noiabria 1825 po 20 noiabria 1850 g.', *SIRIO* 98 (1896), 468–98.

[78] Iu. E. Ianson, *Sravnitel'naia statistika Rossii i zapadno-evropeiskikh gosudarstv*, i. *Territoriia i naselenie* (St Petersburg, 1878), 345; see also K. David Patterson, 'Cholera Diffusion in Russia, 1823–1923', *Social Science and Medicine*, 38 (1994), 1171–91 at 1176–9.

[79] Quoted in John Saville, *1848: The British State and the Chartist Movement* (Cambridge, 1987), 164.

than they solved. By other criteria—financial, social, ethnic—the consequences of the regime's conduct of affairs in 1848 were disastrous. All the Russian empire really achieved by trying to shut itself off from the revolutions of 1848 was the prospect of many more substantial threats to its well-being in the not too distant future.

FURTHER READING

The principal study of the Russian empire at the time of the revolutions of 1848 remains A. S. Nifontov's classic, *Rossiia v 1848 godu* (Moscow, 1949). In English, the best introduction is chapter 8 of W. Bruce Lincoln, *Nicholas I* (London, 1978). On diplomatic and military affairs see especially Ian W. Roberts, *Nicholas I and the Russian Intervention in Hungary* (Basingstoke and London, 1991). On the regime's ideological outlook see Nicholas Riasanovsky, *Nicholas I and Official Nationality in Russia, 1825–55* (Berkeley, 1959); chapter 9 of Richard S. Wortman, *Scenarios of Power: Myth and Ceremony in Russian Monarchy*, i (Princeton, 1995); and, for the years 1848–55 in particular, chapter 6 of Sidney Monas, *The Third Section: Police and Society in Russia under Nicholas I* (Cambridge, Mass., 1961). Isaiah Berlin's 'Russia and 1848', repr. in his *Russian Thinkers* (London, 1978), deals almost exclusively with the effect of the 1848 revolutions on the views and prospects of dissident Russian intellectuals. Other studies in this well-worked part of the field include Joanna Seddon, *The Petrashevtsy* (Manchester, 1985), and Judith E. Zimmmerman, *Midpassage: Alexander Herzen and European Revolution, 1847–52* (Pittsburgh, 1989). On the regime's conduct of economic affairs see Walter McKenzie Pintner, *Russian Economic Policy under Nicholas I* (Ithaca, NY, 1967). On peasants see David Moon, *Russian Peasants and Tsarist Legislation on the Eve of Reform: Interaction between Peasants and Officialdom, 1825–1855* (Basingstoke and London, 1992), and chapter 3 of Olga Crisp's *Studies in the Russian Economy before 1914* (London and Basingstoke, 1976). On bureaucratization see chapters 8–9 of *Russian Officialdom*, ed. Walter McKenzie Pintner and Don Karl Rowney (Chapel Hill, NC, 1980). Relations among Poles, Ukrainians, and Russians in the south-western part of the empire crop up in chapter 7 of Edward C. Thaden, *Russia's Western Borderlands, 1710–1870* (Princeton, 1984).

8

The United States and
the Revolutions of 1848

TIMOTHY M. ROBERTS

DANIEL W. HOWE

IN 1848 most Americans did not believe that their own country needed the kind of revolution Continental Europe was having,
about which they read in their newspapers. Their reactions to the
revolutions nevertheless reveal much about their own society, their
political culture, and their prejudices. This is an essay about the
way people in the United States responded to the European revolutions of 1848. It seeks to take account not only of diplomatic
history but also of American domestic politics, social structure,
and legal institutions. More than anything else, it is an examination
of American public opinion.

Before the completion of the transatlantic cable in 1867, news
from Europe arrived in the United States by steamship. Once
the news arrived—usually in New York—it was then disseminated
rapidly by telegraph. The steamships brought the news in bunches,
which the American press would digest and broadcast at once, so
that on occasion weeks of European events would be reported on
the same day in the United States. Reports from the British press
were especially influential because they were conveniently written
in English. The first news of the February Revolution in Paris arrived on 20 March 1848.[1] It had been less than two weeks since
the United States Senate had ratified the Treaty of Guadalupe

---

[1] On the state of journalistic communication in this era see Menahem Blondheim,
*News over the Wires: The Telegraph and the Flow of Public Information in America,
1844–97* (Cambridge, Mass., 1994).

Hidalgo, ending a victorious war against Mexico that brought huge territorial acquisitions, including everything from Texas to California. What looked at first like the disintegration of the European political order was welcomed by the public of a triumphant United States. Just when the United States had confirmed its supremacy over the North American continent news arrived of turmoil in reactionary Europe. America's greatness, ideological superiority, and providential destiny seemed to be confirmed. Once they learnt of the momentous events taking place in Europe, the American newspapers rushed correspondents of their own to the scene, so that for the later phases of the revolutions there are first-hand accounts by American journalists, not just American newspapers reprinting and reshaping British reports.[2]

As time went on, the news of the European revolutions became more ambiguous. Different groups in American society then seized upon different aspects of the revolutions to validate their own objectives and preconceptions. Various groups of Americans, including ethnic minorities, radicals and conservatives, Protestants and Catholics, antislavery crusaders, pro-slavery expansionists, and proponents of rights for women, all advanced their own viewpoints on the European revolutions and their outcomes.[3]

The United States had a paradoxical relationship to the revolutions of 1848. On the one hand, the nation had been born out of a revolution, and Americans were extremely proud of this revolutionary heritage. It disposed them to welcome the European revolutions in 1848 and wish them success. On the other hand, however, most Americans also felt somewhat detached from the events they read about. To them, the issues involved in the European revolutions did not seem to be live political issues in the United States. In many parts of central and southern Europe the revolutions of 1848 reflected the national aspirations of ethnic groups. American citizenship, however, was defined in terms of republican ideology, not in terms of national origin. Although many white ethnic groups published newspapers in their ancestral language and ethnic block voting was common, there was no impulse towards political auto-

[2] New York, Washington, and New Orleans newspaper reports on the events in Paris are edited and translated into French in Guillaume de Bertier de Sauvigny, *La Révolution parisienne de 1848 vue par les Américains* (Paris, 1984).

[3] See Timothy M. Roberts, 'The American Response to the European Revolutions of 1848' (diss. Oxford, 1997).

nomy for particular ethnic groups. Any European immigrant could become a naturalized United States citizen relatively easily.

Serfdom and manorial restraints, such as still existed in the Austrian and Russian empires, were unknown in the United States; the white labour force was free to move about and frequently did so. Of course, there was chattel slavery in the southern half of the country. Slavery in the United States was a special case of oppression, more intractable even than serfdom in central and eastern Europe. One of the durable achievements of the revolutions of 1848 was the emancipation of the slaves in the French and Danish West Indies. Parliament had abolished slavery in the British West Indies back in 1833. Yet only a few Americans saw any connection between the revolutions of 1848 and their own institution of slavery. Acceptance of slavery in the United States was based on the assumption of white racial supremacy. But within the white race and the male gender, social and economic opportunities were widespread. Careers were open to talent in the United States, provided the careerist was white and male.

Under the July monarchy in France, perhaps one man in thirty had the vote. In the United States in 1848 laws regulating the suffrage were set by the individual states, but overall these states provided the most widespread suffrage in the world at that time. Universal white manhood suffrage had become the norm throughout the union. There were still controversies over the franchise, but they involved marginalized minority groups. Some states allowed immigrant men to vote even before they became naturalized citizens, and this was controversial. A few states allowed free black men to vote on equal terms with white; most states did not. New York allowed black men to vote if they met a property qualification that was not imposed on whites. Native Americans and African Americans were by definition outsiders; indeed contemporaries seldom referred to them as Americans. In their case, however, it was not so much their nationality as their humanity itself which was being questioned. If a man was fully human—that is, if a man was white—he could become an American and express himself politically, regardless of his national origin; all it took was meeting a residency requirement. To be a loyal American citizen was to be of the white race and to subscribe to the ideology of republicanism.

Political participation was the central action of this republican ideology, for it gave concrete expression to the ideal of government by consent. Voting was a civic ritual, and men took it seriously. Voting was not secret. The ballots were long, with many offices—state and local as well as federal—to be filled by the electors. There were two major parties, the Democrats and the Whigs, and a number of minor parties. Ballots were printed by the parties, not by the government, and they typically listed only that party's own candidates. Not surprisingly under these circumstances, most men voted a straight party line for all offices. Elections were frequent, terms of one or two years being common for many offices. Every state set its own dates for elections, with the result that election returns were being reported from some place or other during most months of the year. (The first time that all voters across the country went to the polls on the same day was the presidential election of 4 November 1848.) Voter participation was high; in the presidential election of 1840 over 80 per cent of the legally qualified electorate had cast ballots.[4] This would stand as an all-time record, because voter participation in the United States has declined throughout the twentieth century from its nineteenth-century highs.

The United States in 1848 was an open society, in the sense that people were generally free to try out new ideas and frequently did so. This openness was most conspicuous in religion. Although individual states were constitutionally free to have established churches if they wished, in fact there was no longer an established church in any of the states; the last establishment of religion had been abolished in Massachusetts in 1833. Americans throughout the union were free to have any religion or none: in effect the country enjoyed a free marketplace in religion. Under this voluntary system, the churches and their clergy were supported entirely by the freewill offerings of their laity. Except for colleges, very few religious institutions had endowments of any significance. There was a high degree of local parish autonomy and lay control, even in those denominations, like the Anglican and Roman Catholic, that were hierarchically organized. The country thought of itself as Protestant, and the most popular Protestant sects were Methodism, Baptism, Presbyterianism, and Congregationalism. All in all, American religious life was even more diverse, democratic, and egalitarian than American po-

---

[4] The exact percentage is 80.2: US Bureau of the Census, *Historical Statistics of the United States* (2 vols.; Washington, 1975), ii. 1072. On American political life in this period see Michael Holt, *Political Parties and American Political Development from the Age of Jackson to the Age of Lincoln* (Baton Rouge, La., 1992).

litical life. People excluded from political life, such as women and African Americans, could and did play significant roles in religious life.[5]

The vast size and empty spaces of the North American continent provided a safety-valve for certain kinds of discontent and an opportunity for diversity to flourish even against public intolerance. Just about anything could be tried, including drastic innovations in marriage and family structure, if people could be found who were willing to participate in the experiment and make enough personal sacrifice. When socialism was introduced into the United States from France, its followers were able to found communities of their own without political interference. The Utopian socialism of Charles Fourier enjoyed an extensive vogue in the United States during the 1840s. The American followers of Fourier were known as Associationists and led by a man named Albert Brisbane. Between 1841 and 1848 there were operating in the United States no fewer than thirty-five phalanxes, as these socialist communities were called. The phalanxes were scattered around the country, mostly in the area stretching from New England westward between the Great Lakes and the Ohio River. When the revolutions of 1848 broke out, the American Associationists eagerly sent representatives to France to see how the cause of socialism could best be furthered. They were disappointed in their French counterparts, whom they found impractical, and the American Associationists were generally not willing to embrace the Marxian variant of socialism with its call for violence. In 1849 the California gold rush distracted adventurous souls away from experimental communes and towards treasure-hunting in the high Sierra. The Fourier movement in the United States went into decline.[6]

The political participation white male Americans enjoyed in the mid-nineteenth century had not been won entirely painlessly. In several states—notably New York, Massachusetts, and Virginia—the democratization of the electoral franchise had been gained only after serious political struggles, and conventions had to be held to rewrite the state constitutions. But in only one case had there

[5] See Nathan O. Hatch, *The Democratization of American Christianity* (New Haven, 1989).
[6] Carl Guarneri, *The Utopian Alternative: Fourierism in Nineteenth-century America* (Ithaca, NY, 1991).

been insurrectionary violence. This occurred in the state of Rhode Island in 1842. It is called the Dorr Rebellion. Like the uprising in Paris of June 1848, the Dorr uprising in Rhode Island represented the grievances of discontented urban workers. In 1842 the state of Rhode Island was the only state that had not rewritten its constitution since the Revolution; it was still operating under its colonial charter of 1663. Within this legal framework fewer than half the white men qualified for the elective franchise and the new industrial urban areas around Providence had little representation in the state legislature. Disfranchised urban artisans and working men bore most of the burden of taxation. While the colonial charter would not have been conspicuously undemocratic in Europe in the 1840s, it was so in the America of the time. Furthermore, the charter made no provision for its own amendment, since it had been assumed that the Privy Council in London could change it, which was now obviously out of the question.

In 1840 a Rhode Island Suffrage Association began to hold demonstrations, and the following year the association sponsored an unauthorized convention which drew up a document called by them the 'People's Constitution'. This 'People's Constitution' was ratified by a referendum in which all white men in the state were allowed to vote. The referendum had no legal status, although the authorities allowed it to occur. Its supporters claimed they were exercising popular sovereignty, as authorized in Locke's philosophy that government owes its authority to the consent of the people. In 1842 the radicals presumed to nominate Thomas Dorr for governor and other men for other state offices, and called an election under the 'People's Constitution' to put them into power. This time the legal authorities took the challenge seriously enough to pass a law forbidding such extralegal elections. On 18 April the election took place anyway, and on 3 May Thomas Dorr's supporters inaugurated him as governor, along with a 'People's Legislature'. Since the state capitol building was barred to them, the 'People's Legislature' met in a deserted factory. Armed conflict began on 18 May when the rebels tried to capture a state arsenal and failed. The radicals' support melted away quickly thereafter, partly as a result of weak leadership by Dorr, and partly because the legal authorities made it clear that they were willing to change the charter form of government. A number of radical leaders were rounded up and tried. Dorr himself was convicted of treason against the state of

Rhode Island and sentenced to life imprisonment; he was released after serving twenty months. Meanwhile the charter government had authorized a legal constitutional convention, which drew up a frame of government called the 'Law and Order Constitution'. This constitution greatly broadened the franchise, including black men, who had not been enfranchised by the 'People's Constitution'. However, the Law and Order Constitution imposed a property qualification on immigrant whites for voting, and it left the new urban areas still under-represented in the state legislature. This constitution was approved and implemented. Within a few years the political conflicts represented by the Dorr rebellion were being carried on by normal party politics: the former rebels pursued their interests through the Democratic party, and the former defenders of the old charter pursued theirs through the Whig party.[7]

Perhaps the Dorr Rebellion can be considered the closest counterpart in the United States to the European revolutions of 1848. To be sure, it had been a small-scale event and was easily contained. But memories of it were still vivid in 1848, and in fact the issues of the uprising were being reheard because of a legal case arising from the rebellion. The case of *Luther* v. *Borden* was being argued before the United States Supreme Court, beginning in January 1848. The case had been brought by one of the Dorrite rebels whose house had been broken into by state militia under colour of martial law, which the charter government had declared after violence had broken out. The plaintiff claimed that the 'People's Constitution' had been the valid constitution of Rhode Island at the time. The United States Supreme Court rejected that claim, vindicating the legality of the charter government and upholding its legal right to declare martial law.[8] This decision ironically aligned the United States Supreme Court with prescriptive authority against the claims of popular sovereignty, even at the very moment when American public opinion was most enthusiastically embracing the cause of the European revolutionaries. The two sides of American society, the revolutionary and the non-revolutionary, were illustrated simultaneously.

[7] See Marvin Gettleman, *The Dorr Rebellion: A Study in American Radicalism, 1833–1849* (New York, 1973); and George M. Dennison, *The Dorr War: Republicanism on Trial, 1831–1861* (Lexington, Ky., 1976).

[8] 48 US (7 Howard) 1–88 (1849).

In America the first reaction to the February revolution in Paris was most enthusiastic. The United States minister to France, Richard Rush, acted on his own authority when, on 28 February, he precipitately extended recognition to the provisional government in Paris; no other foreign power had yet done so. But his action was readily confirmed by the presidential administration of James Knox Polk when news of it finally reached the city of Washington twenty-six days later.[9] The feelings of the American public were captured by the popular poet James Russell Lowell, in his 'Ode to France':

> And down the happy future runs a flood
> Of prophesying light;
> It shows an earth no longer stained with blood,
> Blossom and fruit where now we see the bud
> Of brotherhood and Right.[10]

A meeting of newspaper editors and publishers held in Washington on 5 April, representing a wide spectrum of opinion, extended the collective congratulations of Americans to the people of France. The American journalists commended the French for having respected on the one hand 'the rights of private property' and on the other 'the rights of labor'.[11] In the long run, however, it would not prove possible for Americans to view events in Europe as confirming both these two ideals.

Americans rejoiced when the spirit of revolution spread to Germany. In July 1848 a private American citizen took it upon himself to act as envoy from the United States to the liberal Frankfurt assembly. This audacious act was disavowed by the president as soon as he learnt of it; however the administration was prepared to authorize a representative to Frankfurt of its own choosing. An experienced diplomat, Andrew Jackson Donelson (nephew of his namesake), was duly—if somewhat prematurely—appointed 'Min-

---

[9] Henry Blumenthal, *A Reappraisal of Franco-American Relations, 1830–1871* (Chapel Hill, NC, 1959), 13–14.
[10] James Russell Lowell, 'Ode to France: February 1848', in his *Poetical Works* (4 vols.; Boston, 1890), i. 258.
[11] *National Intelligencer*, Washington (7 Apr. 1848).

ister Plenipotentiary to the Federal Government of Germany'.[12] During the months to come many Americans, including prominent politicians, took great interest in the drafting of a written constitution for Germany, offering advice and criticisms to the Frankfurt liberals. The Polk administration went so far as to send an American warship, the *USS St Lawrence*, to Bremerhaven, to demonstrate official good will. Later, two officers of the US Navy were allowed to give advice to the fledgling German navy, facing war with Denmark, and arrangements were made for a German warship to be outfitted in the Brooklyn Navy Yard.[13]

Typical of the early American enthusiasm for the revolutions was the Great Demonstration (as it was called) in New York in April 1848. Three stands were set up, an 'American stand', a 'German stand', and a 'French and Italian stand'. Orators on the first of these delivered speeches, recited poetry, and conducted songs in English; orators on each European stand performed the same in the native languages—German, Italian, French, and Polish (this last from the French–Italian stand). Some speeches were given in two or three languages. The *Marseillaise* was sung.[14] As this demonstration suggests, American sympathies had not only an ideological basis, but also an ethnic one. Americans took a keen interest in what went on in their ancestral homelands, especially if they were first-generation immigrants.

There was also a religious basis for American interest in the revolutions of 1848. Some evangelical spokesmen seized upon events as heralding the overthrow of the papacy, the long-deferred fulfilment of the Protestant Reformation. Alexander Taggart McGill, a Presbyterian minister, recalculated the significance of the number 1848 to bring it into conformity with biblical prophecies concerning the final overthrow of the Antichrist. Baptist and Methodist journals featured reinterpretations of the book of Revelation and the unfolding of the apocalypse. But biblical literalists were by no means the only clergy to welcome what they imagined would be the downfall of the papacy. Even clergy with liberal theological views, like Horace Bushnell of Connecticut, welcomed evidence that America's example was redeeming Europe in both political and

<hr/>

[12] Arthur James May, *Contemporary American Opinion of the Mid-century Revolutions in Central Europe* (Philadelphia, 1927), 15, 26.
[13] See Günter Moltmann, *Atlantische Blockpolitik im 19. Jahrhundert* (Düsseldorf, 1973), esp. 133–75.   [14] Roberts, 'American Response', 125–8.

religious affairs.[15] For their part, American Catholics naturally took an even keener interest in the fate of the European Catholic church, and the papacy in particular. American Catholics remained loyal to Pius IX both in his reformist and in his conservative phases. America's leading Catholic intellectual, Orestes Brownson, condemned the European uprisings and distinguished them sharply from the American Revolution of 1776. John Hughes, the Irish American archbishop of New York, took the same position. He interpreted the failure of the 1848 revolutions, when it came, as exemplifying their fundamentally irrational and irresponsible nature. From the vantage-point of 1850, he contrasted the abortive, secularist European uprisings with the American revolution, a deliberate act, well grounded in precedent, by 'a fair majority of the reasoning part of the community'.[16]

One way that Americans paid public tribute to events in Europe was in their decisions to name or rename their places and possessions after revolutionary heroes. The favourite of all these celebrities was the Hungarian leader Louis Kossuth. (Since they could not manage the Hungarian pronunciation of this name, Americans called him 'Kus-SOOTH'when he visited the United States in 1851 and 1852.) Towns in Indiana, Mississippi, and Ohio were named after him, as was the largest county in Iowa. (Today a visitor to the Kossuth County courthouse in Algona, Iowa, sees the Hungarian coat of arms displayed.) Towns in Arkansas and Wisconsin named themselves after the French poet-revolutionary Alphonse de Lamartine. Pennsylvania ended up with towns named after both Kossuth and Lamartine. Revolutionary enthusiasm manifested itself in fashions of dress as well, such as the liberty cap of the French, the red attire of the Italian *carbonari*, or the fur hats and boots popularized by Kossuth.[17]

Only in a few cases did Americans actually volunteer to intervene in European uprisings. Of course, the revolutions came to an end so quickly that there was only a brief window of opportunity for Americans to act. Lieutenant Mayne Reid, a veteran of the Mexican War,

---

[15] Alexander Taggart McGill, *Popery the Punishment of Unbelief* (Philadelphia, 1848); Horace Bushnell quoted in John R. Bodo, *Protestant Clergy and Public Issues, 1812–48*, (Princeton, 1954), 237.

[16] Orestes Brownson, 'Legitimacy and Revolutionism', in his *Essays and Reviews Chiefly on Theology, Politics, and Socialism* (New York, 1852), 389–415; John Hughes, *The Church and the World* (New York, 1850), quotation from p. 25.

[17] Roberts, 'American Response', 90–3.

assembled 500 Germans and Hungarians in New York and armed each with a colt revolver, intending to pursue the struggle overseas, but in the event nothing came of his venture. George B. McClellan, future Union general in the Civil War, arranged to join the Hungarian army as a military adviser, but the Hungarian surrender put an end to his plans.[18] Probably the most significant attempt by people in America to intervene actively involved the abortive Irish rebellion of 1848. Groups calling themselves 'Young Ireland' distributed propaganda to the effect that the Continental revolutions would spread to Ireland. Unrealistic expectations among the Irish American community were fed by rallies in New York City during August of 1848. After the failure of a pitifully small and inept uprising, British authorities in Ireland arrested a group of Irish Americans. The men were United States citizens, and the American minister in London had to intervene to secure their release in return for an American apology. The episode left a bitter taste in the mouths of many Irish Americans, who felt that they had been deluded into thinking that the 1848 rebellion in Ireland was much more viable than it turned out to be.[19]

Private armed interventions in Latin America based in the United States were common throughout the nineteenth century, so common that they even had their own name, 'filibustering'. The revolutions of 1848 stimulated some of this activity, giving it a cloak of republican respectability. One Narciso López tried to mount an invasion of Cuba from American soil, seeking to overthrow Spanish rule on the island and annex it to the United States. López enjoyed widespread popular support among Americans, especially with Democrats and territorial expansionists, but his repeated expeditions between 1848 and 1851 were frustrated, either by the Spanish themselves or by the embarrassed Whig administration in Washington.[20] Another filibusterer, William Walker, professed to want to liberate Nicaragua with a crew of mercenaries drawn from the United States; what he really seems to have intended was to set himself up as dictator and eventually secure Nicaragua's admis-

---

[18] Ibid. 93–4.

[19] John Belchem, 'Republican Spirit and Military Science: The "Irish Brigade" and Irish-American Nationalism in 1848', *Irish Historical Studies*, 29 (1994), 44–64; id., 'Nationalism, Republicanism and Exile: Irish Emigrants and the Revolutions of 1848', *Past and Present*, 146 (1995), 103–35.

[20] See Tom Chaffin, 'Narciso López, Filibustering, and US Nationalism, 1848–51', *Journal of the Early Republic*, 15 (1995), 80–108.

sion to the Union as a slave state. Walker ended up being captured in Central America and facing a firing squad there in 1860. The use made of revolutionary precedent to justify such undertakings was open to the charge of hypocrisy, and contemporaries as well as posterity levelled that charge.

The year of revolution was also a presidential election year in the United States, and the American reception of events in Europe was coloured by domestic political allegiances. Among the Americans who greeted the revolutions most enthusiastically were the supporters of a minor party called the Free Soil Party, which argued that Congress should pass legislation abolishing slavery in all of the territories, i.e. those areas belonging to the United States which had not yet been admitted to statehood and consequently were still under the direct legislative authority of the central government. The Free Soil Party drew what strength it had from northerners who had become impatient with the reluctance of both the Democratic and the Whig Parties to offend southern slave-holding interests. Supporters of the Free Soil Party saw themselves as challenging the political status quo in the United States and welcomed the revolutions in Europe as heralding a worldwide change in public opinion, one that might sweep away all established tyrannies, including American racial slavery. Ideologically, the Free Soil Party of 1848 celebrated equal opportunity and self-help, ideals that it saw exemplified in at least some aspects of the revolutions in Europe. Free Soil spokesmen emphasized the role of the United States as a beacon of liberty to the rest of the world, and pointed out that America could play this role convincingly only if it restricted the spread of slavery as a step towards its ultimate abolition.[21]

However, the two major parties were not disposed to allow the little Free Soil Party to monopolize the lessons to be derived from the European uprisings. The Democratic Party pointed with pride in its national party platform, adopted in May 1848, to 'the sovereignty of the people'. Evidently in imitation of the United States, Europeans were 'erecting republics on the ruins of despotism in the Old World', the platform noted. The party convention tendered 'fraternal congratulations to the National Convention of the Repub-

[21] See Frederick J. Blue, *The Free Soilers: Third Party Politics, 1848–54* (Urbana, Ill., 1973).

lic of France'.[22] To Democrats, the principle of popular sovereignty vindicated the destruction of the national bank by their heroic former president Andrew Jackson. Popular sovereignty also provided an alternative method of dealing with the potentially explosive issue of slavery in the territories. Let the people, i.e. the white settlers in the territories, decide the issue of slavery for themselves. This was the programme of the Democratic candidate for president in 1848, Lewis Cass.

Within the Whig Party, feelings about the European revolutions were more mixed. The Whigs were a middle-class party that tended to represent the prosperous and respectable social elements in all parts of the country. There was a strong streak of humanitarian sentiment among the Whigs that manifested itself in sympathy for middle-class reformers in Europe. Whig newspapers like the *New York Tribune* reflected this attitude. On the other hand, reports of violence and anarchy dismayed middle-class Americans, and this was reflected in the reporting of the *National Intelligencer*, the Whig newspaper printed in Washington. Whigs showed less enthusiasm than their Democratic colleagues for the effusive resolution which Congress sent to the French people in April congratulating them 'upon their success in their recent efforts to consolidate liberty'.[23] When the presidential election came in the autumn, it was the Whig candidate, Zachary Taylor, who won. Taylor had been a successful general in the Mexican War. The party with the weakest sympathy for the European revolutions, the party with the most significant reservations about those revolutions, had won the votes of the American free electorate. The response of the Whig administration to events in Europe during the coming years would reflect conflicting attitudes.

There were also reservations expressed about the revolutions, even at the outset, by some of the most pro-slavery political leaders in the Democratic Party, such as South Carolina's two senators, John C. Calhoun and Andrew P. Butler. Spokesmen for a minority white regime in their state, these men had good reason to be especially sensitive towards constitutional governments being overthrown by domestic insurrection. The decision by the new French republic to abolish slavery in the French West Indies only con-

---

[22] 'Democratic Platform of 1848', in *National Party Platforms*, ed. Kirk Porter and Donald Bruce Johnson (Urbana, Ill., 1966), 12.

[23] *Congressional Globe*, 30th Congress, 1st session, p. 549.

firmed the fears of these defenders of the institution.[24] Calhoun had
more sympathy with Frankfurt than with Paris. When German liberals sought his opinion on a draft constitution, he cautioned them
against delegating too much power to the central government and
urged them to preserve state rights.[25]

The revolution of the Magyars in Hungary had aroused strong
sympathy in the United States. On 18 June 1849 President Taylor
secretly appointed Dudley Mann as a special envoy to the Hungarians and dispatched him on a mission to meet Kossuth. Mann never
reached the Hungarian headquarters because the whole movement
was crushed before he got there. Nevertheless, his mission had consequences, because the Austrian government eventually found out
about it. On 30 September 1850 the Austrian envoy in Washington,
J. G. Hülsemann, presented a very strongly worded protest to the
administration. The United States secretary of state, Daniel Webster, decided not to apologize for interfering in the internal affairs
of the Habsburg empire, but instead composed a long and stri-
dent defence of American sympathy for the principle of national
self-determination. Some of Webster's rhetoric was deliberately
insulting: 'The power of this republic, at the present moment, is
spread over a region one of the richest and most fertile on the
globe, and an extent in comparison with which the possessions of
the House of Hapsburg are but a patch of the earth's surface.'[26]
Webster released his letter to Hülsemann to the public because he
intended his manifesto as much for domestic as for international
consumption. He feared sectional divisions in the United States,
and hoped by inflaming patriotic passions to quell any talk of the
break-up of the Union.[27] After Webster made a speech repeating
his insults, Hülsemann demanded his dismissal. When this was not
forthcoming, Austria severed diplomatic relations with the United
States for more than a year.

But Webster's flamboyant rhetoric only served to obscure what

---

[24] On both Whig and southern Democratic reservations see Richard C. Rohrs,
'American Critics of the French Revolution of 1848', *Journal of the Early Republic*,
14 (1994), 359–77.
[25] Calhoun's advice is reprinted in Merle Curti, 'John C. Calhoun and the Unification of Germany', *American Historical Review*, 40 (1934–5), 476–8.
[26] Daniel Webster, *Writings and Speeches* (18 vols.; Boston, 1903), xii. 170.
[27] He confided his motives in a letter to George Ticknor of 16 Jan. 1851: *Writings
and Speeches*, xvi. 586.

was really going on in American foreign relations. For the most part, the United States administration had no difficulty reconciling itself to the practical realities of the failure of the revolutions of 1848. As soon as it came into office, the Whig administration began backing away from its predecessor's covert involvement with the Frankfurt assembly.[28] Even before Webster's bombastic pronouncement to the Austrians, the United States had already (in September 1849) suppressed Donelson's diplomatic mission to the defunct central government of Germany and (in November) replaced Richard Rush in Paris with a new minister friendly to Louis Napoleon. To understand the ready American acceptance of the reimposition of conservatism in Europe, and particularly the attitude of the commercial-minded Whig Party, one must look at the impact the revolutions had had on American business.

In so far as the United States had a tangible interest in the affairs of Europe in 1848, it was one of commerce and finance. American business interests in Europe were far different from American ideological sympathies. The leading American export to Europe was cotton, produced largely by slave labour. Demand for American cotton plunged in the spring of 1848 when European buyers became uncertain of the availability of credit facilities during times of turmoil. But as authoritarian governments reasserted their control by 1849, business confidence returned and the demand for cotton soared. On 5 November 1849 the *New York Herald* aptly commented that although Americans could not condone the brutalities of either the revolutions or their suppression, 'we can console ourselves with a rise in the cotton market, [creating] as great a sensation in Wall Street and in New Orleans as the recent revolutions did among speculators in the destiny of the human race'. Financial markets, like the cotton market, experienced a dip and recovery. The American investment banking firm of Corcoran & Riggs was the counterpart of Baring Brothers in London. Corcoran & Riggs had been having difficulty selling in Europe the United States government bonds that had been issued to finance the Mexican War. When the revolutions broke out, demand for American securities dried up altogether. Corcoran & Riggs had sold bonds valued at only $3 million out of a stock worth $14 million which they had acquired for resale. Only a temporary respite granted by the US Treasury in the autumn of 1848 kept the firm from going under. But

<hr />

[28] See Moltmann, *Atlantische Blockpolitik*, 236–63.

soon the reaction in Europe had proceeded far enough for British and Continental investment markets to recover. By the spring of 1849 Corcoran & Riggs had not only sold all their inventory of US Treasury bonds but were marketing American state and corporate obligations as well.[29] The behaviour of trade and financial markets showed that the practical interests of the United States lay, at least for the short term, more in European stability than in European liberty.

A final orgy of interest in the by now failed revolutionary movements was associated with the visit to the United States of the Hungarian leader Louis Kossuth. After the collapse of the Hungarian revolution, Kossuth took refuge in Turkey, from which Austrian authorities tried to extradite him. The American government intervened and offered Kossuth asylum in the United States. Accordingly, he was transported through the Mediterranean and Atlantic aboard a naval vessel, the *USS Mississippi*, arriving in New York on 5 December 1851. There he received a tumultuous welcome and embarked upon an extensive tour of the United States in the hope of rallying support for his cause.[30] What Kossuth sought was American diplomatic and financial help for Hungarian independence, backed up by threats of military or naval intervention against Russia and Austria. What he received, on the other hand, were expressions of sympathy, together with private financial help that the Hungarian mostly dissipated in publicity and poorly planned arms purchases. Some of the money was also embezzled by the men around him.[31]

Within a month of his arrival Kossuth was visited by a delegation of African Americans who wanted him to endorse the antislavery movement and perhaps even racial equality. Kossuth was unwilling to give them such a statement, fearing to jeopardize his objectives with southern politicians, some of whom, as we have seen, harboured a suspicion of the European revolutionaries. Thereupon the abolitionist press denounced the Hungarian revolutionary as a hypocrite.[32] This proved to mark the beginning of a decline in Kossuth's popularity. Southerners and Catholics had never warmed to

[29] Roberts, 'American Response', 159–65.
[30] See Donald S. Spencer, *Louis Kossuth and Young America: A Study of Sectionalism and Foreign Policy, 1848–52* (Columbia, Mo., 1977).
[31] Ibid. 166–7.
[32] William Lloyd Garrison, 'Letter to Louis Kossuth', *The Liberator* (20 Feb. 1852), was reprinted in expanded form as a pamphlet.

him. Francis Bowen, writing in the *North American Review*, exposed the Magyars' treatment of ethnic minorities.[33] It gradually became clear that the American public regarded him as a celebrity, but not as a mentor in foreign policy. The Hungarian misinterpreted the crowds who came to see him as expressions of support for American intervention in eastern Europe. When Kossuth waited upon the most eminent of American elder statesmen, Henry Clay, the old man warned his visitor not to expect that the United States would compromise its accustomed isolation from European affairs. 'Far better is it for ourselves, for Hungary, for the cause of liberty,' declared Clay, that 'we should keep our lamp burning brightly on this Western shore as a light to all nations, than to hazard its utter extinction, amid the ruins of fallen or falling republics in Europe.'[34] Having decided that the Democratic Party was more inclined to pursue an aggressive foreign policy than the Whigs, Kossuth attended the Democratic national convention during the summer of 1852. But the party was unwilling to go beyond the rhetoric of sympathy to make any commitments of aid. Although the editor of a prominent newspaper, the *Democratic Review*, became enthusiastic for intervention in the Hungarian cause, all this accomplished was to discredit that newspaper's favourite candidate for president, Stephen Douglas. Disillusioned at length with American politicians and their people, Kossuth left the United States with his wife, both of them incognito, on 14 July 1852. He took up residence in Britain, along with Garibaldi, Mazzini, and other defeated revolutionaries, and periodically published embittered denunciations of American hypocrisy. He did, however, manage to live the rest of his life in comfort on the remaining proceeds (some $90,000) of his American fund-raising.

Louis Kossuth's visit seemed to indicate the transitory quality and superficial nature of American interest in the revolutions of 1848. In reality, however, there were some more durable legacies of the revolution. Notwithstanding the disappointment experienced by Kossuth, the revolutions did have some significant effects in the United States.

The Free Soil movement to restrict the spread of slavery went

---

[33] [Francis Bowen], 'The War of Races in Hungary', *North American Review*, 70 (Jan. 1850), 78–136.
[34] Henry Clay, *Works*, ed. Calvin Colton (10 vols.; New York, 1904), iii. 223–4.

into a temporary decline following the sectional compromise of 1850. However, it quickly rebounded after the Kansas–Nebraska act of 1854 reopened the question of the expansion of slavery. American critics of slavery did draw some encouragement from the act of the Second French Republic in emancipating the slaves in the French West Indies. More directly important, however, was the substantial migration to the United States of German liberals following the failure of the 1848 revolutions in the German states. A few radicals, such as the communist Wilhelm Weitling, settled in New York City, and for a brief time led native and immigrant labourers to organize trade co-operatives and achieve better working conditions.[35] Most Germans, however, settled in the upper midwest, on farms and in the cities of Chicago and St Louis. There the 48ers, as they were called, became influential advocates of preserving the west for free settlement and preventing the spread of slavery. Sometimes they made common cause with British Chartists who had migrated to the United States during the years since 1841, but mostly they were identified with German language and German culture. Bound together by double ties of ideology and ethnicity, the German 48ers made themselves a distinctive force in American politics. Under the leadership of Karl Schurz, they played a prominent role in creating the Republican Party in 1855 on a Free Soil programme. Contemporaries considered them a significant force in both Abraham Lincoln's campaign for the senate in 1858 and in his election as president in 1860.[36] After the abolition of slavery, some of the mid-western 48ers turned next to socialism and the labour movement of the late nineteenth century. The German-language newspaper press, based principally in the mid-west, remained an important forum of radical opinion until the forcible suppression of German-language publications at the time of the First World War.[37]

Another effect of the revolutions of 1848 came from the various calls for American military intervention, especially in Ireland and Hungary. These calls provided encouragement for Americans to think of themselves as having a mission in the world that could jus-

[35] Sean Wilentz, *Chants Democratic: New York City and the Rise of the American Working Class* (New York, 1984), 354–87.

[36] Bruce Levine, *The Spirit of 1848: German Immigrants, Labor Conflict, and the Coming of the Civil War* (Urbana, Ill., 1992).

[37] See Elliott Shore *et al.*, *The German-American Radical Press* (Chicago, 1992).

tify aggressive international behaviour. Actually, Americans needed little such encouragement in the New World, where bellicose policies towards Spain, Mexico, and the American Indians had been consistently rewarded with territorial expansion. The Democratic administration of Franklin Pierce, elected to succeed the Whigs in 1852, catered to American imperialism, particularly the wishes of southern political leaders to expand the area open to slavery. They pursued the possibility of annexing Cuba, which already had a flourishing slave-based economy. In 1854, at Ostend in Belgium, three American diplomats made an unofficial offer of $100 million for Cuba to the Spanish government. (The Spanish were not interested in selling.) The Pierce administration did succeed in purchasing an additional slice of northern Mexico from a Mexican government that had been thoroughly intimidated by defeat in the recent war. The particular objective of this purchase was a southern route for a transcontinental railway to link Los Angeles with New Orleans. In all of its imperialist schemes, ironically, the Pierce administration was able to invoke the liberal and idealistic rhetoric of what was called the 'Young America' movement. Young America claimed to invoke the spirit of the European revolutions of 1848. The movement, which in effect constituted an arm of the Democratic Party, argued that since the United States was a liberal democracy, it should expand whenever possible and take an active interventionist role in foreign affairs, since by doing so it was enhancing the influence of liberal democracy. Presumably there were some of the journalists and spokesmen for the movement who sincerely believed this, but Young America certainly provided a convenient cover of hypocrisy for the pro-slavery expansionists of the 1850s. If the German 48ers helped the cause of Free Soil, Young America had the opposite effect: it exploited the memories of the revolutions to help the forces of slavery expansion.[38]

The year 1848 was also important in the history of American feminism. One of the greatest of American feminist intellectuals, Margaret Fuller, was sent to Rome to cover the revolution there for the *New York Tribune*, edited by the reformer Horace Greeley. There she made herself America's first ever war correspondent—male or female. Her accounts of events are those of an engaged participant, not a detached observer, for she identified wholly with what she viewed as a revolution against oppression, tradition, and obscu-

[38] See Spencer, *Louis Kossuth and Young America*.

rantism on behalf of republicanism, national self-determination, and human potential.[39] In romantic defiance of convention, Fuller had a love affair with an Italian revolutionary nobleman quite a bit younger than herself, Count Giovanni Ossoli, and bore him a child. On her way back to the United States in 1850 Fuller, her count, and their child all perished when their ship sank in a storm. The manuscript of her history of the Italian revolution was lost for ever. Though she lived but forty years, Margaret Fuller had made a lasting mark in the history of American feminism.[40]

During Fuller's absence from America there had been a convention in Seneca Falls, New York, on behalf of women's rights. It marks the beginning of the agitation that eventually led to the Nineteenth Amendment to the Constitution, giving women the right to vote. The convention met on 19 and 20 July 1848, one week after news had arrived of the Bloody June Days in Paris. In Germany, the democratic clubs began to include women in their meetings during that month, and later in the year the Frankfurt assembly would discuss rights for women in connection with its proposed constitution for a unified Germany. Interestingly enough, however, the American women meeting in western New York State did not claim to be part of a contemporary transatlantic movement. Of course, the revolutionary context was all too apparent, and frequently pointed out, but invariably by outside observers. The *New York Herald* editorialized as follows:

This is the age of revolutions. To whatever part of the world the attention is directed, the political and social fabric of the world is crumbling to pieces, and changes which far exceed the wildest dreams of the enthusiastic Utopians of the last generation, are now pursued with ardor and perseverance. . . . By the intelligence, however, which we have lately received, the work of revolution is no longer confined to the Old World, nor to the masculine gender. The flag of independence has been hoisted, for the second time, on this side of the Atlantic, and a solemn league and covenant has just been entered into by a Convention of women at Seneca Falls. . . . Little did we expect this new element to be thrown into the cauldron of agitation which is now bubbling around us with such fury. . . . Though we have the most perfect confidence in the courage and daring of . . . our lady acquaintances, we confess it would go to our hearts to see them putting on

[39] They have been reprinted in Margaret Fuller, *These Sad But Glorious Days: Dispatches from Europe, 1846–50*, ed. Larry Reynolds (New Haven, Conn., 1991).

[40] The definitive two-volume biography, not yet complete, is Charles Capper, *Margaret Fuller: An American Romantic Life* (New York, 1992–).

the panoply of war, and mixing in scenes like those at which, it is said, the fair sex in Paris lately took prominent part.[41]

The bemused, patronizing tone affected by the *Herald* was typical of the press coverage received by the convention.

The women of Seneca Falls did indeed call for a revolution; years later the leaders would found a journal named *The Revolution*. But the example they invoked was not the revolutions that were going on while the Seneca Falls meeting was in session: rather, they took inspiration from the revolution of 1776 and Jefferson's Declaration of Independence. (The 'Declaration of Sentiments and Resolutions' which they produced is printed at the end of this chapter.) The rhetorical choice made by the women of Seneca Falls to recur to the declaration of 1776 in presenting their grievances has been a characteristic one for Americans. This is the revolution that endures for Americans, the one that has remained their inspiration.[42] Despite Margaret Fuller's sympathetic accounts of 1848, the events of that year could not compete with 1776 for persuasive, authenticating rhetorical power.

As the years passed, most Americans looking back upon the unsuccessful revolutions of 1848 came to emphasize the differences between those failed events and their own successful revolution of 1776. The European working classes had been uneducated, not only individually but collectively and historically. They had not been schooled for liberty by the gradual development of free institutions that Americans had experienced during their own colonial period. The American Revolution had been no mere sudden outbreak of desperation but the logical fulfilment of generations of preparation. When the European revolutions broke out in 1848, Americans were encouraged briefly to suppose that Europe and America might be drawing closer together. The eventual failure of the revolutions, however, led to the conclusion that America was really alone in the world.

Although the United States was often said to be a Protestant country, it turned out that the American Catholic interpretation of

[41] Quoted in Larry J. Reynolds, *European Revolutions and the American Literary Renaissance* (New Haven, 1988), 55.

[42] For a recent discussion of the invocation of natural rights and American constitutional rights at Seneca Falls see Nancy Isenberg, 'Women's Rights and the Politics of Church and State in Antebellum America', *Journal of American History*, 85 (June 1998), 98–128, esp. 104–8.

the revolutions became the prevailing view in the United States. As the Catholic Americans had pointed out, revolution in America and Europe meant different things. The one worked; the other didn't. The one was compatible with Christianity, private property, right reason, and good order; the other wasn't. The failure of the 1848 revolutions constituted a major event in shaping belief in American exceptionalism.

APPENDIX

Declaration of Sentiments and Resolutions
Women's Rights Convention, Seneca Falls, July 1848[43]

When, in the course of human events, it becomes necessary for one portion of the family of man to assume among the people of the earth a position different from that which they have hitherto occupied, but one to which the laws of nature and of nature's God entitle them, a decent respect for the opinions of mankind requires that they should set forth the causes that impel them to such a course.

We hold these truths to be self-evident: that all men and women are created equal; that they are endowed by their Creator with certain inalienable rights; that among these are life, liberty, and the pursuit of happiness; that to secure these rights governments are instituted, deriving their just powers from the consent of the governed. . . .

The history of mankind is a history of repeated injuries and usurpations on the part of man toward woman, having in direct object the establishment of an absolute tyranny over her. . . .

He has never permitted her to exercise her inalienable right to the elective franchise.

He has compelled her to submit to laws, in the formation of which she had no voice. . . .

He has made her, if married, in the eye of the law, civilly dead.

He has taken from her all right in property, even to the wages she earns. . . .

He has so framed the laws of divorce . . . as to be wholly regardless of the happiness of women—the law, in all cases, going upon a false supposition of the supremacy of man. . . .

[43] From Elizabeth Cady Stanton *et al.*, *History of Woman Suffrage* (6 vols.; New York, 1881), i. 70–3.

He has monopolized nearly all the profitable employments, and from those she is permitted to follow, she receives but a scanty remuneration. . . .

He has denied her the facilities of obtaining a thorough education, all colleges being closed against her. . . .

He has created a false public sentiment by giving to the world a different code of morals for men and women, by which moral delinquencies which exclude women from society, are not only tolerated, but deemed of little account in man. . . .

He has endeavored, in every way that he could, to destroy her confidence in her own powers, to lessen her self-respect and to make her willing to lead a dependent and abject life. . . .

Resolved, That all laws which prevent woman from occupying such a station in society as her conscience shall dictate, or which place her in a position inferior to that of man, are contrary to the great precept of nature, and therefore of no force or authority. . . .

FURTHER READING

Timothy M. Roberts, 'The American Response to the European Revolutions of 1848' (diss. Oxford, 1997), is the most comprehensive treatment of its subject.

The notes to this chapter include most of the relevant secondary works. Two that are especially helpful are Henry Blumenthal, *A Reappraisal of Franco-American Relations, 1830–1871* (Chapel Hill, NC, 1959), and Donald S. Spencer, *Louis Kossuth and Young America: A Study of Sectionalism and Foreign Policy, 1848–1852* (Columbia, Mo., 1977). Interesting if not always convincing cases for the revolutions' influences on American literati are made in Larry Reynolds, *European Revolutions and the American Literary Renaissance* (New Haven, 1988). Reynolds also edited Margaret Fuller's reports from Italy to the *New York Tribune* in *These Sad but Glorious Days: Dispatches from Europe, 1846–1850* (New Haven, 1991). For the American fascination, both positive and negative, with the Roman republic of 1848, see also William L. Vance, *America's Rome*, ii. *Catholic and Contemporary Rome* (New Haven, 1989).

Most works on American interaction with the German revolutions of 1848 deal with the political refugees from Germany and their influence on American politics; the best of these is Bruce Levine, *The Spirit of 1848: German Immigrants, Labor Conflict, and the Coming of the Civil War* (Urbana, Ill., 1992).

9

1848–1849 in the Habsburg Monarchy

R. J. W. EVANS

NEWS of the fall of the monarchy in France reached a Vienna in intercalary mood, on 29 February at the height of Fasching, or carnival. For the next fortnight it generated a rising ferment, heightened by the announcement that Monday, 13 March, would be the date for a meeting of the local estates, a kind of assembly of notables, at which Metternich's absolutist regime was expected to make some concessions. Students at the university especially, having heard a fiery sermon on the Sunday by a radical priest and composed a petition (which was presented, with due propriety, by their professors), were now ready to press the case for change more strongly. So were thousands of workmen, clustered expectantly in the narrow streets of the inner city. They surrounded and then stormed the gathering of the estates, forcing deputies from the latter to take a broad list of grievances to the nearby royal palace, the Hofburg.[1]

The first response from there was defiant: it unleashed serious bloodshed, with fifteen or so killed around the nearby barricades and dozens more in the suburbs. Turbulence only grew and by evening conciliatory counsels prevailed. The 74-year-old Metternich—after a last windy and wordy self-justificatory oration—was persuaded to withdraw: he slipped out of the city in disguise and made for England. Thus the reactionary Field Marshal Windischgrätz (of whom more later), having gone home to put

---

[1] Heinrich Reschauer, *Das Jahr 1848: Geschichte der Wiener Revolution* (Vienna, 1872), and Maximilian Bach, *Geschichte der Wiener Revolution im Jahre 1848* (Vienna, 1898), both contain exhaustive accounts of the March days.

on his uniform for action, returned to find the court in disarray and himself seriously overdressed. Metternich's pupil Hartig summed it up laconically as his diary entry for the day: 'wolkig [cloudy], Revolution.'[2]

These celebrated events sent out shock waves across the monarchy, by post-coach and peasant messenger, by railway and steamboat. Just across the Hungarian border they catalysed an existing movement of diet opposition: ten days earlier the lower house, in session at Pressburg, had already unanimously embraced an eloquent call of its principal tribune, Lajos/Louis Kossuth, for constitutional and national rights throughout the Habsburg lands. That speech, read out to crowds, had a decisive impact in Vienna too. Now the impetuous youth of the chief urban centre, Buda-Pest, rioted for a fuller programme of such rights, beginning with press freedom, which they proceeded to assert by default.[3] In Bohemia too reform was already in the air. A gathering at the Wenceslas Baths in Prague had agreed on a petition, which was promptly copied out by inmates of the local lunatic asylum.[4] In Milan tensions centred on tobacco, forsworn some weeks earlier by Italian patriots as a protest against the state monopoly in the substance. Now barricades sprang up, and the government lost control of the entire city within a few days.[5]

These were only the main initial flashpoints. The monarchy quickly appeared fractured like a broken jigsaw. The year 1848 in the Habsburg dominions presents far the most complex of contemporary revolutionary scenarios, both in its intricate domestic

    [2] Heinrich von Srbik, *Metternich: Der Staatsmann und der Mensch* (3 vols.; Munich, 1925–54), ii. 275–90. Ronald E. Coons, 'Reflections of a Josephinist', *Mitteilungen des Österreichischen Staatsarchivs*, 36 (1983), 204–36 at 212 n. (Hartig). Later Count Hartig was much more forthcoming: in his 'Genesis . . . of the Late Austrian Revolution' (see Further Reading), 161 ff., he stresses the dignity of Metternich's withdrawal.

    [3] Kossuth's speech of 3 Mar. is printed in his *Írások és beszédek 1848–9-ből*, ed. T. Katona (Budapest, 1987), 12–26. Its Viennese version is in Bach, *Wiener Revolution*, 12–20. Cf. R. J. W. Evans, 'Hungary and the Habsburg Monarchy, 1840–67: A Study in Perceptions', *Études danubiennes*, 2 (1986), 18–39 at 25–6. For Pest: Deák (see Further Reading), 68 ff.

    [4] Classic descriptions—including the initial impact from Paris—in the memoirs of Josef Václav Frič, *Paměti* (3 vols.; Prague, 1885–6), ii. 210 ff., and Alfred Meissner, *Ich traf auch Heine in Paris*, ed. R. Weber (Berlin, 1973), 155 ff. (p. 170 for the lunatics).

    [5] Fervently Italian view of these events in G. F.-H. and J. Berkeley, *Italy in the Making* (3 vols.; Cambridge, 1940), iii. 73–96; cf. Ginsborg (see Further Reading), 127–41.

canvas and in its interaction with all the unrest beyond Austria's borders, from France to the Balkan lands, from Italy to the confines of Poland. The Habsburg capital Vienna played a key role; but a considerable number of other places took major parts as well. Some acted as substitutes of a kind for Vienna, in that Innsbruck, Olmütz, Kremsier, and in a different way Frankfurt am Main temporarily assumed surrogate official functions. Others featured in their own right as rival focuses of regional and ethnic sentiment, or as staging-points in the multilateral contestation: they included Buda-Pest, Prague, Lemberg and Cracow, Milan and Venice, Zagreb and Temesvár, Kolozsvár and Hermannstadt, even picturesque backwaters like Blaj or Karlovci, and a string of fortresses and battle-sites.[6]

Narrative skills stand at a premium for the historian of these rapidly shifting events (with 'meanwhile' as his phrase of last resort). But we should bear in mind that contemporaries could hardly cope either, even though most had merely a few facets of the kaleidoscope to contend with. Only one institution was necessarily involved in all convolutions and actively responsive to most of them: the dynasty itself—a clue to its own eventual survival, and to that of its territorial possessions as an undivided whole. The Habsburgs, as 1918 would definitively confirm, represented the only common bond for all these separate realms; and precisely the bonding process legitimated their rule, the mandates for distinct sovereignties over individual pieces, though extant in their family titulature, having long expired (and, as events would show, there was no desire on the part of the dynasty to renew them). But before any *restitutio in integrum*, the area suffered the most searingly disruptive movements anywhere on the continent—for months the future of a European great power appeared to hang in the balance—and the longest-lasting, since the crisis of state reached its denouement only in 1849, long after the main lines of a settlement were clear elsewhere.

[6] I have used the place names most familiar in the literature on 1848. Olmütz is Olomouc in Czech; Kremsier is Kroměříž in Czech; Lemberg is Lwów in Polish and L'viv in Ukrainian; Cracow is Kraków in Polish; Temesvár is Timișoara in Romanian; Kolozsvár is Klausenburg in German and Cluj-Napoca in today's Romanian; Hermannstadt is Sibiu in Romanian and Nagyszeben in Hungarian; Blaj is Blasendorf in German and Balázsfalva in Hungarian; Karlovci is Karlóca in Hungarian and Karlowitz in German. Buda-Pest was still two separate cities which, though increasingly felt to be a single conurbation, especially by virtue of the great chain bridge completed during 1848–9, united only in 1873.

March 1848 in Habsburg Europe began as part of an international, even universal, movement, with two kinds of overall cause. The first was the decay of central authority during the Vormärz or 'Pre-March' period, as the eve-of-revolution years are known in Austrian history. The grasp of Metternich proved increasingly limp or contested from within, and indecision was exacerbated by the fact that although a regency council had been installed since the accession of the feeble-minded Ferdinand in 1835, the latter remained nominally responsible for decisions.[7] At least this famously affable emperor was also highly quotable: 'I like ruling; the only hard bit is signing my name.' The very wealth of such aphorisms, genuine or apocryphal, testifies to popular indulgence of the person of the hapless ruler, but growing disdain for the system which he embodied.

Chronic budgetary difficulties were now exacerbated by the economic weakness of the mid-1840s: harvest failures and industrial slump which brought many taxpayers to the verge of penury, besides aggravating the miserable conditions of a flood of new immigrants to the towns, especially Vienna. A perceived need for military enhancement combined with this in leading the government to seek further substantial loans. It looked to Russia, which was unable or unwilling to offer much, and wished to attach undesirable strings anyway: shades of later events. It also looked to a consortium of Viennese bankers, which would oblige only while the currency remained creditworthy. This was the immediate reason for summoning those estates' representatives, putatively to support the regime, on 13 March.[8]

The second cause—and reason for the summons—was liberal opposition, which fed upon a European mood, and drew particularly on German example. It operated powerfully already from the 1830s within semi-constitutional Hungary, where the authorities' persecution of its extremer manifestations—including imprisonment of the young Kossuth—proved counter-productive. By the mid-1840s full-scale diet opposition had taken root there, based on the activities of county gentry and intellectuals, with a precise schedule of liberties demanded ('Twelve Points'). Similar, though more muted, ventures started to emerge in Lower Austria and

---

[7] On Ferdinand see Lorenz Mikoletzky in A. Schindling and W. Ziegler (eds.) *Die Kaiser der Neuzeit, 1519–1918* (Munich, 1990), 329–39, a valuable sketch.

[8] Adolf Beer, *Die Finanzen Österreichs im 19. Jahrhundert* (Prague, 1877), 163 ff.

Bohemia.[9] The impact began to be felt within the administration. There were even official sops to this *parti de mouvement*, if gestures like the foundation in 1847 of a learned academy, to bring together intellectuals from throughout the monarchy, can be accounted such.[10] Thus we find widespread sentiment for change in the Vormärz. Once the ice was broken, everywhere programmes were formulated with slightly variant numbers of reform points. The Hungarian twelve would quickly be radicalized in Pest; when the time came the Serbs at Karlovci were ready with ten, the Croats at Zagreb with eleven, the Poles at Lemberg with thirteen, the Slovaks at Turčiansky Svätý Martin with fourteen, the Romanians at Blaj with sixteen . . . All demanded peasant emancipation, civic freedoms, legal equality, and so forth. National guards and student legions sprang up on all sides. Yet hardly anyone had expected total upheaval. 'I have lived long enough in Vienna, and had sufficient opportunity to observe its population,' wrote a foreign observer in 1843, 'to know that its artisans and workmen, i.e. those groups without which politically motivated and educated people cannot hope to bring about revolutionary alterations in state and government, live too well and are too contented and fortunate ever to become their tools.' The writer was William Wilde, father of Oscar.[11]

The revolution's deeper origins were largely hidden to contemporaries, as they are all too (and deceptively) obvious to posterity. Metternich alone did predict it, crying wolf for decades, creating self-fulfilling expectations by his very denial of moderate remedies.[12] By the same token, oppositions, even in Hungary, remained temperate and loyal, on the whole. Moreover, the more advanced

[9] János Varga, *A Hungarian Quo Vadis: Political Trends and Theories of the Early 1840s* (Budapest, 1993). For Vormärz contacts between Austria and Hungary, or the lack of them, cf. Evans, 'Hungary and the Habsburg Monarchy', 21–5. For diets in Austria and Bohemia: Viktor Bibl, *Die niederösterreichischen Stände im Vormärz* (Vienna, 1911); Antonín Okáč, *Český sněm a vláda před březnem* (Prague, 1947); Christine L. Mueller, *The Styrian Estates in Transition, 1740–1848* (New York, 1987), ch. 7.
[10] Richard Meister, *Geschichte der Akademie der Wissenschaften in Wien* (Vienna, 1947).
[11] *Oscar Wildes Vater über Metternichs Österreich*, ed. Irene Montjoye (Frankfurt a.M. and Berne, 1989), 95. Wilde took a positive view of many aspects of Austrian life, especially (technical) education.
[12] Srbik, *Metternich*, esp. ii. 180 ff.; G. de Bertier de Sauvigny, *Metternich et son temps* (Paris, 1959), 65–80.

ones had already fractured, and such public debates as could be conducted during the Vormärz—perforce through pamphlets printed abroad—had begun to yield internecine feuds, especially over issues of (perceived) cultural hegemony.[13] The Galician events in 1846, when peasants cut down their noble masters as soon as the latter rose for the Polish national cause, intensified a sense of need for change, but also the insecurity of élites before any wider challenge.

My own sketch of the course of the revolution likewise falls, for convenience of exposition, into twelve narrative points.

(1) The fall of Metternich was followed, after two more turbulent days, by the promise of a 'Constitution'—the very word implying a strange foreign import—for the Austrian lands.[14] This was widely understood by German Austrians as part of a German-led transformation of political circumstances in central Europe. As the court agent of their furthest-flung compatriots, the Transylvanian Saxons, reported as early as the following day, 'With 15 March 1848 there begins for the Austrian monarchy a new era of her political life and history. The immediate results will quite certainly be a closer link with Germany and a strengthening of German national feeling.'[15] Those immediate results represented a compromise between reformist bureaucrats and the liberal movement; but the bureaucrats' concept of a strong central ministry and weak legislature was soon vitiated.

The Austrian ministry found its authority circumscribed ever more in the first months; at times it hardly seemed to stretch beyond Vienna. Plans for a Reichstag, or parliament, drawn up by a long-serving official, Franz von Pillersdorf, who was soon to become head of government, had to be modified under the pressure of the crowd within Vienna. Eventually a unicameral body assembled

[13] The fullest study of this for Austria and Bohemia remains Jan Heidler, *Čechy a Rakousko v politických brožurách předbřeznových* (Prague, 1920); for Hungary cf. below, n. 28.

[14] *Die Constitution: Tagblatt für constitutionelles Volksleben und Belehrung*, a daily founded in Vienna on 20 Mar., is a mine of information. On 'constitution' as a magic term cf. Pech (see Further Reading), 66–8; later, native coinages—*Verfassung, ústav*, etc.—took over. The Hungarians had already devised the term *alkotmány*, on which cf. László Péter in R. Robertson and E. Timms (eds.), *The Habsburg Legacy: National Identity in Historical Perspective* (Edinburgh, 1994), 13–26.

[15] *Revoluţia de la 1848–9 din Transilvania*, ed. Ş. Pascu and V. Cheresteşiu, i (Bucharest, 1977), No. 8.

in July. It was to be a focus for important debates, but inconclusive ones—except for the issue raised by a young rural radical, Hans Kudlich, of the terms for peasant emancipation.[16] Moreover, the German liberals, too, quickly lost out further. They found themselves in a minority at the Reichstag, which was elected by something close to universal (albeit indirect) male suffrage. Meanwhile a further stage in the revolution yielded what proved to be awkward and debilitating results for the new regime: the imperial family, terrified by street demonstrations—or was there *arrière-pensée?*—fled Vienna for traditionalist Innsbruck, chief town of the Tyrol, in mid-May.

(2) In Hungary, Austria lost almost all authority. From March constitutional developments proceeded there in parallel, but more ordered and consistent, fashion. A responsible ministry was instituted under Lajos Batthyány, which incorporated all shades of *Vormärz* political reformism: it brought together, *inter alia*, the great innovator of Hungary's recent past, István/Stephen Széchenyi, with both the man of the moment, Kossuth, and the great leader of the near future, Ferenc/Francis Deák. They presided over an organic transition from the old noble diet to a new national assembly (also summoned in July), and an extensive legislative agenda initiated by the April Laws, the last act of the diet. This classic enactment of individual civil freedoms introduced a phase of deceptive calm when the Hungarian regime seemed close to untrammelled parliamentary sovereignty.[17]

Yet the uneasy separation from Austria generated elements of genuine confusion. How were responsibilities for what was still a single imperial army, stationed all across the monarchy on no 'national' principle—but also without any clear denial of it—to be divided between Vienna and Buda-Pest? What about 'common' finance, including tariffs, currency, debts, etc.? Did Hungary have power to take diplomatic initiatives? A conservative *grand seigneur*, Pál Esterházy, long-time Austrian ambassador to the Court of St

---

[16] On the Reichstag: Rath (see Further Reading), 275 ff.; *Protokolle des Verfassungsausschusses im österreichischen Reichstag, 1848–9*, ed. Anton Springer (Leipzig, 1885); Roman Rosdolsky, *Die Bauernabgeordneten im konstituierenden österreichischen Reichstag, 1848–9* (Vienna, 1976).

[17] Deák (see Further Reading), 91–106, whose title, *Lawful Revolution*, is most apposite; Aladár Urbán, *Batthyány Lajos miniszterelnöksége* (Budapest, 1986). Important documentation in Árpád Károlyi, *Az 1848-diki pozsonyi törvénycikkek az udvar előtt* (Budapest, 1936).

James, joined Batthyány's government as a kind of liaison officer with the crown, but was freely spoken of—even by Austrians—as 'Hungarian foreign minister'.[18] These, and other sore points, some of them self-inflicted wounds, would progressively fester. Arguably this was the most competent of all the 1848 regimes in Europe over the territory where it was effectively sovereign; but it was crippled, as we shall see, by disputed authority in the south and east of the country, parts of which had actually been long settled as Austrian military colonies.

(3) Meanwhile other parts of the Austrian monarchy also asserted themselves. 'The Five Days of Milan' saw Lombardy and simultaneously Venetia almost wholly lost to makeshift Italian administrations; the main Habsburg army under Field Marshal Radetzky, garrisoned there, retreated into its fortresses, the famous Quadrilateral, and allowed active intervention from Piedmont to seek to confirm the dissociation of the two provinces. Whereas Milan, home to some of the most progressive elements in Italian political and economic life, remained—like Hungary—largely under the control of the local nobility, Venice, seriously neglected since coming under Austrian rule at the turn of the century, fell into the hands of a radical party led by the lawyer, Daniele Manin.[19]

Further north, a Bohemian movement, Czechs and Germans working together at the outset, asserted the autonomy of the lands of St Wenceslas. By 8 April they were offered a home-rule package for Bohemia, with linguistic and other kinds of equality. Something similar seemed to be on the way for Galicia, where Polish insurrectionaries led the demands, in an effort to bind in domestic advances with the international cause of reconstituting the former republic, while averting any backlash from the underclass akin to that of two years before. Even Ruthenes in the north-east and Slovenes in the south-east advanced programmes; but these, lacking any firm territorial basis, were, like some of the issues in Hungary to be discussed below, from the start more heavily 'ethnic' in emphasis.

[18] István Hajnal, *A Batthyány-kormány külpolitikája* (Budapest, 1957), esp. 20 ff. These issues of common affairs are too complex to be discussed here, but there is a scrupulous introduction to them in Deák (see Further Reading), 132 ff. For the policy towards nationalities in the army: Sked (see Further Reading), 44 ff.

[19] For Lombardy: Clara M. Lovett, *Carlo Cattaneo and the Politics of the Risorgimento, 1820–60* (The Hague, 1972), esp. 37–63. On Venice: Ginsborg (see Further Reading).

(4) Meanwhile too, a further great 'international' complication for the Austrian authorities had emerged: the claim of the parliament at Frankfurt am Main to legislate for the whole German people, at least for the populations inhabiting the Confederation, conceived as successor to the old Reich. That meant a goodly part of the Habsburg lands: all that was not Hungary, Lombardy-Venetia, or Galicia, realms which many German liberals were therefore disposed to leave to their own devices anyway.[20] Elections were duly called for May in all relevant parts of the Monarchy. Like so much else during 1848 in central Europe, they created as many problems as they solved, as will very shortly appear; nevertheless, we might marvel at the efficiency of their execution.

Would Austria be 'absorbed into Germany', as the Prussian ruler had already rhetorically proclaimed for his kingdom? There was a widespread expectation, not just among Germans, of something of the kind, and Austrians become increasingly active both in the assembly debates and in the new government at Frankfurt. But most of them did not conceive of this prospective 'Grossdeutschland' as dissolving all the bonds of their existing Austrian Reich, still less as relegating Vienna to merely peripheral status. The full ambiguities of the situation on all sides stood revealed by the end of June, when the 'regentship' of Germany was by a majority of the parliament freely offered to, and accepted by, a Habsburg archduke, Johann.[21]

(5) By this time the Frankfurt issue had opened wide another division within the 'revolutionary' camp: the clash of Czech and German ambitions. Invitations to prominent Austrians to join a steering Committee of Fifty at Frankfurt included one to the author of a well-known German-language history of Bohemia, František Palacký. His reply, delivered almost by return of post, and then printed in over 100,000 copies, was the moment when the ethnic worm turned in central Europe. One phrase said it all: 'I am a Bohemian/Czech of Slav race [Ich bin Böhme slawischen Stammes/ Jsem Čech rodu slovanského]': a startling declaration from one widely thought a thoroughly Teutonic scholar. Thus 'Franz' re-

[20] Hagen Schulze, *The Course of German Nationalism . . . 1763–1867* (Eng. trans.; Cambridge, 1991), 70 ff. and *passim*; Wolfram Siemann, *Die deutsche Revolution von 1848–9* (Frankfurt, 1985), 76 ff., 146 ff.

[21] Siemann, *Deutsche Revolution*, 131 ff. His title was *Reichsverweser*, a term which sounded venerable but lacked any clear meaning.

vealed himself as 'František'. Those petty-nationalists Marx and Engels wilfully failed to see the point, calling Palacký a 'knave', and claiming, quite falsely, that he could not even speak Czech properly.[22]

Czech assertiveness was heightened by the fervent and eloquently patriotic journalism of Karel Havlíček, passionate disciple of Daniel O'Connell, who had recently electrified the public by using the Repeal movement as a transparent cover for criticism of Austrian constitutional arrangements and the Irish people as exemplar for the revival of oppressed and forgotten nations.[23] The result was a successful campaign for abstention from the elections to Frankfurt throughout the non-German parts of Bohemia. But their need for more political clout inclined Czech leaders to espouse calls from lesser Slav groups for a congress of Slavonic peoples, which duly assembled at Prague at the beginning of June, attracting over 300 participants, some of them—supposedly as mere observers—from outside the Habsburg lands, most notably the Russian anarchist Bakunin.[24]

(6) Here we come nearest to a clear focus and firm outcome in these still early months of the great 1848 imbroglio. Not the congress itself, whose importance was largely symbolic. Rather Windischgrätz, now military commander in Bohemia, took some associated disorders as the pretext for intimidation, and bombarded Prague into submission, although hardly any real rebellion was afoot (and that may have been fuelled by *agents provocateurs*). This tactic had in fact already been tested just weeks earlier by local army commanders at Cracow in Galicia. A month later, in the same vein, Radetzky, having ignored conciliatory soundings on the Italian front from his own government, defeated a motley Piedmontese army at Custoza, on the border of Lombardy with Venetia.

---

[22] Jiří Kořalka, first in *Husitský Tábor*, 6–7 (1983–4), 239–360, then summarized in his *Tschechen im Habsburgerreich und in Europa, 1815–1914* (Vienna and Munich, 1991), 175–200, argues that Palacký's Czechness—but not of course its new political thrust—was known to some of those who invited him; certainly, he had just begun publishing his history in Czech. On the other hand, it was true that his family tended to speak German. For Marx and Engels see Ernst Hanisch, *Der kranke Mann an der Donau: Marx und Engels über Österreich* (Vienna, 1978), 92, 152, 172. Close analysis of the whole Czech–German schism in R. Maršan, *Čechové a němci r. 1848 a boj o Frankfurt* (Prague, 1898).

[23] Barbara Reinfeld, *Karel Havlíček, 1821–56* (Boulder, Colo., 1982), 25–6.

[24] Lawrence D. Orton, *The Prague Slav Congress of 1848* (Boulder, Colo., 1978).

At a stroke this brought many Germans into line with the success of their 'national' army. The ensuing cult of Radetzky marched *pari passu* with an ebbing of liberal opposition from that quarter.[25]

Custoza also gave scope to redeploy units elsewhere: in Hungary as things proved, where the Hungarian regime simultaneously forfeited its chance to use Habsburg embarrassment in Italy as a bargaining counter. The Frankfurt experiment too began to lose steam at precisely this juncture, despite—or because of—the activity of Austrians there, especially of Anton von Schmerling as chief minister of the provisional executive. On 6 August Austrian troops dutifully donned *schwarz-rot-gelb*, the colours of the proposed new unitary state, to show their nominal adherence to the German idea—but they obeyed only their own chain of command. In September Austrian deputies at Frankfurt faced a dilemma over the requirement—narrowly endorsed—for territories within and outwith the forthcoming 'greater Germany' to be linked by nothing more than the person of their joint monarch, even if the rest of the Parliament was still loath to exclude 'Austria' as a whole.[26]

(7) As belligerence subsided—for a time—in Austria, it rose across the Hungarian border, where the relation of the reconstituted kingdom to the rest of the monarchy was already, *de facto* at least, largely a personal union, although complicated by the role of the Palatine, a kind of viceroy, as officially designated *alter ego* within the ruling family.[27] Hungary thus formed a wholly separate theatre of events during 1848–9—its traditions, after all, were quite distinct,

---

[25] Rath (see Further Reading), 264–5; Siemann, *Deutsche Revolution*, 150–1.

[26] Siemann, *Deutsche Revolution*, 133; cf. Árpád Károlyi, *Németújvári grof Batthyány Lajos . . . főbenjáró pöre* (2 vols.; Budapest, 1932), i. 258 ff. Günter Wollstein, *Das Großdeutschland der Paulskirche: Nationale Ziele in der bürgerlichen Revolution, 1848–9* (Düsseldorf, 1977), and id. in R. Jaworski and R. Luft (eds.), *1848/49: Revolutionen in Ostmitteleuropa* (Munich, 1996), 79–302, on the Frankfurt debate.

[27] The holder of the office in 1848 was the freshly appointed Archduke Stephen, a cousin of the king born and bred in Hungary. He played a crucial role as mediator in the preparation of the April Laws, and at subsequent junctures; but he was placed in an increasingly impossible position when the court, while refusing to give him clear instructions, began to repudiate his actions on the grounds that he had exceeded his authority. There is no biography of Stephen, but very careful study of his relations with the Hungarian ministry in Urbán, *Batthyány miniszterelnöksége*.

and its integration into Austrian absolutism had remained fairly superficial—but an equally fissiparous one. From mid-April other national groups within Hungary mostly turned against a government which they perceived to be Magyar- and noble-dominated, its political benefits outweighed by a cultural-linguistic agenda of 'Magyarization' already contentious during the Vormärz.[28]

Croats were agitated and agitating from the start. By the end of March they had installed a fiercely patriotic ban (viceroy) of their own with civil and military powers over their distinct realm. Josip Jellačić's appointment to this position was denounced as illegal by the government in Buda-Pest, and half-heartedly rescinded for a time by Ferdinand as king; but the Croat separatist movement proceeded unabated, and soon found its focus in a (no less illegal?) diet.[29] Serbs took to arms already from April: they later proudly and pointedly proclaimed that they were the first to do so.[30] Many of them, like some Croats, were frontiersmen (*Grenzer*) on the Austrian-run military border anyway. At their metropolitan see of Karlovci they likewise formulated separatist, or at least autonomist, demands, which were promptly condemned— and requited—as 'treason' by the Hungarian government and then by the Hungarian assembly, not least because thousands of volunteers poured across the border from the independent principality of Serbia. The Banat (called Vojvodina by Serbs) fell into complete disorder by June.[31] A majority of Romanians in Transylvania followed suit, roused by their own extraordinary manifestation of

[28] Spira (see Further Reading) summarizes a mass of historiography on this aspect of 1848 in Hungary. The chief documentary collections are cited in the next nn. Rival approaches, with source materials, to the pre-1848 contest: Gyula Szekfű (ed.), *Iratok a magyar államnyelv kérdésének történetéhez, 1780–1848* (Budapest, 1926); and Ján V. Ormis (ed.), *O reč a národ: Slovenské národné obrany z rokov 1932–48* (Bratislava, 1973).

[29] A murky and thorny set of issues beyond the scope of this essay. There is no remotely adequate life of Jellačić: the latest, Walter Görlitz, *Jelačić, Symbol für Kroatien* (Vienna, 1992), being as shallow as its precursors, while Rudolf Horvat, *Ban Jelačić* (2 vols.; Zagreb, 1990), is no more than a national chronicle actually compiled almost a century earlier. Useful short survey by Gunther E. Rothenberg, *The Military Border in Croatia, 1740–1881* (Chicago, 1966), 143–57. Cf. documents in Stephan Pejaković, *Aktenstücke zur Geschichte des kroatisch-slavonischen Landtages und der nationalen Bewegung vom Jahre 1848* (Vienna, 1861).

[30] József Thim, *A magyarországi 1848-49-iki szerb felkelés története* (3 vols.; Budapest, 1930–40), iii. 233, an immensely detailed account, with massive documentation prepared from a Magyar standpoint. For a more Serbophile view: [Emile Picot], *Les Serbes de Hongrie* (Prague, 1873), 218–74.

[31] All this is chronicled in Thim, *Szerb felkelés*, and Picot, *Serbes de Hongrie*. Cf.

popular democracy at Blaj and by a decision to unite their province to the rest of Hungary, a measure enacted by the local diet, at which they had next to no representation.[32] So did the bulk of Saxons, inhabiting their tightly regulated communities on the south-eastern border, and some of the Slovaks, whose claims, by contrast—in the absence of any kind of demarcated territory historically occupied by themselves—represented an extreme 'ethnic' slate.[33]

(8) From late August to early October there took place the breakdown of the Austro-Hungarian relation, i.e. that between the Hungarian regime, on one hand, and both the government in, and the dynasty just returned to, Vienna on the other, though these two were still distinct entities. In response to Batthyány's pleas for support against an insurrection by parts of the Habsburg army, the Austrian cabinet issued a memorandum arguing that the April Laws, thus the whole constitutional credentials of its Hungarian equivalent, were themselves unlawful. Attempts at reconciliation, on a personal, governmental, or parliamentary level, proved abortive.[34] Batthyány and his colleagues resigned, or tried to; several of them, including the deranged Széchenyi, fled, as did the Habsburg Palatine; and radicals took over in the Hungarian capital. The king sent a native-born mediator, General Lamberg, a widely respected figure who, by tragic mischance, still lacked proper accreditation on his arrival there and was lynched by an enraged, misguided

also Michael B. Petrovich, *A History of Modern Serbia* (2 vols.; New York, 1976), i. 239–46.

[32] Introduction in Bodea (see Further Reading). Documentation in Cornelia Bodea (ed.), *1848 la români: O istorie în date și mărturii* (2 vols.; Bucharest, 1982). Note that Romanians living elsewhere in Hungary, mainly in the Banat, were much more divided in their loyalties: I. D. Suciu, *Revoluția de la 1848–9 în Banat* (Bucharest, 1968).

[33] For Saxons: Carl Göllner, *Die Siebenbürger Sachsen in den Revolutionsjahren 1848–9* (Bucharest, 1967). Ethnic Germans elsewhere in Hungary mostly sided with the Hungarian government. Useful introduction to the Slovak cause in 1848 by Ronald V. Baumgarten, 'Slovakia's Role in the 1848 Revolutions' (diss. Florida State University 1982). The main documentary collections are Daniel Rapant, *Slovenské povstanie roku 1848–9* (12 vols.; Martin and Bratislava, 1937–67), from the Slovak side, and Lajos Steier, *A tót nemzetiségi kérdés 1848–9-ben* (2 vols.; Budapest, 1937), from the Magyar.

[34] The key document is printed in Ferdinand Fenner von Fenneberg, *Geschichte der Wiener Oktobertage* (2 vols.; Leipzig, 1849), i. 32–50; cf. Redlich (see Further Reading), i/1. 188 ff.; i/2. 48 ff. Cf. also, on the September negotiations, Evans, 'Hungary and the Habsburg Monarchy', 26–8.

mob on the bridge of boats across the Danube between Buda and Pest.

Jellačić now marched on the twin cities, but was countered by a hastily assembled Hungarian army, with parliamentary and popular support ably co-ordinated by a new Committee of National Defence under Kossuth. It possessed few resources until Kossuth and others created them, with recruitment campaigns, new currency, improvised weaponry, and so forth.[35] The Habsburgs and their domestic allies had resources, but little co-ordination. Jellačić and his troops proved feeble; the Serbs were now rent by internal feuding, and embarrassed by the questionable status of their foreign volunteers; some Romanians proved to have different priorities and exhibited questionable loyalties.[36] The ruler sought to impose his own head of government on the country, but could find only a bewildered, semi-retired, 73-year-old cavalry general prepared to do his bidding. This four-days' wonder, one Ádám Récsey, allegedly signed the dynasty's declaration of war on its Hungarian subjects in return for settlement of his debts.[37]

(9) This impasse provoked a new revolutionary outbreak in Austria, more spectacular and more socially radical than all the preceding ones: insurrection in Vienna. Its immediate cause was an order from the minister of war, Latour, for troops to be sent into Hungary. This touched a nerve of sympathy on the Austrian left for the Hungarian cause, which was fanned by open and covert activities on the part of spokesmen for the latter in Vienna.[38] There was a background of growing worker and student unrest in the city

[35] Ferdinand Hauptmann, *Jelačić's Kriegszug nach Ungarn, 1848* (2 vols.; Graz, 1975). For Kossuth: István Barta, 'Kossuth alföldi toborzó körútja 1848 őszén', *Századok*, 86 (1952), 149–66.

[36] The Serb patriarch, Rajačić, was soon at daggers drawn with his military commander, Stratimirović: cf. the latter's account in *Was ich erlebte* (Vienna and Leipzig, 1911). There were also the repercussions of the dynastic squabbles between Obrenovićes and Karadjordjevićes. Romanian insubordination is illustrated by e.g. Silviu Dragomir, *Avram Iancu*, 2nd edn. (Bucharest, 1968); cf. Suciu, *Revoluţia . . . în Banat*.

[37] Récsey was installed on 3 and resigned on 7 Oct. He actually had to countersign his own appointment. Heinrich Friedjung, *Österreich von 1848 bis 1860*, 4th edn. (2 vols.; Stuttgart and Berlin, 1918), i. 78–81, is corrected by Károlyi, *Batthyány*, i. 406 ff.; cf. Urbán, *Batthyány miniszterelnöksége*, 722–4.

[38] The extent of such activities is still a subject of some dispute: cf. Károlyi, *Batthyány*, i. 450 ff.; István Barta in *Századok*, 85 (1951), 443–85; *Magyarische Rebellenbriefe, 1848*, ed. Friedrich Walter (Munich, 1964).

as public-works programmes initiated in the spring were cut back and the authorities attempted to subdue mass organizations. Latour was slain and his body hung from a lamp-post. The court fled again, this time to Moravia, to the episcopal see of Olmütz and its nearby residence town of Kremsier, where it was joined by most of the Reichstag. Power in the capital, such as could be exercised, passed to extremists; radical deputies arrived from Frankfurt (Karl Marx had visited earlier); an itinerant Polish general, Józef Bem, tried to mobilize for defence. But there was hesitation on both sides about military liaison with the Hungarians, although their forces were massed on the nearby border.[39]

Windischgrätz again advanced to restore order, again exceeding his own instructions in the process. Then the carnage was aggravated by a tardy and thus futile decision of the Hungarians to invade after all. Thousands died, and tough reprisals included the execution of an official representative of Frankfurt, Robert Blum. Key political changes took place in the aftermath: a new Austrian regime was installed under Prince Felix Schwarzenberg (Windischgrätz's brother-in-law), which re-established harmony between government and court, largely by playing the court's tunes; and a new emperor sealed the bargain. The young Franz Joseph, untrammelled by all the concessions which his uncle had made over previous months, or—fresh from military service in Italy—by any scruples about the further use of violence, ascended the throne on 2 December. Ferdinand, put out to grass by his nearest and dearest just when ruling had become better fun than ever, jibbed at first, but then seems to have taken it all in good part. 'God bless you, be good [bleib nur brav]', he apparently told his 18-year-old successor, 'God will protect you; you're welcome [es ist gern geschehen].'[40]

(10) Now Windischgrätz took over the main field army to settle accounts with the Hungarians. His invasion soon reached Buda-Pest and forced a scrambled retreat in the last hours of the old year by the Kossuthist administration and parliament on the new

[39] Fenner von Fenneberg, *Wiener Oktobertage*, by a leading rebel; Alexander von Helfert, *Geschichte Österreichs vom Ausgange des Wiener Oktober-Aufstandes 1848* (6 vols.; Leipzig and Prague, 1869–86), vol. i, hostile to the revolution.
[40] Ferdinand's words have been retailed in a variety of forms. For the ceremony and attendant circumstances: Helfert, *Geschichte*, vol. iii, pro-dynastic; Friedjung, *Österreich*, i. 92–118, critical; cf. Jean-Paul Bled, *Franz Joseph*, Eng. trans. (Oxford, 1992), 47–9.

railway east towards Debrecen, whither Hungarian troops also
withdrew, tactically, though in some disarray. But simultaneously
Bem reappeared in Transylvania to take over command of the insurgents (or the army loyal to the legally instituted government
of 1848, according to one's point of view). In two extraordinary
months this charismatic foreigner, who spoke not a word of Hungarian, cleared the Austrians and their local allies out of the province. While refusing mediation by moderate Magyars, including
Batthyány and Deák ('I don't treat with rebels', was his notorious
comment), Windischgrätz remained almost equally suspicious of
the other nationalities, and inclined to a restoration of the *status quo
ante*.[41]

However, his hand was forced from Austria. There, the Reichstag
had resumed its debates at Kremsier, now with a clear Slav but still
liberal-minded majority. Deterred by official rebuke from pressing
its claim to be founded on the principle of popular sovereignty,
the assembly nevertheless continued to enjoy much credibility as a
constitutional focus.[42] By March, Schwarzenberg and Franz Joseph
felt sufficiently uneasy about its impending recommendations and
confident of the government's position to dissolve the chamber by
force. In its place they dictated a constitution of their own, now
with authority for the whole monarchy. Was it really designed only
to deprive the Hungarians of theirs, as wits proclaimed?[43] A wave
of protests followed in the Austrian lands. Attempts at more serious
opposition were easily mastered by the regime, which was boosted
also when an ill-conceived revival of Piedmontese hostilities could
be seen off by Radetzky within a few days at Novara (though Venice
still held out). Yet the ministry's legitimacy remained an issue, and
the liberal intentions of several of its members continued to reflect
both conviction and expediency.[44]

(11) This 4 March Constitution, often called after its chief architect, Count Franz Stadion, was wholly centralist, and therefore

---

[41] For Windischgrätz see Helfert, *Geschichte*, vol. iv; Friedjung, *Österreich*, i. 129–
34 and *passim*.
[42] Classic treatment of the Kremsier debates in Redlich (see Further Reading), i.
221–323.
[43] Walter Rogge, *Österreich von Világos bis zur Gegenwart*, i (Leipzig and Vienna,
1872), 77 ff.
[44] Friedjung, *Österreich*, i. 255–91. Cf., most recently, Gunther Hildebrandt,
Österreich 1849: Studien zur Politik der Regierung Schwarzenberg (Berlin, 1990),
19 ff.

unacceptable to practically all shades of opinion within Hungary, above all to the Magyars. Ironically, it coincided with a drastic shift of military fortune there: led by a brilliant young general, Artúr Görgey, the Hungarian armies threw Windischgrätz out of the country, mopped up most domestic rebels, and recovered Buda-Pest after a protracted siege which was perhaps wasteful too, since Vienna, still seething with suppressed discontent, lay vulnerable to a pre-emptive strike. Meanwhile Kossuth seized the occasion to burn the revolution's bridges, depose 'the perjured house of Habsburg-Lorraine', and install himself as governor president. But inner squabbles about political aims and military strategy, which included intermittent clashes between Kossuth and Görgey, jeopardized Hungarian success. Both sides looked for allies. Hungary's only real chance lay in mending fences with the local nationalities; and some negotiations—albeit rather desultory—resulted, even with elements among Romanians and Serbs.[45] The Austrians had Russia up their sleeve.

An appeal to the tsar had long been mooted (recall the financial talks on the eve of the revolution); limited intervention had already taken place in Transylvania—it was promptly seen off by Bem; and Nicholas feared especially the Polish dimension of the Hungarian war. Now Schwarzenberg swallowed a grievous penalty in prestige, and a huge Russian army marched down from the north.[46] The fighting was over by mid-August. Kossuth handed over civil authority to Görgey, who then controversially but inevitably capitulated. He surrendered not to the Austrians, for whom Field Marshal Haynau had just worsted the last remaining effective Hungarian field troops under Bem and himself, but to Paskevich. Russia insisted on a pardon for Görgey (thus fuelling the legend of his treason), but handed over the remaining military leaders to Haynau, who butchered as many as he could and added in a large number of politicians, including the blameless Batthyány. This vindictiveness—like British policy in Ireland in 1916—proved a dramatic miscalculation.

(12) The revolution was now over bar the shouting, and that mainly happened abroad. Manin's Venice conceded later in Au-

---

[45] Surveyed in Spira (see Further Reading), 151–91.
[46] Roberts (see Further Reading). Important documentation (mainly in French) on the background to the decision in Erzsébet Andics, *A Habsburgok és Romanovok szövetsége* (Budapest, 1961).

gust; the last Hungarian garrison came to terms in October; the final nails were hammered into the Frankfurt coffin over the summer, with the interment of unitary German institutions by the end of the year. Those radically compromised sought exile where possible, especially thousands of Magyars (and of course an old-new wave of Poles). A phased return to absolutism took place throughout the monarchy. Liberals gradually deserted or were forced out of government. We should not, however, exaggerate the speed or inevitability of this. Alongside evidence of continuing unrest, which caused martial law to be maintained in several territories, there were also continuing expectations.

Despite the spoiling tactics of conservatives, headed by the semi-disgraced Windischgrätz, the implementation of constitutional forms proceeded in some areas, with comprehensive plans for elective local government on several levels, a new legal system, and so forth.[47] Things might well have gone further, but for the sudden derangement of Stadion in the summer of 1849. And equal rights, in culture, language, or religion, were much invoked, even if few could be satisfied: the rewards accorded to some looked remarkably like the punishments meted out to others, as another *bon mot* had it.[48] Only in the last hours of 1851, in the aftermath of Napoleon III's coup in France, did Franz Joseph finally opt officially for the revival of a purely absolute form of government. Thus Vienna aped Paris, at the end of the troubles as at the beginning. Did that outcome render Austria a land again fit for Metternich? The old chancellor had indeed returned a few months previously. Yet by that time—to anticipate the conclusion of my essay—much of the message of revolution had been firmly incorporated, either into the business of Austrian government or into the ideology of some future opposition to it.[49]

Such, in all brevity, was the trajectory of the unprecedented upheavals unleashed in Habsburg central Europe by the bankruptcy

---

[47] Carl von Czoernig, *Oesterreichs Neugestaltung, 1848–58* (Stuttgart and Augsburg, 1858), esp. 80 ff., is detailed self-justification by the new regime.

[48] For an early formulation of this aphorism, in the *Neue Rheinische Zeitung* of Marx and Engels, see Hanisch, *Der kranke Mann*, 152.

[49] Metternich's last years are described in Srbik, *Metternich*, ii. 422–515. For post-1849 official reform see Czoernig, *Neugestaltung*, and Friedjung, *Österreich*, i. 292 ff. Cf. R. J. W. Evans, 'From Confederation to Compromise: The Austrian Experiment, 1849–67', *Proceedings of the British Academy*, 87 (1994), 135–67.

of its *ancien régime* in March 1848. The remainder of this chapter is devoted to analytical comments which may help to give some shape to the flux of the events just described.

(*a*) Surprise when the monarchy revived, even in a potentially strengthened form, by the end of 1849 matched surprise at its revolutionary near-collapse in the previous year. But the recovery had equally fundamental causes. The monarchy's survival was widely attributed at the time, as it has been by many historians, to the army and its commanders (particularly the insubordinate ones).[50] That is surely a misconception. Very few people sought a break-up of the Habsburg lands. Germans remained largely loyal, fired indeed to some extent—though hardly coerced—by the achievements of Radetzky. The Austro-Slav programme was likewise loyal: devised especially by Palacký and other Czechs, it was also embraced by Croats, Ruthenes, Slovenes, some Slovaks, and Poles. To Palacký we owe a still more famous remark (from the same Frankfurt letter) that if the Habsburg monarchy did not already exist, it would be necessary to create it—actually not an original formulation, which is itself significant: the sentiment was widespread in 1848.[51] Some Serbs and Romanians are hard to judge, but cultural and political unity with their ethnic kin probably mattered more to them than independence. Italian resentments, at least in Lombardy-Venetia, were more ingrained, but ultimately peripheral: some sagacious Austrians, even in government, thought the Italian provinces a liability anyway. The Magyars were firm, but mostly royalist enough, a majority of the Batthyány cabinet conspicuously so, unless pushed to a breach. So, overwhelmingly, were assimilationist Jewish circles throughout the monarchy, despite— or because of—the evidence of anti-Semitism during some of the revolutionary disturbances.[52]

Correct constitutional attitudes often prevailed within the army too, and much heart-searching was caused by the labyrinthine dilemma of whether individuals were subordinate to Austrian or

---

[50] Most recently James J. Sheehan, *German History, 1770–1866* (Oxford, 1989), 697–702; Jonathan Sperber, *The European Revolutions, 1848–51* (Cambridge, 1994), 206–9.

[51] Kořalka's detective work, loc. cit. (see n. 22); cf. R. J. W. Evans in Robertson and Timms (eds.), *Habsburg Legacy*, 27–8.

[52] Survey in William O. McCagg, *A History of Habsburg Jews, 1670–1918* (Bloomington and Indianapolis, 1989), 83–101. Cf. Béla Bernstein, *A negyvennyolcas magyar szabadságharc és a zsidók* (Budapest, 1898).

Hungarian authority.[53] The exceptions indeed proved decisive. Yet the case is really that initiatives taken by certain conservative commanders, with the connivance or clear support of the Austrian war ministry, forestalled civilian settlements; then made states of siege self-fulfilling; and finally saddled the Habsburgs with an ultimately indefensible Lombardy-Venetia and with an irreconcilable Hungary, whose estrangement gained its symbolic manifestations in the victims of Haynau. Arguably the legend of the army's saving role in 1848–9 cast a long shadow over the future, in conditioning the views of Franz Joseph above all, and damaging the Habsburg dynasty in the eyes of all those who perceived its retreat from reformist programmes as a breach of faith.[54]

(b) Evidently the fortunes of the Habsburgs and their subjects through 1848–9 depended also on the international situation. A strong and coherent großdeutsch outcome at Frankfurt would necessarily have confirmed new power structures within the monarchy. An effective Polish movement—however unlikely—might have meant the loss of Galicia. Real commitment to a uniform conception of the Italian cause could have rendered Radetzky's position politically untenable. The presence of foreign co-nationals within the insurrectionary Serb and Romanian legions probably did these movements more harm than good.

Most important was the attitude of the great powers. Republican France could have been troublesome, had her actual diplomacy matched some of the advanced pronouncements of her government spokesmen. Yet at no point did the critical mass of international radicalism encourage her to try.[55] British official attitudes during and after the revolution were uniformly supportive of the Habsburgs' authority, Palmerston advising merely, and privately, that it might be wise to cede Lombardy. Metternich felt thoroughly at home in England ('We couldn't have found things better in London if we had been John Bull in person').[56] Perceptions of the European

[53] Good examples in Deák (see Further Reading), and id. in East-Central European Society (see Further Reading), 393–418.

[54] Franz Joseph and the army: Harm-Hinrich Brandt in Schindling and Ziegler (eds.), Kaiser der Neuzeit, 345 ff.; Bled, Franz Joseph, 37 ff.; Steven Beller, Francis Joseph (London, 1996), 45 ff., esp.59–6. Good material in Antonio Schmidt-Brentano, Die Armee in Österreich: Militär, Staat und Gesellschaft, 1848–67 (Boppard a.R., 1975).

[55] Cf. James Chastain, Liberation of Sovereign Peoples: The French Foreign Policy of 1848 (Athens, Oh., 1988).

[56] Constantin de Grunwald, La Vie de Metternich (Paris, 1938), 328; cf. Srbik,

balance of power worked to limit any scope for constitutional re-ordering in the centre of the continent.

Eventually the Austrians themselves invoked that balance of power, but also upset its equilibrium, by calling in the Russian army. That has occasioned endless dispute. Was intervention necessary, or desirable from the Austrian viewpoint? Some have argued that the Habsburgs would have won the war anyway (but probably not on such terms as they were later able to impose).[57] Certainly the Russians' presence, and their comparative magnanimity in victory (which they could afford), made Austrian retribution in Hungary seem worse—though the tsar himself did not scruple elsewhere. Most importantly, Russian involvement catalysed a belated mood of repugnance in western countries at Habsburg counter-revolutionary activity, especially in Hungary. Now the United States actually ventured a diplomatic mission, to put pressure on the oppressive empire.[58] Thus was generated the climate in which *émigrés* could be first protected from Austrian demands for extradition, then fêted and welcomed as victims of tyranny: not just Kossuth, received as a hero in Britain and America, but also, for instance, Kudlich, living out his days—till 1917—in Hoboken, New Jersey.

(*c*) What had the revolutions actually been about: liberal or national goals? For most participants this would have appeared a false antithesis. Few thought as deeply as Palacký. For him the nation was a quasi-religious bond and guarantor of liberal values against the uniformity of the centralist state, which had now reached the limits of its usefulness as an instrument of democratization; and the Habsburg monarchy, as guarantor of nations, would need to be created (to round off his celebrated aphorism) in the interests 'of humanity itself'.[59] Even without theory, plenty of representa-

Metternich, ii. 303–31. For British policy: Charles Sproxton, *Palmerston and the Hungarian Revolution* (Cambridge, 1919); R. W. Seton-Watson, *Britain in Europe, 1789–1914* (Cambridge, 1937), 241–71; A. J. P. Taylor, *The Struggle for Mastery in Europe, 1848–1918* (Oxford, 1954), 1–45.

[57] e.g. Alan Sked, *The Decline and Fall of the Habsburg Empire* (London, 1989), 94–108, esp. 102.

[58] Arthur J. May, *Contemporary American Opinion of the Mid-century Revolutions in Central Europe* (Philadelphia, 1927); cf. Roberts and Howe in this volume. It arrived too late to make any impact.

[59] See especially his essays reprinted in *Radhost: Sbírka spisůw drobných*, iii (Prague, 1873), 43–70; and cf. M. Otáhal in Jaworski and Luft (eds.), *Revolutionen in Ostmitteleuropa*, 47–56.

tives of smaller nations could see the need to secure cultural values, above all freedom of language use, by liberal legislation. Hence the inevitable fragmentation of a universal idea or ideal. There is a good example in the practice of the Austrian Reichstag. It engendered an interminable wrangle over the *Parlamentssprache*, the language of debate: the *de facto* use of German faced practical or ideological objections from other nationalities and raised massive problems of intelligibility.[60] Against that, the unyielding attitude of Magyars towards all 'ethnic' objections to, or restraints upon, their reform programme can easily be understood, as can the reluctance of non-Magyar groups to accept such discrimination against their cultures.

The issue tended to pit two kinds of nation one against the other: those with a clear territorial foundation for constitutional claims and a firm social base for the individual rights bestowed by liberal reform; and those which lacked them. 'Historic' and 'unhistoric' nations, in other words, a formula devised by Marx and Engels at this time precisely with reference to the Habsburg lands, and with unabashed prejudice in favour of the former: 'The next world war will also cause whole reactionary peoples to disappear from the face of the earth. And that is no bad thing.'[61] Small wonder that smaller, mainly Slav, nationalities resisted so fiercely the (pseudo-) liberal embrace of dominant groups; though as the Czech case best demonstrates, in its equal reliance on the rights of peoples and on the historic liberties of the Bohemian crown, these categories, like other Marxian and Engelsian ones, were never satisfactory in the first place.

(*d*) All this had been fairly clear already before 1848. There was no serious room for doubt that the Czechs possessed a developed language-based culture during the Vormärz; a full-scale polemic about 'Magyarization' had unfolded with intensifying venom since the 1820s. What the revolution did was to engage the masses in these conflicts, and thus to propel the latter with broader currents

---

[60] Paula Geist-Lányi, *Das Nationalitätenproblem auf dem Reichstag zu Kremsier, 1848–9* (Munich, 1920), 91 ff.

[61] 'Der nächste Weltkrieg wird . . . auch ganze reaktionäre Völker vom Erdboden verschwinden machen. Und das ist auch ein Vorteil': Engels (13 Jan. 1849), quoted in Hanisch, *Der kranke Mann*, 176. This was not an isolated comment. 'The Austrian army, which conquered Prague, Vienna, Lemberg, Cracow, Milan and Buda-Pest— that is the real and active [fruit of the] Slav Congress. . . . A war of extermination of the Germans against the Czechs now remains the only possible solution' (ibid. 92, 94).

of social radicalism. Popular involvement is evident in the urban upheavals; but hardly less so in the countryside, where peasants downed tools on much seigneurial land at the first hint of the abolition of labour service and protested intermittently against the limits of the emancipation package. Women, too, began to emerge into the public eye, mainly as activists for a given national cause.[62]

It is important to recognize that such political mobilization of the masses was almost wholly new to the area, and assumed a variety of forms both constructive and destructive. A vast and quite unprecedented bulk of journal and pamphlet literature appeared during 1848. The conduct of elections, most on a genuinely broad suffrage, proceeded remarkably rapidly and smoothly. They yielded a significant number of popular tribunes, especially in Austria, where dozens of Reichstag deputies were illiterate. Military recruitment comprises the other side of the same coin: witness the extraordinary success of Kossuth's call to arms, begun in autumn 1848 in the areas nearest to Buda-Pest and accessible by train. Perhaps one in two of Magyar families supplied someone to the war effort in one way or another.[63] Some anti-Magyar campaigns attracted almost equal participation; the result was guerrilla and irregular tactics on a vast scale and some extreme brutality, probably unmatched elsewhere in contemporary Europe, on both sides.[64]

Not that popular nationalism contributed as much to this as its ideologues, then and later, sought to claim. It was a complex brew of old resentments and new visions. As the colourful Slovak patriot

---

[62] Marxist historians have supplied massive documentation on popular participation. See esp. Rosdolsky, *Die Bauernabgeordneten*. Cf., for Austria, Wolfgang Häusler, *Von der Massenarmut zur Arbeiterbewegung: Demokratie und soziale Frage in der Wiener Revolution von 1848* (Vienna and Munich, 1979), and id. in Jaworski and Luft (eds.), *Revolutionen in Ostmitteleuropa*, 173–95; for Hungary the earlier classic analysis of Ervin Szabó, *Társadalmi és pártharcok a 48-49-es magyar forradalomban*, 2nd edn. (Budapest, 1949), and the fascinating memoir of the people's tribune, Mihály Táncsics, *Életpályám*, ed. J. Czibor (Budapest, 1978), 304 ff. The role of women needs further exploration; there is a good piece on Czech patriotic women by Mirjam Moravcová in Jaworski and Luft (eds.), *Revolutionen in Ostmitteleuropa*, 75–96.

[63] Antal Mádl, *Politische Dichtung in Österreich, 1830–48* (Budapest, 1969), 228 ff. On elections: Peter Burian, *Die Nationalitäten in 'Cisleithanien' und das Wahlrecht der Märzrevolution, 1848–9* (Graz and Cologne, 1962); Rosdolsky, *Die Bauernabgeordneten*, 42–83. For Kossuth: Barta, 'Kossuth . . . körútja'. The 50% estimate was made by András Gergely at a conference in Vienna, Mar. 1998.

[64] Cf. my article 'Religion und Nation in Ungarn, 1790–1849', in Zs. K. Lengyel and U. A. Wien (eds.), *Siebenbürgen in der Habsburgermonarchie . . . 1690–1867* (Cologne, 1999), 13–44.

and agitator Jozef Miloslav Hurban, haranguing labourers from his horse, complained: for centuries they had been obsessed with the sod, dung, cattle; if they only secured national rights, social and economic ones would follow.[65] Often the result was a quandary of loyalties. As the ethnically diverse inhabitants of Fehértemplom, i.e. Bela Crkva, i.e. Weißkirchen, i.e. Biserica Albă, in the Banat, lamented to the king in June 1848: 'What in one place is right and lawful appears in another as treason to the good cause, and whatever one may do, one simultaneously infringes Your Majesty's laws, even while one fulfils them.' Within months the place was witness to some of the worst massacres of the whole civil war in Hungary.[66]

(e) Finally, what were the consequences? In a word: momentous, for this supposedly 'failed' revolution—as such it has so often been presented—was actually a great and lasting success. Precisely because it was so innovative, intensive, and comparatively tenacious at the time, its legacy proved incalculably great. I have already hinted at the subsumption of major reform initiatives into the government programme of the 1850s. The most fundamental was peasant emancipation: announced for Austria on 28 March 1848, to become effective within a year, legislated for in Hungary by the April Laws, then debated at length in both parliaments, mainly to settle the matter of compensation, it was actually implemented in all its bewildering complexity only by the restored absolutist regime. Others lay in the economic, social, legal, technical, educational, and further spheres. Even political and constitutional agendas were merely frozen during the 1850s, re-emerging almost at a stroke thereafter. The Reichstag was re-established in 1860–1 (albeit called 'Reichsrat', the name earlier given to an advisory body actually set up under the provisions of 4 March 1849), as was the rest of the Austrian constitution, by Stadion out of Kremsier, with its origins in Pillersdorf.[67]

In Hungary the April Laws were an exact blueprint for much of the compromise legislation of 1867. In fact the *Ausgleich* formally in large measure just reasserted them, in line with the long and staunch Magyar campaign, orchestrated by Deák, of passive

[65] Rapant, *Slovenské povstanie*, i. 270–1.
[66] Quoted in Thim, *Szerb felkelés*, ii. 390; cf. ibid. i. 161 ff.
[67] The most authoritative and brilliant treatment of these developments remains Redlich (see Further Reading), i. 460 ff. and ii.

resistance in the name of constitutional principle (which, to recall repercussions nearer at hand, did so much at the turn of the century to inspire Arthur Griffith's ideal for Sinn Féin).[68] The associated system of 'dualism' had already been a fact of the whole 1848–9 experience, which subsequent centralization actually only enhanced, because it sobered Hungary's non-Magyars up from their newly found Austrophilia. More generally, the programmes of all the national movements in the monarchy rehearsed those formulated in 1848. Even if their deployment during the revolution did not itself ensure their subsequent revival, it reinforced them precisely by the memory of (temporary) failure, and by the mythopoeic force of sacrifice. Even the final parting of the ways in Germany, that climax of the most elemental and ancient of Habsburg power struggles, was decisively shaped by 1848, as Austrians found themselves forced to establish a relationship with the rest of Germany, rather than simply subsisting as part of it. We may leave the last word to ex-Emperor Ferdinand, 'the Kindly', darling of the revolutionaries, to whom he granted so much, contemplating central Europe on the morrow of the decisive battle at Königgrätz/Sadowa from his enforced retirement in Prague Castle and observing, in his broad Viennese: 'Des hätten mir a zsambracht [Even I could have done as well as that]'.[69] And so, in a way, he had.

FURTHER READING

The multifarious episodes which constitute the 1848–9 revolution in the Habsburg lands were widely commented upon at the time in both Britain and America. Lives of its great men—above all Kossuth—and accounts of its wars and tumults predominated, but more thoughtful, even analytical, work also appeared, such as Count Franz Hartig's 'Genesis, or Details of the Late Austrian Revolution', which came out in translation as an additional volume in the numerous re-editions of William Coxe's *History of the House of Austria* from the early 1850s. However, this flood of writing rapidly subsided, and the events themselves largely faded into oblivion in the Anglo-Saxon world. Recent decades have brought a renewed surge of

[68] Introduction to Deák in Béla K. Király, *Ferenc Deák* (Boston, 1975). On the Irish connection: Arthur Griffith, *The Resurrection of Hungary: A Parallel for Ireland* (Dublin, 1904); cf. Tamás Kabdebó in *Századok*, 125 (1991), 309–31.

[69] Quoted by Mikoletzky in Schindling and Ziegler (eds.), *Kaiser der Neuzeit*, 332.

interest, spurred initially by the hundredth anniversary of the revolution, which yielded a pioneering collection edited by François Fejtő under the title *The Opening of an Era: 1848, an Historical Symposium* (London, 1948), with several chapters on central Europe. This note therefore largely restricts itself to original work in English, as well as important translations into English, on the main themes.

The most outstanding overall survey remains the brilliant conspectus in C. A. Macartney, *The Habsburg Empire, 1790–1918* (London, 1968), 306–432. For Vienna see R. J. Rath, *The Viennese Revolution of 1848* (Austin, 1957). For Bohemia see Stanley Z. Pech, *The Czech Revolution of 1848* (Chapel Hill, NC, 1969). Josef V. Polišenský, *Aristocrats and the Crowd in the Revolutionary Year 1848*, Eng. trans. (Albany, NY, 1980), is quirky, but contains valuable material. The Hungarian lands are the subject of a superb, even-handed narrative by István Deák, *The Lawful Revolution: Louis Kossuth and the Hungarians, 1848–9* (New York, 1979). Cf. György Spira, *The Nationality Issue in the Hungary of 1848–9*, Eng. trans. (Budapest, 1992), with detailed bibliography but residual Magyar bias. Ian W. Roberts, *Nicholas I and the Russian Intervention in Hungary* (London, 1991), treats the key diplomatic issue for the Habsburgs. Cf. A. J. P. Taylor, *The Italian Problem in European Diplomacy, 1847–9* (Manchester, 1934), on Italy. For the Italian provinces see also Alan Sked, *The Survival of the Habsburg Empire: Radetzky, the Imperial Army and the Class War, 1848* (London, 1979), and Paul Ginsborg, *Daniele Manin and the Venetian Revolution of 1848–9* (Cambridge, 1979). There are useful articles on military aspects in Béla K. Király (ed.), *East-Central European Society and War in the Era of Revolutions, 1775–1856* (New York, 1984). For guidance on the German question, in which Austria bulked so large, see elsewhere in the present volume.

The bulk of the literature, including most eyewitness accounts, is available only in central European languages. I have made some comments on the historiographical traditions of the subject in '1848 in Mitteleuropa: Ereignis und Erinnerung', forthcoming in the conference proceedings G. Klingenstein *et al.* (eds.), *1848: Ereignis und Erinnerung in den politischen Kulturen Mitteleuropas* (Vienna, 2000). And two brilliant, still unsurpassed, analyses of the political and constitutional significance of 1848–9 for the long-term development of the area demand to be mentioned, though neither has ever been made available in English and their titles may not betray their relevance to this subject: Louis Eisenmann, *Le Compromis austro-hongrois de 1867* (Paris, 1904), and Josef Redlich, *Das österreichische Staats- und Reichsproblem* (2 vols.; Leipzig, 1920–6).

10

1848 in European Collective Memory

ROBERT GILDEA

OUR perspective on any historical event is conditioned not only by historical scholarship but also by collective memory, by the collective construction of the past by groups or subgroups which has more to do with political controversy and power struggles than the scholarly scrutiny of historical documents. I shall explore, in sketchy fashion admittedly, the ways in which the revolutions of 1848 have been remembered in common, through the commemoration of chosen actors and events by funeral rites, erecting statues, naming public places, processions to shrines, and mass rallies, and political debates which crystallized around the celebration of key anniversaries. The commemoration of heroes, martyrs, and events often serves to elaborate a founding myth of a political movement, a story of its origin and purpose, in order to define it against competing movements, to bind it together, and to establish the legitimacy of its claims. Here myth is understood, of course, not as fiction or fairy-tale, but as a shared construction of the past that fulfils these political purposes of definition, binding, and legitimation.

There was no single, objective view of the 1848 revolutions but only competing views, constructed and sustained by different political communities seeking to justify their own agendas. For democrats, 1848 was a democratic revolution *par excellence*, which, through the processes of democracy, ensured liberty, equality, and fraternity. For socialists, on the other hand, 1848 represented the

This is a revised version of a paper originally given in Würzburg, Germany, in 1996, and also appears in Dieter Dowe *et al.* (eds.), *Europe in the Revolutions of 1848* (Berghahn: forthcoming).

betrayal of democratic ideals by a bourgeoisie intent only on main-
taining its class domination at the expense of the proletariat. For
patriots, 1848 was the springtime of peoples, when emergent nationalities threw off the yoke of the old multinational empires.
For emancipationists, finally, 1848 meant the emancipation of slave
labour, at least in the French colonies.

The paradox of these myths, by which politicians and activists
found in 1848 the heroes and defining moment of their own movements, was that in all cases 1848 failed them. It was a year full of
promise, but the promise was not realized. The democrats lost their
liberty and sometimes democracy too; the socialists were crushed
and persecuted; the champions of national liberation were sacrificed
at the altar of *Realpolitik*; and the emancipationists were confronted
by colonial oppression and racism. At best, 1848 continued to hold
out a mirror to their aspirations, presented them with an ideal that
might one day be fulfilled. At worst, it saddled political communities with a historical burden which outweighed the benefits of
legitimation afforded by the founding myth and encouraged them
to seek a principle of legitimation elsewhere.

It must be said, of course, that changing events altered the way
in which the revolutions of 1848 were regarded by any or all of
these political movements. Ideals that were shattered at one moment nevertheless remained ideals, with a power to inspire, and
in different circumstances the realization of those ideals might become feasible. This final chapter seeks to trace changes in collective
memory over the 150 years that followed the revolutions, concentrating on the fiftieth, hundredth, and—in so far as it is yet possible
to judge—the hundred and fiftieth anniversaries of 1848.

The first myth constructed around the revolution of 1848 was the
democratic one. Democratic movements traced their foundation
to 1848 and argued that the central achievement of that year was
to find a path to democracy between stifling authoritarianism and
violent revolution. The emphasis was different from country to
country. In France the democratic myth proclaimed that the revolution of 1848 fulfilled the promises of the Revolution of 1789 and
yet was the antithesis of the Terror of 1793. In Germany, where
fear of French-style revolution was so intense that revolution was
virtually prevented from breaking out at all, 1848 was cultivated as

a reminder by democrats that even in authoritarian and then Nazi Germany there was still an indigenous democratic moment.

For French democrats, democracy meant bringing back the republic that had originally been founded in 1792; but republicanism was discredited in the early part of the nineteenth century in France by its identification with revolutionary dictatorship, the guillotine, the Terror, and civil war. French republicans, an endangered species, understood that they would have to demonstrate that the Republic was compatible with liberty if it were ever to gain acceptance at a future date. They argued therefore that democracy in the form of universal suffrage would make the violent seizure of power unnecessary, and that if the people were consulted, political strife would subside as the people came together in fraternal union in support of the Republic. That Republic, they insisted, would not terrorize its opponents, but establish a regime of liberty, justice and respect for rights, and seek to win over doubters by weight of numbers and force of argument.

The agenda of the republicans was clear even before the Revolution of 1848. François Raspail, who was born under one republic and wished to die under another, told his opponents in 1835: 'The republic we desire is not that of '93. It is the republic where discussion will replace war and the improvement of mankind will make the scaffold redundant.'[1] Shortly after taking power in 1848, the Provisional Government of the republic announced the abolition of the death penalty for political crimes and called elections under universal manhood suffrage to a Constituent Assembly. Victor Hugo, in his manifesto to the electors of the Seine, said that the republic must not restart 'those two fatal and inseparable machines, the *assignat* printing-press and the pivot of the guillotine', which had discredited the First Republic, but become 'the holy communion in the democratic principle of all French people now, and of all peoples one day'.[2]

Whether to trust in free elections and fraternity to secure the republic was not rather naïve is open to debate. The elections of 1848 returned a majority of conservatives and class war broke out in the streets. On the anniversary in 1848 of the proclamation of the first French republic of 1792, Raspail told Ledru-Rollin, who had been minister of the interior in the Provisional Government:

[1] *Le Réformateur* (10 Jan. 1835).
[2] Victor Hugo, *A ses concitoyens* (Paris, 1848).

'All your policy is based on fraternity, and the policy of a people of brothers has only to lift a finger and thrones collapse.'[3] Ironically Raspail was speaking from prison, Ledru-Rollin would be driven into exile the following year, and the much-vaunted people threw themselves into the arms of Louis-Napoleon Bonaparte. The democratic agenda failed to understand that universal suffrage would not necessarily play into the hands of republicanism. It failed to deal adequately with its enemies, royalists or Bonapartists. And it failed to see that as the working classes became disillusioned and class struggles sharpened, the rhetoric of fraternity would look increasingly threadbare.

Despite these errors of judgement, republicans of 1848 clung to the view that the regime of 1848 was an immense improvement on that of 1793 and that democracy would replace repression by liberty, civil strife by fraternity. Ledru-Rollin, elected to the National Assembly of the Third Republic in 1874, praised the 'republic of clemency' of 1848, so unlike the First Republic, which had become an armed camp, and blamed the monarchists and Bonapartists for not giving it a chance.[4] Louis Blanc, who had chaired a commission on labour questions in 1848, likewise stressed the 'magnanimity' and 'generosity' of the revolutionaries of 1848.[5] He admitted, when a monument to Ledru-Rollin was unveiled in 1878, that the Provisional Government had not had enough faith in the republic and had sometimes lacked boldness and energy. But he insisted that universal suffrage was 'the saving principle which checks insurrections and riots, and dispenses from violent efforts'.[6] 'Before this powerful voice of the country', he reiterated at Raspail's funeral, 'all parties must withdraw and fall silent. We expect this act of patriotism from them. The country wishes it; the country commands it.'[7]

The men who founded the Third Republic, and steered it between the reefs of popular revolution and monarchist and Bonapartist reaction, took a more realistic view of the ethos of 1848. In 1904 a

---

[3] F. Raspail, 'Remerciements', in *Discours du citoyen Ledru-Rollin prononcé au banquet du Châtelet, 22 sept. 1848* (Paris, 1849), 19.

[4] Ledru-Rollin, *Discours politiques et écrits divers* (2 vols.; Paris, 1879), ii. 483.

[5] Louis Blanc, speech on revolution of Feb. 1848, 24 Feb. 1877, in his *Discours politiques, 1847–81* (Paris, 1882), 247; 'Caractère généreux de la Révolution de février', *Histoire de la Révolution de 1848* (2 vols.; Paris, 1880), vol. i, ch. 6.

[6] Blanc, speech of 24 Feb. 1878, in *Discours politiques*, 299.

[7] Speech of 13 Jan. 1878: ibid. 291.

Société d'Histoire de la Révolution de 1848 was founded, sponsored by Henri Brisson and Armand Fallières, respectively speakers of the Chamber of Deputies and Senate, socialist deputies Alexandre Millerand and Jean Jaurès, and the in-house historian of the Radical Party, Alphonse Aulard. At its general assembly in the Sorbonne on 24 February 1905 the society's president, Adolphe Carnot, member of a great republican dynasty, brother of the assassinated president, and a leader of the centre-left Alliance Démocratique, provided a perceptive but critical defence of 1848:

There were at that time surges of universal fraternity which were ahead of their time but had an influence on the development of the aspirations of modern peoples towards harmony and general peace. We must not lose the lessons of a period so full of generous hopes, which were often illusions, but which also sometimes led to great reforms and beautiful creations. Swept along by their own generosity, the emancipators of 1848 were too ready to believe the hypocritical promises of their opponents. The republic and liberty fell victim to this confidence and, during a cold December night, were strangled by the prince president who had sworn an oath to defend them. The present republic has returned in part to the great ideas of the Second Republic. But it must not forget to learn the lessons of history. On the one hand it must take precautions against the manœuvres of reaction, while on the other it must moderate dangerous impatience and unrealizable Utopias by expanding both general and civic education.[8]

History cruelly demonstrated that the manœuvres of reaction would easily get the better of the generous ideals of 1848. The democratic myth, as we shall see, was appropriated by reformist socialists such as Léon Blum, who opposed joining the Third International in 1920 on the grounds that Bolshevism represented the dictatorship of the proletariat, the eclipse of liberty, and a return to the Terror. Yet the noble ideals that had inspired the republic did not prevent its abolition by the Vichy regime in 1940 and Blum himself spending five years in the prisons of Vichy and Nazi Germany. When he delivered a lecture at the Sorbonne for the hundredth anniversary of the Revolution in 1948, he was in pessimistic vein: 'We are still confronted by the same problems, the same difficulties, the same anxieties, and sometimes without the same hopes,' he said, 'so that one might say that [in 1848] humanity never lost such an

---

[8] 'La Révolution de 1848', *Bulletin de la Société d'Histoire de la Révolution de 1848*, 2 (1905–6), 2.

opportunity, that it never toppled from so high up.' He criticized the members of the Provisional Government of 1848 for being the 'victims of a psychosis', for being so obsessed by the need to exorcize the memory of the Terror that they lacked the confidence to take decisive action, called elections before educating the masses in republican ways, and, in their fear of alienating the bourgeoisie by social reforms, alienated the working classes, who were their staunchest supporters.[9]

By the time of the 150th anniversary in 1998, the republic was politically secure and its survival not in doubt. Celebration of the revolution was a low-key affair, centring on an exhibition in the National Assembly inspired by its speaker, Laurent Fabius, and organized by the leading historian of the Republic, Maurice Agulhon. Fears of 1793 had long been laid to rest. Commemoration was confined to the grand setting of the Palais-Bourbon and did not spill on to the streets. Fabius echoed Blum's reproach of the 'generous and sometimes unrealistic idealism' of the revolutionaries, their 'magnificent surge of fraternity' halted by the June Days and coup of 2 December. Yet the brief of the exhibition was not reality but image, and the image of the republic given maximum prominence was the neo-classical Marianne of Jean-Léon Gérôme honoured by the Provisional Government of the republic in 1848: statuesque, more crown of laurels than red bonnet scarcely visible, sword pointing down and raised arm offering an olive-branch in the other.[10] The issue in 1998, however, was not whether the republic was still violent, but whether it could still stimulate any enthusiasm among the French people.

While for a long time the main purpose of the democratic myth of 1848 in France was to purge the heinous associations of the republic of 1793, in Germany it served to recall that Germans were capable not only of revolution but of freedom. Revolutions in France throughout the nineteenth century and then in Russia in 1917 drove Germans into the arms of authoritarian and repressive governments for eighty-one of the ninety-seven years between 1848 and 1945. Democrats searching for a founding myth were

[9] Léon Blum, lecture of 24 Feb. 1948, in *L'Œuvre* (Paris, 1963), 420–8. On the commemoration of 1848 in France see Timothy Baycroft, 'Commemorations of the Revolution of 1848 and the Second Republic', *Modern and Contemporary France*, 6/2 (May 1998), 155–68.

[10] Assemblée Nationale, *Les Révolutions de 1848: L'Europe des images* (Paris, 1998). I am grateful to Tom Gretton for this reference.

loath to turn to the violent revolution of 18 March 1848 in Berlin, which was, as we shall see, appropriated by the socialists, but the opening of the National Assembly in the Paulskirche of Frankfurt on 18 May 1848 offered an altogether more respectable heritage. When imperial Germany collapsed in the defeat of 1918, Friedrich Ebert, the Social Democratic chancellor of the new republic, announced that 'the great German revolution will bring Germany neither a new dictatorship nor servitude, but will firmly establish German freedom. . . . Political freedom is democracy on the secure foundations of a constitution and the law.'[11] Weimar democracy in fact hovered between Communist revolution and Nazi counter-revolution, and in May 1923, as civil war threatened, Ebert went to the Paulskirche with the leading politicians of the republic to head the commemoration of the seventy-fifth anniversary of the opening of the assembly. Greeted by a crowd of 30,000, he argued that on 18 May 1848, escaping from reactionary government, 'the German people took its destiny into its own hands'. Although the revolution was defeated, he asserted, the ideals of 'Einheit, Freiheit und Vaterland' lived on, so that when the German people once again took control of its destiny in 1918, it was to the Frankfurt assembly that the architects of the Weimar Republic like himself turned for inspiration.[12]

The purpose of Ebert's speech was to establish the legitimacy of the constitutional, parliamentary republic and to give honour and respectability to the revolution of 1848. Needless to say, the Nazis and Communists rejected both: the monument to Ebert placed on the façade of the Paulskirche in 1926 was demolished by the Nazis in 1933, and the church was reduced to rubble by Allied bombing. The postwar mayor of Frankfurt, Walter Kolb, interpreted the destruction of the church as a divine punishment for Germany's betrayal of democracy and had it rebuilt in time for the centenary of 1848 with materials brought from all over the country as a 'credo of German democracy'. It was thought fitting that the speeches should be made by a German poet, Fritz von Unruh, who had fled the Third Reich in 1933 and campaigned for democracy in the United States, and by the chancellor of the University of Chicago,

[11] Friedrich Ebert, *Schriften, Aufzeichnungen, Reden* (2 vols.; Dresden, 1926), ii. 120–1.

[12] Dieter Rebentisch, *Friedrich Ebert und die Paulskirche: Die Weimarer Demokratie und die 75-Jahrfeier der 1848er Revolution* (Heidelberg, 1998), 10. I am grateful to Hartmut Pogge von Strandmann for this reference.

who greeted the reintegration of Germany with the 'spiritual life of the world'.[13]

The idea that democracy in Germany was not home-grown, but was imposed by victorious foreigners after 1945, died hard. Speaking in the Paulskirche for the 150th anniversary of the opening of the National Assembly, however, Federal President Herzog riposted that there was indeed an indigenous democratic tradition in Germany, symbolized by two great events, the Frankfurt Assembly and the collapse of the Berlin Wall. He admitted that 'the history of freedom in our nation has often been one of experiment, losing the thread, of mistakes and defeats'; but for their own self-confidence and identity Germans must honour the right tradition. In this respect 1848 was central, as the moment when all the principles underpinning Germany's current political existence—the rights of man, democracy, and the common will to unite the diverse regions and movements—had been laid down. Though Germans were suffering the dislocations and disappointments of reunification, he urged, they should not throw in their lot with extremist parties which had already destroyed German democracy once, but learn the lesson of 1848, when people also in crisis put their faith in parliamentary leaders and democratic solutions.[14] In both France and Germany democratic republics were firmly established, but the appropriation of the democratic myth of 1848 by the political establishment ran the risk that ordinary citizens would no longer respond to it.

The socialist view of the 1848 revolutions held that the democratic claim that liberty and fraternity could be established purely by the democratic process was nothing but a political illusion. It argued that the democratic rhetoric of fraternity concealed the reality of bourgeois class interests and that democratic revolution against absolutism and feudalism became bourgeois betrayal and bourgeois repression when the working classes started to assert their own interests. For socialists the defining moment of the 1848 revolution was the June Days in Paris, when the working classes were provoked into insurrection and then ruthlessly suppressed by the fraternity-preaching bourgeoisie. Pierre-Joseph Proudhon recalled that two weeks after his election to the French Constituent As-

[13] *Frankfurter Neue Presse* (19 May 1948).
[14] *Frankfurter Allgemeine Zeitung* (19 May 1998).

sembly in June 1848, the proletarians who had returned him were brutally massacred. 'The memory of the June Days will leaden my heart with an eternal remorse,' he wrote. It was a 'disastrous apprenticeship', both for himself and the workers, which dispelled illusions about the political process. 'Fighters of June!' he warned, 'In March, April, and May, instead of organizing yourselves for labour and liberty . . . you ran to the government, you asked it to provide what you alone could give yourselves, and postponed the revolution by three stages.'[15]

The young Jules Vallès, who witnessed columns of June insurgents being marched off in chains for deportation, was haunted for the rest of his life by the June Days. He was obsessed by the idea of writing a history of it, but so great was his emotion that he was never able to put pen to paper. The hero of *L'Insurgé*, Vallès's fictional account of the Commune (1886), is also trying to write a history of the June Days. As a journalist in Paris in 1871, Vallès interpreted the revolutionary ferment in Paris that led up to the Commune in the light of the June Days:

It was in June and the same men who have just dishonoured Paris, the Jules Favres, the Pagèses, all the traitors, trotted through the barricaded and smoking streets behind Cavaignac's mare and spat on the wounds of the defeated. In the cellar of the Tuileries, beneath the barracks, in the Panthéon, the prisoners were swimming in blood and excrement. Sometimes they were asked through a skylight, 'Who wants bread?' And when a pale face appeared it was blown apart by a rifle shot.[16]

The suppression of working-class revolution served the elaboration of the founding myth of socialism. Socialism sprang from the June Days, said Vallès, like the ball from a cannon. A brief alliance between middle and working classes had been constructed in Paris, bringing in the republic and a number of social reforms, but was not even attempted in Germany, where the middle classes threw themselves into the arms of monarchy, army, bureaucracy, and aristocracy at the first whiff of popular revolution. Workers' demands were rejected, workers' insurrections were crushed, and socialists were able to define 1848 as the martyrdom of the proletariat, which must according to the logic of the socialist gospel eventually result in its resurrection.

[15] P.-J. Proudhon, *Les Confessions d'un révolutionnaire* [Oct. 1849], in *Œuvres complètes*, ed. C. Bougle and H. Moysset (13 vols.; Paris, 1923–36), vii. 167–9.
[16] *Le Cri du Peuple*, (22 Feb. 1871).

The ferocity of the repression of the June Days served the French socialist myth well; by contrast Engels regretted that the people of Berlin, far from putting up a fight, had opened the gates of Berlin to the Prussian army in November 1848:

A well-contested defeat is a fact of as much revolutionary importance as an easily-won victory. The defeats of Paris in June 1848, and of Vienna in October, certainly did far more in revolutionizing the minds of the people of those two cities than the victories of February and March. The Assembly and the people of Berlin would probably have shared the fate of those two towns above-named; but they would have left behind themselves, in the minds of the survivors, a wish of revenge, which in revolutionary times is one of the highest incentives to energetic and passionate action.[17]

As a result of this non-event, socialists looking for a revolutionary episode in Berlin to commemorate fastened on the initial insurrection of 18 March 1848, when crowds gathering in the castle square to applaud concessions made by the king were cleared by royal troops and artisans who threw up barricades were fired upon.

The elements of the socialist collective memory were thus democratic illusion and bourgeois betrayal, the martyrdom of the proletariat, and lastly the socialist revolution that had remained unfulfilled in 1848 but now became the goal for all future revolutions. For Karl Marx, as for French socialists, the Paris Commune was seen as popular retribution for the repression of the June Days carried out by the men of order. On 18 March 1871, he asserted, 'the ghosts of the victims, assassinated at their hands from the Days of June 1848 down to 22 January 1871, arose before their eyes'.[18] Unfortunately the bourgeoisie was again triumphant and, for Marx, as far as the repression they indulged in was concerned, '1848 was only child's play compared with their frenzy in 1871.'[19]

The June Days were joined by the Paris Commune in the litany of proletarian martyrdoms. The Communard Benoît Malon, in exile in Switzerland, spoke of the 'Third Defeat of the French Proletariat', following the Lyons rising of 1832 and the June Days.[20] Even after the Commune, the French socialist leader Jules Guesde proclaimed that 'the fighters of June were the first to resort to arms

---

[17] Friedrich Engels, *Revolution and Counter-revolution in Germany in 1848* (London, 1896), 96 (written in Mar. 1852).
[18] Karl Marx, *The Paris Commune of 1871*, ed. Christopher Hitchens (London, 1871), 86.   [19] Id., *The Civil War in France* (London, 1933), 10.
[20] Benoît Malon, *La Troisième Défaite du prolétariat français* (Neuchâtel, 1871).

for the social republic. Their glorious and bloody defeat marks the violent entry of the proletariat, as a distinct party, on to the stage.'²¹ It was not until his newspaper, *L'Égalité*, went into a second series in 1880 and he started to build the Parti Socialiste Français that he concentrated on the cult of the Paris Commune rather than on the June Days. In Germany the Berlin barricades of March 1848 were briefly joined by the Paris Commune in the *Märzfeier* organized by the Social Democratic Party to define its ideals and legitimacy, but by the 1890s the cult of the Paris Commune weakened in Germany and 1848 once again became the sole object of the March festivals.²² Only the socialists remained loyal to the cult of 1848 as a violent and popular revolution. Franz Mehring claimed in *Die Neue Zeit* in 1898 that the ruling classes had tried to eliminate 'the extraordinary year [1848]' from the history books and pretended that concessions in 1848 had been made out of the goodness of Frederick William's heart rather than wrung out of him by the people on the barricades of 18 March. 'The now class-conscious proletariat is the sole true heir to the legacy of the March fighters, and this class alone dares to celebrate the fiftieth anniversary of the March revolution as it deserves to be: candidly, unreservedly, bearing in mind all its consequences.'²³

At precisely the same time as the fiftieth anniversary of the 1848 revolution was being celebrated by socialists, however, doubts were being expressed in socialist circles about the lessons of 1848. Questions were raised first, given the spread of democracy throughout Europe in the shape of elections under universal manhood suffrage, as to whether fighting on the barricades, 1848–style, was the best way to achieve a socialist revolution; and second, whether 1848 and indeed 1871 were not premature and reckless and demonstrated the need to build organization and class-consciousness among the proletariat to be certain of success. In all European socialist movements the debate between the revolutionary and reformist strategies was also a debate about the interpretation of the events of 1848.

Engels set the cat among the pigeons on the eve of the fiftieth anniversary with his introduction to the 1895 edition of Marx's *Class Struggles in France*. 'The time of surprise attacks,' he argued,

---

²¹ *L'Égalité*, 1st ser. (25 June 1878).
²² Vernon L. Lidtke, *The Alternative Culture: Socialist Labour in Imperial Germany* (New York and Oxford, 1985), 77.
²³ *Die Neue Zeit*, 16/1. 24 (1897–8), 739.

'of revolutions carried through by small conscious minorities at the head of unconscious masses, is past.' Both 1848 and 1871 had failed because the proletariat was unprepared for revolution. 'Long, persistent work', he said, was necessary to build up class-consciousness and organization among the proletariat. Street battles could never be won by the masses, for though towns had grown, so had armies, and these could now be mobilized more speedily by railway. Moreover, barricades were rendered obsolete by the advent of universal suffrage in Germany since 1848. This, concluded Engels, opened the way for the peaceful, legal advent to power of social democracy.

By 1898 the French had fifty years' experience of democracy, and one wing of the socialist movement was convinced that power could be achieved through elections. Marking the fiftieth anniversary of 1848, the democratic socialist Alexandre Millerand warned that the revolution had at that point been premature and opposed by the mass of the peasantry, who had voted Louis-Napoleon Bonaparte president of the republic. 'Our first task is to teach, to instruct, to enlighten', he warned, while the second (particularly important as the Dreyfus affair raged) was to remain united.[24] Millerand did not carry all socialists with him, particularly when he accepted office in a bourgeois so-called 'government of republican defence' against the forces of anti-Dreyfusard reaction. Jules Guesde argued that 'ministerialism' would alienate the masses, who would then 'allow through the first sabre as, after the collapse of the Second Republic in the blood of June, they permitted the Second December of M. Louis Bonaparte'.[25] For Guesde the unity of the Socialist Party had to be built upon the doctrine of class struggle and revolution, and he continued to cultivate the heroic myth of the June Days and Paris Commune rather than, like the democratic socialists, criticize them as premature.

Engels was cited as an authority by Eduard Bernstein when in 1898 the latter tried to persuade the Stuttgart congress of the German Social Democratic Party (SPD) to abandon the doctrines of violent revolution and the dictatorship of the proletariat. Far from acclaiming the barricade fighters in their anniversary year, he was influenced by the current thinking about crowd psychology of Scipio Sighele and Gustave Le Bon. He argued that crowds were in-

---

[24] *La Petite République* (27 Feb. 1898).
[25] *Congrès général des organisations socialistes françaises tenu à Paris du 3 au 8 décembre 1899* (Paris, 1900), 186.

herently unstable, suggestible, and prone to criminal activities and atrocities like the massacres of St Bartholomew and of September 1792.[26] Appropriating the discourse of evolutionism, he asserted, moreover, that democracy was an inevitable stage in the development of society and must be the instrument of the gradual socialization of society; the dictatorship of classes belonged to 'a lower civilization' and was 'a reversion, a political atavism'.[27] Stefan Born, who had founded the General German Workers' Brotherhood in 1848, but had fled to Switzerland after the Dresden rising of 1849 and started a new career as an academic, concurred that theories of evolution undermined doctrines of class struggle leading to a perfect socialist society, and claimed that ideas were more important than material forces. 'Social revolutionaries become social reformers', he concluded fifty years after the event: 'That is the trend of the times.'[28]

A contrary view was taken by Rosa Luxemburg and Lenin. They argued that democratic concessions were fragile and illusory, granted by reactionary governments and ruling classes and liable to be withdrawn at any moment if it seemed as though the socialist movement might benefit. Moreover, they claimed, an objective reading of Marx and Engels demonstrated that they adhered to a revolutionary interpretation of 1848. Rosa Luxemburg replied to Bernstein that the advent of democracy was not inevitable; on the contrary, it was now being abandoned by the bourgeoisie 'for fear of the growing labour movement'. She accused Bernstein of 'saying goodbye to the mode of thought of the revolutionary proletariat, to dialectics, and to the materialist conception of history'.[29]

The analysis by Lenin, during the 1905 revolution, was likewise based squarely on the purported original reading of the 1848 revolution in Germany by Marx and Engels. Since the German bourgeoisie had thrown itself into the arms of the monarchy, army, and feudal aristocracy, who then turned their bayonets on the people, the same was likely to happen in Russia. The Union of Liberation, inspired by the strategy of French democrats in 1848, had

[26] *Die Neue Zeit* (10 Nov. 1897, 1 Mar. 1898), in H. and J. M. Tudor, *Marxism and Social Democracy: The Revisionist Debate, 1896–8* (Cambridge, 1988), 110–18, 220–1.

[27] Eduard Bernstein, *Evolutionary Socialism: A Criticism and Affirmation* (London, 1909), 146.

[28] Stephan Born, *Erinnerungen eines Achtundvierzigers* (Leipzig, 1898), 295.

[29] Rosa Luxemburg, *Reform or Revolution* [1900] (London, 1986), 64.

launched a banquet campaign in 1904 at which orators demanded a constituent assembly elected by universal suffrage. One of the young lawyers who helped to organize the banquets was Alexander Kerensky.[30] 'Constitutional illusions and school exercises in parliamentarism become merely a screen for the bourgeois betrayal of the revolution,' riposted Lenin in 1905, and bourgeois force would have to be met by the force of a democratic dictatorship of the proletariat and peasantry. Likewise 'petty-bourgeois illusions about the unity of the people and the absence of a class struggle within the people', which ensured that the 1848 revolution was 'not consummated' in a socialist sense, must be avoided. In Russia the workers would be led by an 'independent proletarian party' dedicated to 'the complete victory of the revolution'.[31] In *The State and Revolution*, written in August 1917, Lenin renewed the attack on 'the petty-bourgeois democrats, those sham socialists who replaced the class struggle by dreams of class harmony' and who had betrayed the French revolution of 1848. He cited the *Communist Manifesto* to justify class struggle and the dictatorship of the proletariat, arguing that 'all his life Marx fought against this petty-bourgeois socialism now revived in Russia by the Socialist-Revolutionary and Menshevik parties'.[32]

Whereas for democratic socialists in Germany, as we have seen, the 1918 revolution was the fulfilment of the democratic hopes of 1848, for Rosa Luxemburg no faith could be placed in a national assembly if the bourgeoisie and feudal class decided to defend their privileges by force; existing workers' and soldiers' councils must be transformed into a soviet regime. 'The species embodied by Lamartine, Garnier-Pagès, Ledru-Rollin, namely the species of petit-bourgeois illusionists and babblers of AD 1848, has not died out,' she ranted, 'it has reappeared—without the lustre and talent and allure of newness—in a boring, pedantic, scholarly German edition written by Kautsky, Hilferding, and Haase.'[33] After the workers' and soldiers' councils voted to support a national assembly, Luxemburg helped to found the German Communist Party, claimed the authority of the *Communist Manifesto* of 1848, and ar-

---

[30] Paul Miliukov, *Political Memoirs, 1905–1917*, ed. Arthur P. Mendel (Ann Arbor, 1967), 12; Alexander Kerensky, *The Kerensky Memoirs* (London, 1966), 45.

[31] Lenin, 'Two Tactics of Social-Democracy in the Democratic Revolution' [July 1905], in *Selected Works* (Moscow, 1968), 141–2, 145.

[32] Ibid. 279, 286.

[33] 'Die Rote Fahne' (20 Nov. 1918), in Rosa Luxemburg, *Selected Political Writings*, ed. Robert Looker (London, 1972), 263.

gued that with their aim of destroying capitalism 'we stand on the same ground that Marx and Engels occupied in 1848 and from which in principle they did not deviate'.[34] But Engels had also pointed out that the lack of revolutionary decisiveness manifested in Germany in 1848 boded ill for the success of revolution in the future. After the defeat of the Communist rising of January 1919 and shortly before her murder, Rosa Luxemburg was led to much the same conclusion:

The heroic action of the proletariat of Paris in 1848 has become the living source of class energy for the whole International. The wretchedness of the German March Revolution, by contrast, has weighed down the whole modern German development like a ball and chain. It has produced after-effects extending from the special history of official German Social Democracy up to the latest events of the German revolution—right up to the dramatic crisis we have just witnessed.[35]

For Communists the failed revolution of 1918 was explained by the burden of the failed revolution of 1848, but the defeat of the Third Reich and the patronage of Soviet Communism offered an opportunity in 1948 for realizing the hopes of those who subscribed to the revolutionary message of 1848. In the Soviet-controlled eastern zone of Germany the Dresden Socialist Unity Party, which fused Communists and some Socialists, announced that 'the new Germany has the duty of making up for the neglect of the 1848 revolution', and organized a 50,000-strong demonstration in honour of the March fighters. In contrast to 1848, it argued, the working class was now class-conscious, led by a united Socialist Party, and in a position, linked to wider progressive forces in Germany, to 'undertake the completion of the historical tasks of the March fighters . . . against imperialists and reactionaries'.[36]

French Communists were similarly keen to claim the mantle of the revolutionaries of 1848 from what they called the 'American party' which now ran France, and to assert that the ideals of 1848 were now realized in the Soviet bloc. At a mass rally in Paris André Marty insisted that the Prague coup of the Czech Communist leader Gottwald was only trying to prevent their revolution failing in the same way as the French one had failed in 1848. 'The dream of 1848

[34] Rosa Luxemburg, *Ich war, ich bin, ich werde sein! Artikel und Reden zur Novemberrevolution* (Berlin, 1958), 99.
[35] Luxemburg, *Selected Political Writings*, 305.
[36] *Sächsische Zeitung* (17, 19 Mar. 1948).

has come true', he asserted, 'because in the USSR, over a sixth of the globe, there is no more exploitation of man by man, because the socialist regime has been born. It has crushed the Hitlerian hordes and, over the ruins of Berlin, the Red Army has raised the flag of the insurgents of 1848 that the Fascists stole.'[37] Totalitarian Communism made a bid to appropriate the myth of the failed revolution that needed to be completed by decisive action, and in a short space of time would also seek to appropriate the myth of national liberation for its own ends.

The collapse of Communism in Europe removed the primary exponents of the revolutionary interpretation of 1848. In Germany the sacred date of 18 March was still an issue in 1998, although not for the SPD. The Berlin senate, controlled by a coalition of the Christlich-Demokratische Union (CDU) and the SPD, was extremely reluctant to organize any commemoration at all in 1998.[38] In the end the Prussian minister president Erwin Teufel laid a wreath at the monument to the victims of the March Revolution, but revolutionary protest was confined to the '18 March Initiative' of Günter Grass and Christa Wolf. They paraded 300-strong to demand that 18 March be established as a public holiday and hung signs reading '18 March Square' over those signalling 'Brandenburg Gate Square', since an official renaming had been rejected by the Berlin senate.[39] The French Communist Party marked the 150th anniversary of the publication of the *Communist Manifesto* by a debate in Paris in June on the future path of the Party. Regrets were expressed for the Stalinist period and an address by Ababacar Diop, leader of the 'sans-papier' or non-regularized immigrants under threat of expulsion, gave some indication of new battles to be fought on behalf of 'modern slaves' other than Marx's proletariat. No mention, however, was made of the June Days as the masses bowed to the false consciousness of World Cup hysteria.

One of the most enduring myths of the 1848 revolutions was that it ushered in the springtime of peoples, the liberation of nations from subservience to the great dynastic empires, and that it looked to apply the principle of fraternity to the international community by forming a brotherhood of free nations. In his address to foreign

---

[37] *L'Humanité* (25 Feb. 1948).
[38] 'Blamabel und unwürdig: In Sachen 1848 reagiert der Berliner Senat hilflos': *Die Zeit* (26 Feb. 1998).   [39] *Süddeutsche Zeitung* (19 Mar. 1998).

powers of 2 March 1848 Lamartine declared that the treaties of 1815 were no longer valid and that France would come to the help of peoples who wished to recover their freedom. Unfortunately Lamartine was also keen to lay to rest the ghost of the expansionist First Republic, and in so doing rendered illusory promises of military support to nations seeking independence. 'To return after fifty years to the principle of 1792, to the idea of conquering an empire', Lamartine declared, 'would be to go not forwards but backwards in time. . . . The world and we ourselves wish to march towards fraternity and peace.'[40] As a result the old empires were able to reassert their domination over subject peoples, and the French themselves intervened in 1849 to restore the Pope to Rome, whence he had been driven by revolutionary nationalists under Mazzini and Garibaldi.

A hundred years later Frenchmen who had always defended the liberating and civilizing mission of France were still beating their breasts about the missed opportunity. In his Sorbonne lecture Léon Blum argued that 1848 was a honeymoon period when 'movements for national liberation coincided exactly with movements for democratic liberation', that this was the moment to have created a 'federation of free democracies in Europe'. Since the policy of non-intervention in Spain followed by Blum's government of 1936 had been discredited along with the appeasement of Fascist powers, and the Soviet Union had renewed its grip on eastern Europe, Blum now argued that the French should have intervened decisively in European affairs in 1848, without thought of conquest, but to support democratic and national liberation. Instead of this the Russian tsar and Austrian emperor had been permitted to re-establish their reactionary empires.[41] By extension, he suggested, such an interventionist policy after 1918 might have ensured a benevolent French patronage of nascent democracies in central and eastern Europe, instead of the totalitarian empires of Nazi Germany or the USSR.

The collective memory of national liberation was developed after the victory of the Austrian and Russian empires in 1849 by nationalist leaders such as Mazzini and Kossuth, who had been driven into exile. Mazzini enjoyed the support of the Friends of Italy Society in London, where in 1852 he ranted against the papacy, the nobles,

---

[40] Comité National du Centenaire de 1848, *Documents diplomatiques du gouvernement provisoire et de la commission du pouvoir exécutif* (2 vols.; Paris, 1953–4), i. 8.
[41] Blum, *L'Œuvre*, 425–9.

and the kingdom of Piedmont.[42] Kossuth, who had proclaimed the Habsburg dynasty deposed and issued a Hungarian Declaration of Independence, launched himself on a tour of England and the United States in 1851–2, seeking international recognition for his declaration as well as financial and even military support to make it a reality. In England he flattered the British love of liberty, played on his Protestantism, and saw himself acclaimed as a new Cromwell.[43] In Birmingham he announced to cheers that 'as long as Hungary shall not be restored to its sovereign liberty and independence, as long as Italy shall not become free, the foot of Russia will rest on Europe's neck. . . . The cause of Hungary is the cause of civil and religious liberty.'[44] In the United States Kossuth praised the American Declaration of Independence and republican constitution, but was powerless to persuade the Americans to reconsider the Monroe doctrine and intervene in Europe.[45]

Revolutionary nationalists were brushed aside by the power politics of national unification undertaken from above by the Italian and German states. Mazzini continued to struggle for a popular revolution and constituent assembly to found an Italian republic on the model of 1848–9 and to denounce the 'diplomatization' of the Risorgimento. He languished in prison in 1870 when Rome was finally occupied by Piedmontese armies, refused to accept a royal pardon for his patriotism, and, though acclaimed by the people when he died in 1872, received no tribute from either government or parliament. Kossuth likewise attacked the *Ausgleich* by which Hungary became part of a dual monarchy with Austria, preferring a republic and refusing to accept anything but full independence for Hungary. He was *persona non grata* to Franz Joseph and died in exile in Turin in 1894, and though the crowds turned out in hundreds of thousands for his burial in Budapest, at the wish of the emperor the Hungarian government and parliament did not participate. The street along which the cortège passed was named after him in 1894, but the square outside the parliament building did not take his name until after the First World War.

[42] Meeting of the Society, 24 Mar. 1852: Emilia Morelli, *Mazzini in Inghilterra* (Florence, 1938), 162–6.

[43] Anon., *Kossuth* (London, 1851), pp. iv–v.

[44] Anonymous speech of 12 Nov. 1851: *Authentic Life of his Excellency Louis Kossuth, Governor of Hungary, with a Full Report of his Speeches Delivered in England* (London, 1851), 117.

[45] John H. Komlos, *Kossuth in America, 1851–2* (Buffalo, 1973), 84–6, 150–4.

The gulf between revolutionary nationalism and official nation-building was clearly articulated when the fiftieth anniversary of the 1848 revolutions was marked in 1898. Official Italy celebrated the anniversary of the Statuto, or constitution granted by Charles Albert of Piedmont, which later became the constitution of a united Italy. The socialist leader Turati challenged the official celebrations in Milan by demanding the full realization of the political and civil rights granted by the constitution. Meanwhile the official procession to commemorate the Five Days in March 1848 during which the Milanese drove out the Austrian forces was countered by a popular demonstration.[46] Two months later, popular discontent and strike action in Milan were suppressed by military force in the so-called *fatti di maggio*, precipitating a major constitutional crisis.

In the German Reichstag a confrontation took place on the anniversary of the uprising of 18 March between Robert von Puttkamer, the Prussian minister of the interior, the Socialist leader August Bebel, and the doyen of the National Liberal Party, Rudolf von Bennigsen. Puttkamer declared that the revolution had been caused by a 'foreign rabble' which had stirred up 'our good and loyal people' against their king and had wantonly interrupted the process of reform. Bebel protested at the use of the term 'rabble' to describe those who had died for their ideals on the barricades and argued that 'without 18 March there would be no German Reich, without the German Reich there would be no German Reichstag, and I might add, without the German Reichstag there would be no war minister responsible to it'. He concluded that had King Frederick William kept his promises of 18 March instead of ordering his soldiers to shoot, German unification would have been possible without Bismarck and without the war of 1870.[47] This provoked Bennigsen to intervene, attacking Bebel for opposing the war of 1870, which had been crucial for German unification, and arguing that 18 March had not had the slightest influence on Germany's rise to greatness. 'Its foundations', he said, 'were not the Berlin street-fighting, but the great national movement in which the whole German people participated, including notables, governments, and princes.' He underlined that the Frankfurt assembly, which brought together the

---

[46] Alfredo Canavero, *Milano e la crisi di fino secolo, 1896–1900* (Milan, 1976), 155–7; Louise A. Tilly, *Politics and Class in Milan, 1881–1901* (New York and Oxford, 1992), 260–1.

[47] *Stenographische Berichte über die Verhandlungen des Reichstags*, ix. Legislaturperiode, V. Session, 1897/8 (2 vols.; Berlin, 1898), ii. 1591, 1600–1.

best elements in the German nation, must be credited with the first serious attempt at unification, but that the roles of the future King Wilhelm, who had to flee Berlin after 18 March, and of Otto von Bismarck, who had fiercely opposed the street-fighting, were absolutely central to the success of unification.[48] For most Germans, 1898 was marked less by commemoration of the March 1848 revolution than by celebration of the tenth anniversary of the accession of Kaiser Wilhelm II on 16 June, and the funeral of Bismarck in August. In Austria, to complete the picture, the festivities of 1898 were devoted not to revolution but to the fiftieth anniversary of the accession of Emperor Franz Joseph, praised in one commemorative work as a 'saviour and restorer' who had steered the monarchy away from revolution towards peace and stability.[49]

In imperial Germany the socialists were pilloried as anti-patriotic enemies of the Reich. When they came to power in the Weimar Republic they needed to convince nationalists that they were in a position to protect Germany's interests. In 1923, with the Ruhr occupied by French forces, Friedrich Ebert argued in his Paulskirche speech that the concepts of 'Einheit, Freiheit und Vaterland' that guided the Frankfurt assembly were also 'the essence and guiding star of the struggle for existence we are forced to carry on today on the Rhine, Ruhr, and Saar'.[50] Unfortunately, nationalists and Nazis persuaded the German people that Fatherland and Unity were best secured by sacrificing Freedom, including the existence of the Republic. In 1948, after the collapse of the Third Reich, there was arguably greater harmony between the aspirations of the nationalists of 1848 towards national liberation and international brotherhood and those of the architects of a new Europe. However, there were significant differences from country to country, depending on whether aspirations towards national liberation were on the agenda, had been realized, or were frustrated and remained a painful memory.

In Germany, which was occupied militarily by the Allies and divided by the developing cold war between capitalist west and Communist east, the debate on 1848 was likewise divided. In the

---

[48] Ibid. 1606–7; speech also in Adolf Kiepert, *Rudolph von Bennigsen* (Hanover and Berlin, 1903), 215–17.

[49] Carl Klopfer, *Unser Kaiser: Ein Gedankbuch der fünfzigjährigen Regierung, zugleich ein Lebens- und Charakterbild Kaiser Franz Joseph* (Vienna, 1898), 4.

[50] Rebentisch, *Friedrich Ebert*, 11.

west, intellectuals and politicians looked nostalgically at 1848 as an opportunity that had been squandered to combine the freedom and unity of the German nation. Friedrich Meinecke argued that March 1848 inflicted not just a physical but also a political and psychological defeat on the Prussian military monarchy and that it might have turned the 'authoritarian state' into a 'partnership state', but did not.[51] Theodor Heuss said that repression following the 1848 revolution had favoured only American democracy, as Germans emigrated to the United States, but conceded that the myth of German unity and self-government had been passed down to subsequent generations.[52] The journalist Ernst Friedländer regretted that the Germans had no national day of celebration on a par with the French Bastille Day or American Independence Day. He argued that in 1848 the German people had been united and had the princes on the run, but concluded that deeds had failed to match spirit and that 1848 remained a 'standstill revolution'. Echoing Ebert, he reflected that 'the Germans tried to grasp destiny in their hands and it eluded them'. German unity had come from the hands of Bismarck, for the people but not by the people. The one lesson to learn was that freedom was more important than unity and that current Soviet propaganda ostensibly in favour of a democratic and united Germany in fact promised a 'Soviet totalitarian mass existence and in no sense a German existence'.[53]

For the Communists of the eastern zone, like their Soviet master, the division of Germany was a temporary affair contingent on military occupation. The goal was a democratic united Germany, and in this respect the lesson of 1848 was there to be learnt. The commemoration of 18 March 1848 coincided with the second German People's Congress in Berlin, attended by 2,000 delegates. Otto Grotewohl of the official Socialist Unity Party (SED) called for the delegates to fulfil the vision of those who had fought in March 1848 and found a democratic and united Germany. He rejoiced that some delegates had come from the western zones and argued that German unity served not just a class or a party, but the German nation as a whole.[54] This attempt to appropriate a legitimacy derived from 1848 to set up a Germany that would clearly be a one-party

[51] Friedrich Meinecke, *1848: Eine Säkularbetrachtung* (Berlin, 1948), 9.
[52] Theodor Heuss, *1848: Werke und Erbe* (Stuttgart, 1948), 161–2, 167.
[53] *Die Zeit* (18 Mar. 1948).
[54] *Leipziger Volkszeitung* (18 Mar. 1948); *Sächsische Zeitung* (19 Mar. 1948).

state under the protection of the USSR was necessarily doomed to failure.

The Austrians, who had lost an empire and suffered annexation by the Third Reich, drew few lessons a hundred years on from a revolution that had threatened the integrity and great-power status of that empire. Their main response was amnesia, believing fervently that 'nothing had happened' there in 1848. *Neues Österreich* reported: 'The reminder that a hundred years ago blood was spilt in Vienna for human rights, freedom, and democracy disturbs the operetta-like image we have of the "good old time", in which thirty years ago the "good old" Emperor Franz Joseph died.'[55] From their troubled present they preferred to look back to a golden age of imperial rule.

Nationalities which had struggled to free themselves from the Habsburg empire in 1848 took a very different view. In Italy, the lessons of national unity and independence to be learnt from 1848 were indeed much clearer after the defeat of Fascism and with the challenge of Communism to be faced. The centenary of the Five Days of Milan took on fresh significance after the expulsion of a new wave of Germanic invaders in 1945. A plaque in the piazza della Scala in Milan linked the republican heroes and martyrs of the Five Days, fighting for 'justice, liberty, and independence', to the partisan struggle of 1943–5 which culminated in the 'victorious insurrection of 25 April 1945', an interpretation that neatly brushed aside the Fascist episode as a foreign imposition, not a home-grown product. A new constitution was voted in 1948, on the centenary of the Statuto, taking on a new sheen after the Fascist interlude. The Italian parliament celebrated a hundred years of existence, the speaker of the new chamber of deputies hailing his predecessor, Vicenzo Gioberti, elected speaker of the Turin parliament on 8 May 1848, and praising the parliament's stalwart defence of civil and democratic liberties against the reaction of 1898 and against Fascism.[56] Given that disunity had often left Italy vulnerable to foreign intervention, and that the new threat came from the Communist bloc, Prime Minister De Gasperi, who had built a four-party anti-Communist coalition, opened the Twenty-seventh Congress for the History of the Risorgimento in Milan by insisting

[55] *Neues Österreich* (1 Jan. 1848).
[56] Segretario Generale della Camera dei Deputati, *Il centenario del Parlamento, 8 maggio 1848–8 maggio 1948* (Rome, 1948), 18.

that the lesson of 1848 was that Italians must remain united in their defence of liberty.[57]

Hungary had achieved independence in truncated form in 1918, and the statue erected to Kossuth in Budapest in 1927 depicted him as a defeated leader. Another national hero of 1848, the poet Petőfi, was honoured by a statue in 1882. When the reactionary Hungarian government entered the war against the Soviet Union in 1941, Communists, socialists and trade unionists expressed their opposition to the war and desire for an independent, democratic Hungary by turning to the national heroes. Wreaths were laid at the statues of Petőfi and Kossuth on 15 March 1942, leading to the arrest of 600 Communists, but mass celebrations of the fiftieth anniversary of Kossuth's death planned for 20 March 1944 were curtailed by the German invasion of the previous day.[58]

As in eastern Germany, the Communists who gained influence in Hungary after the war sought to demonstrate that they alone gave expression to the aspirations of 1848 for national liberation and made a bid for the myth of Louis Kossuth. A new statue, surrounded by peasants, workers, and soldiers, was dedicated to him in 1952 and the Communist education minister József Révai, inaugurating it, said that

although he was not a son of his people, he realized that without the libera-tion of the serfs the nation was exposed to oppression. We respect Kossuth for his unshakeable loyalty to the cause of Hungarian independence, for refusing to give way to despair even after the defeat of the revolution and shameful agreement of 1867. We respect Kossuth for the fact that he was clearly aware in 1848 of the relationship between the struggle for free-dom of the Hungarian people and the similar struggle of other peoples in Europe.[59]

What Révai failed to point out was that Kossuth's struggle was as much against the Russians as against the Austrians, so that when the Hungarians rose against Communist and Soviet rule in 1956, they immediately reappropriated their national heroes of 1848 and orchestrated the revolutionary movement around their shrines. The

---

[57] *Corriere della sera* (20 Mar. 1948).

[58] C. A. Macartney, *October Fifteenth: A History of Modern Hungary, 1929–1945* (2 vols.; Edinburgh, 1956–7), ii. 104–5, 247. I am grateful to Robert Evans for information concerning the statues of Kossuth, Petőfi, and Bem in Budapest.

[59] British–Hungarian Friendship Society, *Kossuth, Architect of Hungarian Free-dom, 1802–1894* (London, 1953), 8.

demonstration of 23 October in Budapest began at the statue of Petőfi, where one of his poems was recited. It moved to the statue, erected in 1934, of József Bem, the Polish general who had led the struggle against the Russians in 1849. There another poem of Petőfi was read out:

> Magyars rise, your country calls!
> Meet this hour, whate'er befalls!
> Shall we freemen be, or slaves?
> Choose the lot your spirit craves![60]

As dusk fell the immense statue of Stalin at the entrance to the City Park was brought down, and the crowds marched to Kossuth Square, in front of the parliament building, demanding the return of Imre Nagy to power. From there they went to the radio station, and when security forces fired on them they seized control of the station, subsequently renaming the national radio Radio Kossuth.[61] The crushing of the Hungarian revolution represented for one of the Social Democratic leaders the revenge of the 'red tsars', the heirs of those who had crushed Hungary in 1849.[62]

The reunification of Germany in 1990 provoked widespread fears that the Bismarckian Reich with its militarism and expansionist designs would be resurrected. This spectre the Germans were keen to exorcise, both for others and for themselves. The mantle of the revolution of 1848, when the German nation had sought unity and freedom, and had not (with the exception of a small clash with Denmark) embarked on expansion, was clearly an attractive one. So was the European dimension of 1848, in which subject peoples had to some extent helped each other in the struggle against the authoritarian, multinational empires, for a united Germany contained within the framework of the European Union was felt to be a more acceptable quantity than a great power allying, for example, with Russia. By the same token, those keen on broadening and deepening European integration and popularizing the European idea saw the European vision of 1848 as a rich source of legitimation. Rudolf Scharping, for example, an SPD deputy in the

[60] László Beke, *A Student's Diary: Budapest, October 16–November 1, 1956* (London, 1957), 28.
[61] François Fejtő, *Behind the Rape of Hungary* (New York, 1957), 176–87; Paul E. Zinner, *Revolution in Hungary* (New York and London, 1963), 239–58.
[62] Béla K. Király and Paul Jónás, *The Hungarian Revolution of 1956 in Retrospect* (Boulder, Colo., 1978), 12.

Bundestag, urged the parliament to celebrate 1848 as a 'Europe-wide movement of peoples towards freedom. . . . If, 150 years later, Europe wishes to move close together,' he said, 'it must be a Europe of the people.'[63] In his Paulskirche speech, moreover, President Herzog argued that only in a united democratic Europe would democracy have a chance of meeting the undemocratic challenges of globalization. The fascination of the Frankfurt national assembly with freedom and democracy, he concluded, must now be translated into efforts to democratize decision-making in Europe.[64]

Celebrations of 1848 were scarcely conducted on a European scale in 1998. Besides, commemorations on a national level were challenged by local or regional commemorations claiming the heritage of 1848 for their own. In Germany there was a noticeable difference between south and west Germany, with its democratic tradition, which was keen to mark the event, and Berlin, where, as we have seen, the Senate showed a marked reluctance to do anything. Even sharper was the clash in Italy, where the Five Days of Milan were the subject of two different commemorative events. The official celebration, in the Piazza Tricolore, portrayed them as the first act of popular participation in the 'great struggle for national independence', while in the Piazza XXIV Maggio the Northern League claimed it as the founding act, not of Italian unity, but of Milanese autonomy and Lombard self-government.[65] Explaining the failure of the war against Austria in 1848, the Tuscan radical Montanelli had said: 'We fought as Piedmontese, as Tuscans, as Neapolitans, as Romans, not as Italians.'[66] A century and a half later, in the context of the regionalist challenge to the nation state, that same fragmentation was being celebrated.

The final founding myth of 1848 concerns only one country, France. It relates to the abolition of slavery in the French colonies by a decree of the Provisional Government on 27 April 1848. This was associated with the name of Victor Schoelcher, an Alsatian journal-

---

[63] *Die Zeit* (19 Feb. 1998).
[64] *Frankfurter Allgemeine Zeitung* (19 May 1998).
[65] *Corriere della sera* (18 and 19 Mar. 1998).
[66] Quoted in Robert Gildea, *Barricades and Borders: Europe 1800–1914*, 2nd edn. (Oxford, 1996), 98.

ist and philanthropist who chaired a commission of the Constituent Assembly which pressed for abolition and was later elected deputy for Martinique. Slavery had in fact been abolished by the Convention in 1794, but this date was never celebrated because it was short-lived, abrogated by Napoleon Bonaparte in 1802. Very little was made of the matter in 1898, but to mark the centenary on 27 April 1948 lectures were given at the Sorbonne by three black politicians. They were selected as models of assimilated colonial peoples who subscribed to the myth of the liberating and civilizing mission of a nation that conferred citizenship on all who adopted its values; but while two went through the routine admirably, one was much more critical.

Gaston Monnerville, who originated from French Guiana and was now president of the Council of the Republic (the upper house of parliament), suavely located the emancipation of the slaves in the republican tradition of liberty, equality, and fraternity, and argued that the liberating gesture had been repaid by the rallying of Félix Éboué, Governor of Chad, to the Free French in 1940 and confirmed by the foundation of the French Union in 1946, which was to guide the colonies to democratic self-government. Léopold Sédar Senghor, deputy for Senegal and later its president, said that despite his reservations he had confidence that the constitution of 1946 would be of benefit for colonial peoples. The third speaker, Aimé Césaire, was a Communist deputy for Martinique who was less likely to flatter French self-congratulation because Communist ministers had been expelled from the government the previous year and because demonstrations in the Martiniquais capital Fort-de-France were broken up by the police. Césaire argued that Schoelcher and the decree on emancipation had been systematically marginalized by accounts of the 1848 revolution, which amounted to a form of racism; that slavery demonstrated the coexistence of civilization and barbarism in the French nineteenth century; and that while 'the colonial question has been put, it is a long way from being resolved'.[67] Elsewhere he likened the transport of African peoples to slave plantations in the Americas to deportation of the Jews to Nazi concentration camps, and called the bourgeoisie of France, Spain, Britain and Holland who had

---

[67] Gaston Monnerville, Léopold Sédar Senghor, and Aimé Césaire, *Commémoration du centenaire de l'abolition de l'esclavage: Discours prononcés à la Sorbonne le 27 avril 1948* (Paris, 1948), 22, 27–8, 41–5.

constructed capitalism on the back of slavery 'innocent Himmlers of the system'.[68]

The emancipationist myth aligned the generosity of the French nation with the gratitude of the emancipated black, who having been given his liberty was keen to assimilate French values. It was suggested that emancipated blacks would naturally side with France, given its liberating and civilizing mission incarnate in the Resistance, against oppressive and barbaric powers like Germany. Thus when the remains of Schoelcher were transferred to the Panthéon in 1949 they were accompanied by those of Félix Éboué. Whether the populations of France's empire felt that gratitude in practice is another matter.

For the 150th anniversary of emancipation, Jacques Chirac invited an élite of assimilated French citizens to the Élysée and was pictured with the goalkeeper Serge Lama. He produced a homily on France's liberating and civilizing mission, reminding his audience that the emancipation decree applied the first article of the Declaration of the Rights of Man and the Citizen of 1789: 'Men are born and remain free and equal in rights.' He underlined the 'open and generous attitude' of the French nation, prepared to welcome those who wished to join it and who, in return for the rights of citizenship, despite their own culture and traditions, were prepared to accept the French system of values. This, he said, was 'the French model of integration'.[69]

For the inhabitants of Martinique and Guadeloupe, where the movement for independence from French rule was gathering pace, this restatement of old platitudes was seen as a slap in the face. They were keen to develop their own myth of slavery and emancipation in order to justify their political claims. Thus Martiniquais were keen to point out that on their island abolition had been the fruit of struggle, not generosity, a measure taken by the local French authorities before the arrival of the decree from Paris, in direct response to the slave insurrection of 22 May 1848. Guadeloupians called for a boycott of the commemorative ceremonies, on the grounds that by honouring the virtue of Schoelcher the French were shuffling off responsibility for the crime of slavery, which they had restored and continued much longer than other nations, like the British. More

[68] Aimé Césaire, 'Introduction', in Émile Terson (ed.), *Victor Schoelcher: Esclavage et colonisation* (Paris, 1948), 17–18.
[69] *Libération* (24 Apr. 1998); *Le Monde* (24 Apr. 1998).

forcefully than Aimé Césaire in 1948, the International Committee of Black People, based on Guadeloupe, asked Laurent Fabius, president of the National Assembly, to have the assembly adopt a resolution that slavery was a crime against humanity in the same way that the Shoah was, and to apologize for it. 'Let us be clear', said their spokesman, 'that the genocide of the Jews has been recognized, the crime has been condemned, and the pain of it taken into account. But for the slave there has been nothing. Nothing. The life of a black man does not have the same value as that of the white man.' Visiting the village of Champagney (Haute-Saône), where the *cahier de doléance* in 1789 had called for the abolition of slavery, Prime Minister Jospin admitted that 'in the human tragedy represented by slavery the former colonial powers have to take their share of responsibility'. The inversion of the emancipationist myth, however, thrown back at the French by pro-independence leaders who equated slavery with the Holocaust, illustrates the irreconcilability of collective memories and the fragility of the ideologically inspired interpretations of 1848.[70]

Three general points may be made in conclusion. First, the collective memories of 1848 were diverse, elaborated by a number of political movements—democratic, socialist, and nationalist—which sought to define and legitimate themselves against the authoritarian empires that dominated in Europe. To some extent, while in opposition, they allied with each other; but they were also rivals, and if one movement achieved power it tried to impose its version of events on its competitors as the received wisdom. Thus the democrats sought to win socialists over to the idea of the democratic, not revolutionary, path to power. On other occasions, those already in power appropriated the myth fostered by the opposition and used it for their own ends. In this way the ideal of national liberation was taken up by states such as Piedmont or Prussia for the sake of nation-building, and purged of any revolutionary connotations.

Second, there was a powerful tension between the 1848 revolutions as a rich source of founding myths to define and legitimate political communities, and the burden of failed revolution which threatened to undermine as much as it inspired. Revolutionary

[70] *Le Monde* (25, 26–7, 28 Apr. 1998).

movements were tempted to look alternatively to 1789
1917 as a founding myths, either because they were n
cessful revolutions or because (as with 1871) the martyr
more spectacular. The German people was more likely to
fined with reference to successful moments of nation-state
ing, such as Sedan Day in 1870, than to 1848, when com
national and democratic aspirations ended in failure. Similarl
diverse peoples of the Habsburg monarchy cultivated the acces
of Franz Joseph rather than the revolution that had tried to un
the dynasty and divide the empire. And yet when reunification to
place in 1990 the German nation was happy to revive a democrat
and fraternal nationalist myth that offered an alternative to the mil
itaristic and aggressive national myths of the Second and Third
Reichs.

This brings us to the third point: that collective memories of the
1848 revolutions changed over time. In 1898 the democratic heirs of
1848 had learnt the lessons of failure and were in power in France;
socialists were divided over 1848 according to whether they were
likely to achieve power democratically or not; and national lib-
erationists had been brushed aside by nation-building under the
leadership of existing states. In 1948 democrats in western Europe
reflected on their resurrection from the dead and questioned the
generosity of their predecessors; the socialist myth was taken up
by Communist parties; while the myth of national liberation was
espoused in Italy to whitewash its Fascist past and by Communists
in East Germany and Hungary, where it was hotly contested by
democratic nationalists in 1956. In 1998 both Communism and the
socialist myth were dead; Germans struggled to learn the democratic and nationalist lessons of 1848 afresh; Italians realized that
1848 could sustain regionalist demands; while the French, assum-
ing that they had no more to learn as a democratic nation state, saw
the emancipationist myth blow up in their faces.

List of Contributors

GEOFFREY ELLIS, Fellow of Hertford College, Oxford; author of *Napoleon's Continental Blockade: The Case of Alsace* (1981) and *Napoleon* (1997).

R. J. W. EVANS, Regius Professor of Modern History, Oxford; author of works on Austrian history, including *The Making of the Habsburg Monarchy, 1550–1700* (3rd edn. 1991), and editor, with Hartmut Pogge von Strandmann, of *The Coming of the First World War* (1988; corr. repr. 1998).

ROBERT GILDEA, Fellow of Merton College, Oxford; author of *Barricades and Borders: Europe, 1800–1914* (2nd edn. 1996), and of works on French history, most recently *The Past in French History* (1994) and *France since 1945* (1996).

DANIEL W. HOWE, Rhodes Professor of American History and Institutions, Oxford; author of works on American history, most recently *Making the American Self: Jonathan Edwards to Abraham Lincoln* (1997).

DENIS MACK SMITH, Fellow of Wolfson College, Oxford; author of many works on Italian history, including *Cavour* (1985), and most recently *Mazzini* (1994).

LESLIE MITCHELL, Fellow of University College, Oxford; author of works on British history, most recently *Lord Melbourne, 1779–1848* (1997).

HARTMUT POGGE VON STRANDMANN, Professor of Modern History, Oxford; author of works on German history, including *Walther Rathenau, Industrialist, Banker, Intellectual and Politician* (corr. repr. 1998), and editor, with R. J. W. Evans, of *The Coming of the First World War* (1988; corr. repr. 1998).

TIMOTHY M. ROBERTS teaches at Colorado Christian University; author of 'The American Response to the European Revolutions of 1848' (Oxford D.Phil. thesis, 1998).

DAVID SAUNDERS, Professor at the University of Newcastle; author of *The Ukrainian Impact on Russian Culture 1750–1850* (1985) and *Russia in the Age of Reaction and Reform 1801–1881* (1992).

Index